100 JOBS IN WORDS

100 jobs in Words

Scott A. Meyer

Macmillan • USA

MACMILLAN
A Simon & Schuster Macmillan Company
1633 Broadway
New York, NY 10019

Book design and production by Sandy Bell
100 Jobs in Words is produced by becker&mayer!, Ltd.

MACMILLAN is a registered trademark of Macmillan, Inc.

Library of Congress Cataloging-in-Publication Data

Meyer, Scott, 1961–
    100 jobs in words / by Scott Meyer.
        p.   cm.
    Includes bibliographical references.
    ISBN 0–02–861432–1
    1. Vocational guidance. 2. Occupations. I. Title.
HF5381.M44   1996
331.7'02—dc20   96–9218
                                                  CIP

10 9 8 7 6 5 4 3 2 1

Printed in the United States of America

*To all my teachers who tempered their
criticism with encouragement,
especially Dad, Opa, June, Beth,
Janet, Matt, and Barbara.*

100 JOBS CONTENTS

100 JOBS IN WORDS

JOB 101

WHO AM I to be writing this book? Fair question. In the answer I'll try to suggest what else you'll find in the book.

I am a senior editor at a consumer magazine—before that, I was the magazine's copy/production editor. I came to the magazine with experience as an associate editor of a trade magazine, a writer for a weekly newspaper, and an unpaid intern at a large city magazine. Barbara, a former senior editor of the magazine where I currently work, is now the editorial director of the book packaging firm that developed the idea for this book and marketed it to the publisher. She offered me the chance to write it on a freelance basis. Barbara and I had worked together at the magazine and on a couple of other projects, so she was confident that I would meet the book's deadlines and produce a manuscript that met her quality standards.

Could you have written this book? I'll assume that if you're reading *100 Jobs in Words,* you have strong writing and speaking skills—the primary qualifications for the job. If you are also imaginative and persistent in seeking out sources, and organized and disciplined in creating a manuscript, you can handle the work. But could you have landed the job if you wanted it? That depends equally on your ability to do the work and on whether you could convince the person with the work to assign that you have the ability to do it.

Let's be frank here: Having a connection to the person with a job to offer is often the key to getting the opportunity to do it. Of course, you won't get a job if you can't do the work, but if you can and you've demonstrated that fact to your contact, you've made it easy for that person to give you the job.

Which is why, if you'll forgive the cliché, you must always work with the attitude that no job is too small or unimportant to do well. Here's how it works in a real situation: Jennifer had been an administrative assistant for a programming executive at a television network. When a friend of that executive was searching for an assistant, Jennifer applied for the job and got it with the glowing recommendation of her former employer (whom she never liked, by the way, but she kept that to herself). Jennifer's new job was administrative assistant to the story editor at a major Hollywood movie studio. When that story editor was promoted to vice president at the studio, Jennifer became the new story editor—a job she describes as the bottom rung on the studio executive ladder. (You can read more about Jennifer's career on page 171.)

Like that of the 99 other people in this book, Jennifer's tale is unique. And yet when you read all the stories in the book, you'll see that almost everybody started out doing basic work—in many cases as interns or volunteers—then used those opportunities to make contacts and demonstrate their dedication, enthusiasm, and capabilities. You'll also notice that few of the people had specific training in their field in school; rather, most pursued an education that exposed them to a wide range of topics and taught them where to find information and how to apply it. Finally, you can't help but conclude that great fortunes are not made in these jobs—but with a little experience you can earn a solidly middle-class income. The good news is that with a sound education, determination, and hard work you're virtually assured a livelihood that's challenging and rewarding in many ways.

For those lessons and many others, you and I owe a measure of gratitude to all 100 of these people, who took time out of their schedules to share their insights with us. I repay a bit of my debt with this acknowledgment; we all make good on it when we lend a hand to others getting started in their careers in words.

—Scott A. Meyer

1. Account Executive, Advertising Agency

description: Account executives are the pivot point between the businesses that hire an advertising agency and the creative staff at the agency. Account execs survey the client's needs and communicate them to the copywriters, designers, and other people who devise the advertisements to meet those needs. Account execs contribute ideas to the creation of the ads, help develop public relations strategies with the agency's PR specialists, offer recommendations for placement of the ads, help plan the media mix, and manage each project's budget. Bringing new clients to the agency is also the responsibility of most account execs.

salary: An account coordinator (the entry-level job at midsize to large firms) will start out earning between $18,000 and $22,000 a year. Experienced account executives earn from $26,000 a year and up, depending in most cases on how much business the account exec brings to the agency.

prospects: The rapid expansion of outlets for advertising—cable television, the World Wide Web, direct mail—has heightened the demand for professionals who can help businesses choose and use those outlets to sell their products and services. If you're qualified and hardworking, you'll find work as an account executive in most medium to large cities.

qualifications: An education in marketing, advertising, or business in general will get you an interview at an ad agency, though the talents most critical to doing the job well are the capacity for clear, accurate communications—both written and oral—and people skills.

characteristics: You must be both creative and practical to balance the job of account executive. You also have to function well as the leader of a team and have at least a touch of natural sales ability.

Sue Feringa *is an account executive and producer at an advertising agency in a midsize Midwestern city.*

How did you get the job?

Sue learned the business of the ad agency where she is employed by starting at the bottom, and working her way to the top. She graduated from a small college in the same town with a bachelor's degree in communications arts (and an intensive minor in business), then took a job as the receptionist at the agency. "And in the next 14 years, I climbed the ladder from receptionist to account coordinator, to assistant account executive, to account executive, to account executive and broadcast producer," she says. "I always believed that I had something to learn from every task, no matter how trivial."

Receptionist may not be where everybody has to start, but Sue is convinced that starting near the bottom is useful. "There are so many aspects to an AE's job that I didn't know when I got out of school," she says. "The only way to master the big job is to master the little

ones. You aren't ready to sit behind the big mahogany desk in the leather chair when you get out of school. You've just begun to learn."

What do you do all day?

"About 75 percent of an account executive's job is to get people to work together creatively," Sue says. "I represent the agency to our clients, so I have to get our people to produce exciting ads that will work to show to my client." That means meetings, lots of meetings—with the copywriters and designers, with her agency's public relations department, and with its media planners, who help her determine where to recommend placing the ads. "For some clients, billboards and bus-stop benches are enough exposure to get the response they're interested in," she says. "For others, we produce radio or television commercials."

Sue handles clients with businesses in retail, financial services, pharmaceuticals, higher education, and other industries, even minor league baseball, yet

she approaches each with the same attitude. "I believe, in a sense, that it's my responsibility to represent our client's customers during the creative process," Sue says. "I try to keep everyone focused on what will communicate to the consumers our client wants to reach."

At the same time, Sue is keeping an eye on her client's

> "IN A BIGGER AGENCY I'D BE MUCH MORE LIMITED IN WHAT I'D GET TO DO. I DON'T WANT LESS VARIETY."

bottom line. "I have to answer to my clients for the budgets they give us," she says. "So I'm always considering whether each ad is the most effective use of their money."

Whenever she can, Sue also produces broadcast commercials for her clients and others who

use the agency. "Producing sounds like glamorous work, but it involves 16- to 20-hour days," she says. "I do virtually everything there is to do to make a commercial from the time the copywriter is finished with the script—I order film stock, hire actors, find locations, choose the music, supervise the editing, everything."

Where do you see this job leading you?

Now that Sue has climbed the ladder to the post of account executive, she's enjoying the view. "I like to meet people from all walks of life, and this job keeps bringing them on," she explains. "And I love to see the final product that results from the germ of an idea. We have a great team and I'm happy being a part of it." Sue knows she could go on to a bigger agency in a larger city or she could devote herself simply to producing commercials, but those wouldn't fulfill her anymore than she already is. "I'm lucky because I don't do the same thing every day," she says.

2. Acquisitions Editor, University Press

description: Editors at a university press serve two masters. On one hand, they are part of an academic institution and are bound to seek out and publish books that contribute to our knowledge and understanding and thus enhance the university's reputation. On the other hand, the editors must also find books that have enough commercial appeal to earn back the university's investment in the press. Universities, unlike businesses, can be very secure, stable places to work—they rarely go out of business or are sold. But editors at a university press must be prepared to work within the limits and bureaucracy that are part and parcel of any institution.

salary: Inexperienced editors will start out at about $15,000 a year at a university press (remember, these are often state jobs), while the director can earn $40,000 to $50,000 a year. Of course, discounted—or even free—tuition at the school can compensate for the slightly below average salaries.

prospects: Commercial book publishers are clustered in the country's largest cities, but universities with publishing programs are found in almost every state in the U.S. The staff at a university press is rarely very large (generally two to four editors) and turnover is typically low, but so many universities are publishing books now that opportunities may expand.

qualifications: A postgraduate degree isn't necessary for an editorial job at a university press, but graduate-level coursework in a specialized field can be very helpful. At the least, you'll need a bachelor's degree in liberal arts and sound critical reading skills.

characteristics: If you never wanted to leave school and you enjoy delving deeply into complex subjects, you'll be at home as an editor at a university press. The ability to work well with other people—authors, other editors, faculty members—is also valuable.

Kevin Brock *is an acquisitions editor at a state university press in the South.*

How did you get the job?

Originally Kevin Brock came to pursue a master's degree in history at the university where he now works. But for the past two years he's been a full-time editor at the university's press. He graduated with a bachelor's degree in history from a small liberal arts college, and then worked for two years as the manager of a bookstore that specializes in academic books.

Seeking money for tuition and an opportunity to satisfy a lifelong love of books, Kevin applied for a job as an editor. He was "offered an opportunity to volunteer," he recalls with a laugh, "which I did for three months." When the position of editorial assistant became available, Kevin applied for the job and was hired with full-time pay. Little more than a year later, Kevin was promoted to acquisitions editor.

"I learned so much about how our department works and assumed so many responsibilities as a volunteer. I guess I was at the right place at the right time when the job opened up," Kevin says.

What do you do all day?

The process that brings a scholarly work to print is slightly different from the path for a commercial book. "I read and judge each query or manuscript for both content and writing style," he explains. "If I think it meets our standards and fits our mission—and our editorial board agrees—then I request that the author send a completed manuscript and I'll arrange for two peer readers (experts in the book's particular field of study) who will read and evaluate the work's content for us.

"One negative reading usually kills a book," he goes on, "but with two positive evaluations, we can take the work to our faculty committee, which ultimately decides what we publish."

That process is nearly the sole focus of Kevin's workdays. "I spend a lot of my time identifying appropriate peer readers and writing letters to them about manuscripts they are reading," he says. "I also talk to authors who have manuscripts in progress, copyedit manuscripts, and help keep the interns busy.

"My most consistent duty in any week," Kevin concludes, "is to read query letters and sample chapters from potential authors and evaluate them."

> **"GET TO KNOW SOMEONE ON THE STAFF WHO CAN TELL YOU HOW THE OFFICE WORKS, WHO MAKES THE DECISIONS, AND WHERE THE OPENINGS ARE."**

Where do you see this job leading you?

Kevin Brock had imagined he would become a professor and historian after earning his postgraduate degree, but "I see what the competitiveness of the regular academic life is like," he says, "and that's not for me." Now he sees himself working in university presses and someday becoming the director of a press. "To me, this work seems like an ideal combination—working with academics without being consumed by academia."

3. Administrator for Nonprofit Organizations, Freelance

description: Many nonprofit groups cannot afford full-time staff and yet will never grow with only volunteers handling membership development and communications. The entrepreneur profiled in this entry launched her business to provide professional-caliber services to nonprofits at part-time rates they can afford. She's making a full-time living by performing these functions for several organizations—and by sharing the overhead among them. This work can be managed from a home office and performed within hours convenient to almost any schedule. The long-term success of this enterprise will depend upon attracting many clients in need of these services.

salary: You can charge a 400- to 500-member organization (a small- to medium-size group) up to $20,000 a year, depending on the functions you're hired to fulfill. One full-time person and a part-time assistant can manage four or five organizations' affairs.

prospects: This entrepreneur identified 4,000 nonprofit organizations in the three counties around her home in a medium-size city in the South; the vast majority of them are completely volunteer, she says. Your region will likely have a comparable quantity.

qualifications: Strong writing and editing skills, facility with database management and desktop publishing systems, and event-planning capabilities are the key to doing the job well. Your survival depends on your time management and an ability to sell yourself and your services. Some colleges now offer courses on management of nonprofits; taking them is sure to enhance your appeal to potential clients.

characteristics: To make this kind of operation work, you must be self-motivated, able to shift gears frequently and smoothly, and have the discipline to manage your own business. It helps if you're personable and interested in a lot of different pursuits.

Linda Packard *is the founder and principal of her own business in a midsize Southern city.*

- -

How did you get the job?

Linda has been involved in all sorts of businesses—both for-profit and not-for-profit. "I worked in corporate relations at a local museum," she says. "That's where I learned the fundamentals of successful nonprofit operations.

"But really, all of my experience in business helped me prepare for what I'm doing now," she continues. "I worked for a number of years in real estate and insurance sales; that kind of hard-core business experience is something many nonprofit volunteer groups just do not have."

Linda conceived of her service when she met a local doctor who was launching an association for specialists in his field. "He knew what topics would interest his colleagues and where they could be found," she explains, "but he did not know how to go about reaching them,

nor did he have the time to do it. I gave him a proposal for how I could do it, and he gave me the job."

And so a business was born. Since then, Linda has generated a list of 4,000 nonprofits in the three counties surrounding her home and is researching which among those are good prospects for her to assume their administration. "I'm putting together a presentation for the best prospects," she says. "I think I can handle four or five organizations right now, and if I get more contracts, I can hire a few full-time people and we could handle a lot more."

What do you do all day?

Linda produces an eight-page quarterly newsletter for the organization. "I do everything that needs to be done for the newsletter: I write articles, edit ones written by experts, sell the ads—this newsletter pays for itself with the ads—design the

> "TWO COLLEGES IN MY AREA OFFER CONTINUING EDUCATION COURSES IN NONPROFIT MANAGEMENT— THEY EVEN CERTIFY YOU IF YOU TAKE SEVERAL CLASSES. NO MATTER WHAT YOUR EXPERIENCE, YOU SHOULD GET CERTIFIED IF YOU CAN."
>
> - - - - - - - - - -

pages with my computer's desktop publishing program, and work with the printer on the production of it," she says. "And I maintain the mailing list of members who are to receive it."

Linda also composes direct-mail appeals for new members and funding for the organization, and handles the mass mailings and follow-up. And she plans the group's annual

meeting. "I'm responsible for handling all the details—booking the meeting rooms, coordinating the speakers, everything— for a gathering of 200 to 300 members of the group," she says. "I've hired a part-time assistant to help me with that."

Where do you see this job leading you?

Linda hopes her fledgling business will take off—and believes that it will. "I think we're performing a service that is crucial to the survival of many nonprofits," she says. "And we're making it available to those that need it most—who can't afford to have a staff." Linda has a lot of prospects in her area that she hopes to serve, but she's already thinking about the next step. "I can see taking on groups in any part of the country."

4. Advertising Copywriter

description: Copywriters do more than merely write the words for print or broadcast advertising; they are part of a team that creates entire ad campaigns, producing ideas for themes, images, and sounds as well as words. At an agency, you might be responsible for all of select clients' advertising needs or you may work on specific campaigns for any of the firm's accounts. You may work directly with the client or through your agency's account executives. At times, the deadlines can be very demanding: "Be clever and witty, and make it fast." Even though everybody may know your work—most of us know more than a few advertising slogans—as a writer you will remain anonymous.

salary: The range for entry-level copywriters is vast. At a small agency in a small town, you might start out at just $14,000 a year; at a "hot" agency in a big city, you may earn $35,000 to start. The sharper your learning curve, the more experience you gather, the faster your earnings will rise.

prospects: Almost every business, from the smallest to the largest, and most organizations rely on advertising agencies to help get the message out about their products and services. Advertising copywriters with fresh ideas are in demand all over the country. Competition is fierce for the plum jobs, but opportunities can be had at smaller firms.

qualifications: A portfolio full of attention-grabbing ads you've created is the single best way to convince an agency to hire you. Your training in marketing and advertising helps, but proof that you understand advertising and evidence of your creativity are the keys to landing a job.

characteristics: To succeed in advertising, you must be able to write persuasively but subtly. A sense of humor—both to alleviate the stress and to apply to your work—will help you enjoy the job. Good people skills help make you a better team player and ultimately a better creative person.

Jason Little *is a copywriter at a large advertising agency in a big Midwestern city.*

How did you get the job?

Jason didn't wait for a job to come to him, he went in search of an opportunity. "The summer between my junior and senior years, two friends and I made appointments with creative people at several ad agencies in Chicago, including the one where I now work," says the University of Texas advertising major. "We took the portfolios we had produced at school to ask them to critique, which they were very generous about doing." The following semester, a representative of his current employer—a person he already had met—came to his school to participate in a forum in which professionals judge students' work. "The previous year he had hated my work, but the second time he liked it," Jason reveals. "And he told me before he left the second time that the agency would offer me a job when I graduated. After consideration of other offers, I took it."

From his current perspective, Jason sees what separates the people who get the opportunities at the major agencies from those who don't. "Make your portfolio personal so that it shows your interests, your own sense of style and imagination," he says. "When you have a book that you're confident in, do whatever you can to avoid the gatekeepers—the human resources people—and go right to the decision makers with your portfolio.

"And remember, once you get an interview, that advertising is selling," he adds. "If you can't sell yourself effectively, how can you sell a product?"

What do you do all day?

When he arrives in the morning, Jason gets into his creative mind-set by changing from his work boots to his river sandals. Then Jason and the art director he's teamed with work on the three accounts he was assigned when he started last year: Dewar's Scotch, True Value hardware stores, and Rockport shoes. Together, Jason and the art director develop advertising campaigns for those clients based on outlines of the client's needs supplied to them by the agency's creative directors. "On any given day, I might be writing a script for a television commercial and copy for billboards, auditioning voice talent for a radio ad, and editing the words for a print ad," Jason says. "The best time is when we're competing with other creative teams to come up with the best ideas for a campaign. That's incredibly exciting."

For the most important clients, Jason travels with the agency's account executive to present his team's ideas to the client. "By the time we've finished our process of deciding what's best, we have a good idea of what the client will like and not like," Jason explains. "But there are always changes that the client wants. Our job is to satisfy the client and create ads that will work."

> "ASK ANYONE IN THE BUSINESS TO CRITIQUE YOUR BOOK, AND TAKE THEIR OPINIONS TO HEART. THEY'RE THE BEST WAY TO FIND OUT WHAT YOU'RE DOING RIGHT AND WRONG."

Where do you see this job leading you?

Jason Little has his eye on San Diego or someplace equally endowed with great climate and landscape. "I want to work someplace I love and open my own advertising boutique that does really interesting ads for interesting products and services," he says. "Then I'd like to go back to a great advertising program like the one at the University of Texas and teach." But give him time. "I'm just getting my career going. It'll be a while before I know enough to feel comfortable leaving here."

5. Advertising Media Buyer

description: Companies can choose from more media outlets than ever before—from billboards and bus-stop benches to the Internet's World Wide Web—to advertise their product or service. So companies must rely on media buyers at advertising agencies to help them sort through the media and select the most effective outlet for their message. Media buyers work with the agency's account executives in advising clients, and they interact with the salespeople from newspapers, magazines, radio and television stations, etc. Unlike account executives, media buyers spend most of their time in the office, though they do occasionally go out to meet with clients.

salary: Media buyer can be an entry-level job at an advertising agency. It typically pays $20,000 to $25,000 a year—a little less at small agencies, a little more at large agencies in big cities.

prospects: Virtually every advertising agency of more than a couple of people has media buyers on staff. And because it's an entry-level job, experienced buyers move on to higher-level positions, creating opportunities for new people to get positions as media buyers.

qualifications: Begin with a basic understanding of the various media and an ability to write and speak clearly to a business audience, then add comfort in working with numbers and a familiarity with computers—particularly spreadsheet programs—and you have the fundamental requirements for a media buyer. Top that with classes or experience in business, advertising, and accounting and you'll be a great candidate for a media buyer position.

characteristics: If you enjoy both working alone and being part of a team, collaborating and negotiating, looking at the big picture and managing the details, the job of media buyer will suit you well.

Jim Mathis *is the media director of an advertising agency in a small city in the Midwest.*

- -

How did you get the job?

For many people who don't have experience at an advertising agency, media buyer is the starting point. But that wasn't Jim's path. "I came to this work sort of backwards," he says. "Most people start in the media department and then move on to be an account executive. But I was an account executive first and then went into my position as media director."

Jim's experience working directly with clients helped him gain a perspective on advertisers' needs and the challenges faced by the account executives who help them plan and design their advertising. This awareness is integral to his success as a media buyer, Jim says, but he stresses that there are lots of other avenues for developing a macroview of the business.

"Many media buyers come from other jobs in the media," he explains. "You'll find people with backgrounds in public

"YOU DON'T HAVE TO BE AS MUCH OF A 'PEOPLE PERSON' TO DO THIS JOB AS YOU DO TO BE AN ACCOUNT EXECUTIVE, BUT INTERPERSONAL COMMUNICATIONS SKILLS WILL MAKE YOU A BETTER NEGOTIATOR AS A MEDIA BUYER."

- - - - - - - - - -

relations, journalism, and mass communications. And I think that anyone who has worked selling airtime at a television or radio station will be well prepared to be a media buyer."

What do you do all day?

Jim says that about half his time is spent working alone at a computer and the other half is devoted to meeting with people or talking on the telephone. At the computer, he's working out the recommendations he will bring to those meetings.

"We use standard spreadsheet programs and some specialized media-planning software to create models that help us figure out what will be the most cost-effective way for the advertiser to get its message to the targeted audience," Jim says. "You don't have to be an expert number cruncher to do this—the computer does the crunching and you evaluate the answers."

When Jim and his staff of media buyers reach some strong conclusions for a particular client, they will pass along their findings to the account executive responsible to that client or they will meet with both the client and the account executive. "Each client chooses how much he or she will be involved in the process—some just want to leave it to the agency to han-

dle," Jim says, "but we prefer to talk through our ideas with the client directly and be sure we're all in agreement on how to proceed."

Once the client signs off on the plan, the media buyers begin the negotiations. "Print advertising is relatively easy, because the rates are set for each publication," Jim says. "Broadcast advertising is complicated by the fact that every program on each station has a different rate. But it's in the negotiation of the rates that a good media buyer can provide an invaluable service to the client."

Where do you see this job leading you?

For Jim—who's been both an account executive and a media director—the path is leading to management of an advertising agency. More often, however, media buyers become account executives or they become sales representatives for the media. "All of these jobs help prepare you to do the others," Jim says. "That's why there's a lot of movement back and forth."

6. Advertising Sales Representative, Staff

description: Most newspapers and magazines help pay for the information and entertainment they provide to their audiences with advertising purchased by companies that believe those readers will buy their product or service. That advertising space is marketed by ad salespeople on staff or by independent agencies. The difference is that agencies may represent an array of publications, while staff people sell for just one or maybe a small group of periodicals. Ad salespeople prospect for potential customers, make presentations to them, and in many cases ensure that they produce ads that suit the medium. The ad salespeople tend to focus their efforts on territories: either categories of advertisers or geographical ones. Ad salespeople are usually paid commissions directly correlated to how much advertising space they sell. And they generally travel a lot.

salary: As a new salesperson, you'll get a salary of about $20,000 to $25,000 until you start selling enough to earn commissions which equal that. Then the sky's virtually the limit: the more you sell, the more you earn.

prospects: In a world where new publications are launched almost weekly, you nearly can't fail to find an opportunity to try selling print advertising. And you can do it in almost every corner of the continent.

qualifications: Sales training courses can certainly be helpful in preparing for this work, but persuasive speaking skills, experience selling almost anything, and a basic understanding of the publication's marketplace will land you a job in advertising sales.

characteristics: You must be resourceful and persistent, amiable, and enthusiastic to succeed as an advertising salesperson.

Trish Gapik *is an advertising account executive for a magazine publisher on the West Coast.*

How did you get the job?

Trish was trained as a respiratory therapist and she ran an outpatient rehabilitation department at a hospital for 17 years. "Then I got a job offer from a medical equipment company we dealt with and I decided I was ready to try something else," Trish recalls. "That company went out of business in a year. But I was soon hired by a pharmaceutical company, for whom I was selling for 11 years.

"This pharmaceutical company had great ongoing sales training for its staff and I liked the work, but I was offered a very enticing early retirement, which I took," she continues.

Trish used her newfound free time to pursue her interest in scuba diving. While doing that she met the owner of a publishing company—and he offered her a job selling advertising. "I think the magazines he publishes are great," she says, "and I wanted to be involved with them if I could. So I took the job."

What do you do all day?

Trish tries to find advertisers for the two magazines her company publishes. She looks for prospects in competing magazines, in trade journals and directories, and by networking with people in her industry. That networking consumes a lot of Trish's days—she writes letters, talks on the phone, and meets people face-to-face to ensure that she'll always have a steady supply of potential advertisers on which to call. "You have to spend some time thinking about who your readers are and who wants to reach them, too," she says. "Not every prospect is an obvious choice."

Once Trish has found a sound prospect, she tries to arrange a face-to-face meeting so that she can give a presentation to the people who will be deciding whether or not to advertise. "We present our media kit to the advertiser or the advertising agency they've hired," Trish says. "The kit includes information and demographics about our readers and insight into the dynamics of our industry."

Trish follows up her presentations with telephone calls and letters, hoping the advertiser will commit to an "insertion order," or an agreement to purchase advertising. "I like to develop a rapport with people I'm selling to," she says. "I've never been a hard-sell person—

> ### "IT HELPS BOTH PROFESSIONALLY AND PERSONALLY TO IMPROVE YOUR SALES SKILLS."

I like to talk to people and find out if what I'm selling will help them and their business.

"That's why it helps to care about the product you're selling. You don't want to sell something that you wouldn't want yourself."

Trish sells space for her company's two bimonthly magazines, which means that "we have deadlines almost every week," she says.

Where do you see this job leading you?

"I could keep on working here and making a very nice living," Trish says, "but I might want to work for a larger company, maybe one of our advertisers, and sell its products."

7. Advertorial Director

description: An "advertorial" is an infomercial in print: information (articles, listings, etc.) is provided to the readers that is related to—though not necessarily about—advertisers' products and services. Advertorial directors serve as publishers and editors for these special sections in magazines: they devise themes, assign writers, select designs, coordinate advertising sales, manage production, and solve problems throughout the process.

Some magazines include advertorial sections in every issue—a few, more than one per issue—which sets a nearly feverish deadline schedule. This is not the most glamorous job at a magazine, but it usually pays better than strict editorial work.

salary: An assistant advertorial coordinator—an entry-level job—earns around $25,000 a year; the director can earn up to $40,000 or $50,000 if the sections are consistently profitable.

prospects: More and more magazines are including advertorial sections in their pages, but the full-time staff for these projects is rarely more than a couple of people. Still, with determination and desirable credentials, you can find a job.

qualifications: You must understand and have skills in both the creative and business sides of a magazine, be well organized, and be able to generate ideas that will sell advertising space.

characteristics: This is a management job that requires someone who is persistent, willing to do whatever it takes to get the work done, and able to produce under constant pressure.

Marilyn Plummer *is the special advertising section coordinator for a regional magazine in the Southwest.*

How did you get the job?

Marilyn studied to be a teacher, specializing in English and drama—and worked as a teacher's aide for a year after earning her certification. "But I knew almost right away that I didn't like teaching," she says. "And when I saw a new magazine had started here, I wanted to be a part of it."

She signed on as a secretary just to get on board, then moved to more fulfilling positions, including classified advertising sales representative and promotions manager. "The more points of view you've had from within the magazine, the better prepared you'll be for putting together the special advertising sections," Marilyn says. "It touches on every aspect of producing a magazine—it's sort of like a magazine within the magazine."

When the magazine's publisher decided to launch these special sections to attract adver-

> "WORKING ON ADVERTORIAL SECTIONS IS A GOOD WAY TO FIND OUT WHAT ASPECTS OF MAGAZINE PUBLISHING YOU LIKE AND ARE GOOD AT."

tisers that had not been enticed into the regular editorial pages, he banked on Marilyn's 10 years of experience with the magazine to see them through.

"You have to be detail-oriented, remain calm in all sorts of circumstances, and be persistent but tactful in getting people to meet your deadlines," she says. "I guess he saw that I could do those things or would learn how."

What do you do all day?

Marilyn produces 15 to 20 special sections for the magazine each year, so she's in a constant state of conceiving, preparing,

and executing them. "At any one time I'm finalizing one section before it goes to the printer, assigning and editing stories for the next one, and talking about ideas for the one after that," she says.

And every facet of each section comes under Marilyn's scrutiny. Editorially, she assigns articles to freelance writers (publishing industry guidelines prohibit the magazine's staff writers from contributing to advertorial sections), reviews layouts with designers, collects photographs, coordinates the editing with freelance copy editors, oversees fact-checking, and proofreads. On the business side, Marilyn helps in-house staff develop sales brochures to send to potential advertisers, maintains regular contact with the sales staff to keep up on how many ads will be in the section, and determines where the ads will go in the section. Most of all, she manages the sections' budgets.

"I now have a formula for making a realistic budget for each section," she explains. "The formula's based on my experience, how the section may have done in the past, and our rate card—the amount we charge for advertising.

"Before we even get started, we try to get an accurate guess as to how much money a section will make," she adds. "We go back to the themes that have worked in the past and dump those that didn't. We're also always looking for new ideas."

Where do you see this job leading you?

Marilyn can see a couple of logical next steps: advertising sales or marketing. "If I wanted a job that's fast-paced and exciting, I'd go into sales—but I know that's not for me," she says. "Marketing director may be more up my alley, but I really enjoy the variety in my job. I'd be content to keep getting better at it."

8. Annual Report Editor

description: Perhaps the most important statement a company makes each year is its annual report, which presents not only its financial results of the preceding year but also its image and themes for the upcoming months. The responsibility for conceiving, organizing, writing, editing, developing the graphic ideas, and cracking the whip on the many contributors to the annual report so that it meets its deadline typically belongs to one highly valued member of the corporate communications staff. That person may fulfill other functions at certain times of the year, but the preponderance of the person's time—and all of it for nearly six months—is spent on the annual report.

salary: Entry-level corporate communications staffers start at about $25,000—often with experience in newspaper or trade journalism—but by the time they earn responsibility for the annual report, the salary range is closer to $40,000 or more, depending on the size and profitability of the company.

prospects: Almost all large corporations now have in-house communications departments and all publicly held ones (those that sell stocks) must, by law, produce an annual report. Not everybody on the communications staff, however, will get the chance to edit the annual report.

qualifications: The ability to write clearly in the language and style of business is the primary requirement for a corporate communications job. Knowledge of financial reporting helps, though expertise is not necessary. Experience with the company is almost always a prerequisite for earning the responsibility for the annual report.

characteristics: Strong organization skills are essential for managing a project of this scope and importance. Diplomacy is your ally in pressing people outside the communications staff to meet their deadlines. And your copy will inevitably be edited by the corporation's chief executive officer and possibly by operations managers, too; a thick skin will shield your feelings when people who are not professional writers put their touch to your work.

Christopher Taylor *is the director of communications services and has been the production manager for his corporation's annual report.*

How did you get the job?

Chris Taylor held jobs in book publishing and then in his company's internal communications department before getting the responsibility for the annual report. "I don't know that my path to this job was typical," he confesses. "But then again, I don't know that any path is typical."

Chris does insist that "communications skills are of first and foremost importance" for this work, but that "a general alertness to business" is increasingly critical. "That's especially true of the annual report, which is directed at the investment community."

What do you do all day?

Each autumn, the annual report begins as a proposal for themes, basic structure, and design concepts in the corporate communications department. Once these are approved by the CEO, the massive coordination job begins. "While the editor is writing the letter to the shareholders and the feature material we've decided to include, he's asking the financial reporting department to finalize its statements and working with the designer that's been hired to do the layout and production," Chris explains. "It comes together as a series of parallel efforts." Once all the elements are in place, the CEO again approves the rough layout before it is finished and sent to the printer.

> **"YOU NEED TO BE ABLE TO ARTICULATE YOUR IDEAS WELL TO PEOPLE HIGHER UP THE CHAIN OF COMMAND."**

Unlike many other publications, the deadline for an annual report is immutable. "The Securities and Exchange Commission requires that shareholders receive a company's annual report no more than three months after its fiscal year-end," Chris explains. "Our policy is to have it in the shareholders' hands six weeks before the annual meeting, which is well before the SEC deadline."

Where do you see this job leading you?

Like a good company man, Chris had no answer but to laugh when asked this question.

25

9. Audio Book Abridger

description: To read an average work of fiction or nonfiction aloud for a book-on-tape recording can take 10 or more hours—far longer than most people will listen and costing much more than audio book publishers can afford to produce. So many audio book publishers rely on abridgers, who distill written books into manuscripts that can be read in three to four hours. Abridgers edit the books, excising characters, plot lines, descriptions, and any other elements that can be removed from the text while maintaining the book's essential story, themes, and style. Abridgers are typically hired on a freelance basis and work in their own homes.

salary: Publishers generally pay abridgers by the job rather than by the hour. Fees range from as low as $250 up to $2,000; the average is about $1,000. Bigger publishers tend to pay more, smaller firms (where it's easier to get a start) pay less.

prospects: Audio book publishing is a booming business, so the demand for abridgers is high. So long as the market for audio books—driven in large part by car commuters—remains strong, abridgers will be needed.

qualifications: Experience in abridging is the most important preparation for landing a job as an abridger. How do you overcome this catch-22? Find a small audio book publishing company or an independent audio book producer, emphasize your editing skills and love of books, and beg for an opportunity to try your hand. You must, by the way, also be capable with word-processing software: in almost every case, an abridger must submit the abridged manuscript on computer disk.

characteristics: Abridging is slow, painstaking, meticulous reading and re-reading done by an individual working alone. If that sounds appealing, you'll enjoy working as an abridger.

Beth Baxter *is the owner of a midsize audio book publisher in the Midwest.*

How did you get the job?

Beth got started abridging audio books the hard way: she started her own publishing business. "I had absolutely no experience in publishing—before doing this I ran a windsurfing and sailing-skills school," she admits. "But I've always believed I could do whatever I wanted to do.

"I got into audio book publishing when I got into listening to them," she continues, "and found that there were lots of titles—especially classics—that I wanted to hear but that weren't available."

In the beginning, Beth abridged the books herself as well as performing—along with her husband/partner—nearly every other function necessary for publishing them. Nowadays, Beth hires abridgers and manages the process rather than doing the editing herself.

"Of course, I like to hire people who have experience, because I think you have to do two books before you get the hang of this work," Beth says.

"But I do give people a trial who have never done it before. I look for people who have experience editing in general, who are attentive to detail, and who love to read.

"We produce our books ourselves, but many of the larger publishers are now using producers who hire the abridgers, book studio time, contract the voice talent and engineers, and manage the recording process," she says. "If you're looking for work as an abridger, you might want to call the major publishing companies and ask them which audio book producers they're using, then call the producers about getting an assignment."

What do you do all day?

Of course, an abridger begins with the text. "Each abridger works a little differently," Beth explains. "When I was doing it myself, I carried around a paperback edition of the book I was working on wherever I went and marked it up with a pencil.

"An abridger we use now likes to work on photocopied pages, another has a computer scanner, so she scans the pages in and then edits on-screen," she continues. "However you work, eventually a finished draft has to be typed onto a computer disk."

Beth says that abridging an average novel takes no less than 40 hours of work. "I've tried every shortcut imaginable, and 40 hours is the absolute minimum."

When cutting what amounts to 60 percent or more of a novel, the abridger must find anything in the text that is not absolutely central to the narrative and remove it, but without leaving gaps in the story's continuity that will leave the reader hanging. "Mysteries are the hardest, because you can't take out clues," says Beth. "Some publishers make it even harder on abridgers by forbidding them from changing or adding words—they may only remove them.

"The toughest part of the work is maintaining the style and rhythm of the author's writing," she adds. "But the best part of this work is that you really know the books you've worked on. I abridged Edgar Rice Burroughs' *Tarzan*, for

instance, and I doubt that there's anyone alive who knows that book, inside and out, as well as I do."

Where do you see this job leading you?

Beth plans to continue to publish more audio books from a broader range of titles. Her abridgers can count on more work. "Right now, there's far more demand for abridgers than there are people who can do the job."

10. Book Buyer

description: About 50,000 new books are published each year, while an inexhaustible list of old ones remain in print. Buyers are the people who decide which of those should have space on the shelves at bookstores—and ultimately which will have the chance to find a reading audience. In larger stores, the buyers may specialize in particular types of books; in smaller ones, they are more likely buying for every department.

Book buyers work to get the best discount with distributors and publisher's representatives, participate in marketing decisions, and often travel to trade shows.

salary: Book buying is not entry-level work, but clerks who work their way up to buyer earn $6 to $7 an hour in smaller stores, $20,000 to $30,000 yearly in larger ones.

prospects: Large franchise or chain stores are displacing many smaller, privately owned bookstores. Many buyers are now based out of corporate headquarters in New York or Ann Arbor, where they make purchases for hundreds of their outlets. However, most small proprietors select titles themselves, and most mass merchandisers (Kmart, Wal-Mart, etc.) stock books now, too, and employ buyers to choose what to offer their customers.

qualifications: Experience in retail in general and bookstores in particular is the only qualification necessary to get a job as a book buyer. Most people work their way up from clerk to book buyer. Technical expertise in fields like computers, medicine, and science can be valuable in finding a position, especially at specialty stores.

characteristics: You have to love books, but have a calculating approach to selecting them and a broad knowledge of a lot of subjects, to succeed as a book buyer. Strong negotiating skills will help.

Ron Liggett *is the head buyer for a bookstore in a college town in the Rockies.*

How did you get the job?

Ron owned a small bookstore on the West Coast before moving for personal reasons to the mountain state where he now lives. "I sold my small bookstore because it just could not compete with the chain stores in the area," he says. "Then I decided to move to someplace where I really wanted to live."

"When you have your own business, you work day and night," he continues. "And I wanted to get away from that." But Ron couldn't get away from the book business. He loved bookselling enough to come to apply for a job at the large, independently owned bookstore in his new hometown. His experience as an owner won him the job there.

"The buyer must always consider books based on, bottom line, how well they will sell," he says. "That's something many people new to bookstores don't yet see; as an owner, I learned that lesson well."

> "MOST PEOPLE START AS CLERKS AND WORK THEIR WAY UP TO BOOK BUYER. BUT IF YOU WORK FOR A SHORT TIME AS A SALES REP FOR A PUBLISHER, YOU CAN MAKE THE SWITCH FAIRLY EASILY."

What do you do all day?

"Most of my year is spent sitting across the desk from publishers' representatives, considering new titles, discussing the publisher's backlist, and listening to information and ideas that will help us market the books," Ron says. "Some buyers just take what the reps recommend or buy according to some formula that budgets a certain amount for each type of book, but I do it more by the seat of my pants—I'll take what my experience, knowledge, and instinct tell me will sell to our customers.

"A bookstore, in my opinion, is a compilation of niche markets," he continues. "The buyer must recognize and select books for each of them." Some buyers are required to spend time on the store's retail floor to learn about the customers, but Ron is not. He does keep track of purchasing patterns, inventory, returns, and other data that help him make decisions. He also goes to national and regional trade shows to learn about upcoming releases.

"One of the tricky parts of the job is that ordering must be done seasonally. I'm choosing books for Christmas in June," Ron says. "So you have to be able to anticipate trends and readers' interests well in advance."

While processing all that information and making decisions, Ron has to keep his focus firmly on the ledger. "We try to keep a balance between ordering books from wholesalers—who can get you books very quickly—and directly from publishers, which is less expensive, but takes a fairly long time."

Where do you see this job leading you?

Ron very deliberately chose the place where he is. "I'm at an independent store, I make the decisions I like to make, and I'm living where I want to be," he says. "I'm quite happy right where I am." He says, however, that lots of other buyers become publisher's reps or take other jobs in the book business, perhaps as editors or marketers. "People who work in books tend to love books and to stay in books as much as possible."

11. Book Marketer

description: Salespeople sell books, but marketing specialists guide them in deciding to whom and how to sell them. The publisher's marketing department researches sources of potential customers, develops strategies for reaching them, and creates the advertising and promotional materials that are used in implementing those strategies. Marketing people combine practical business ideas with creative tactics to help the sales department do its job. Because the work is relatively unquantifiable, the marketing department tends to enjoy little glory (or fortune) and suffer little blame for the success of sales efforts. Is that a positive or a negative? Your call.

salary: Entry-level marketing coordinators in book publishing do slightly better than their counterparts in editorial: about $25,000 to start at a modest-size publisher. Marketing directors make $50,000, $60,000, or even more.

prospects: The venues for seeking out customers are ever more complex, so book publishers must rely on marketing departments to keep the sales staff furnished with a healthy supply of leads. That puts people with the uncommon combination of business sense and creative ideas in demand.

qualifications: You don't need a degree in marketing, advertising, or business to work in marketing, but it will help you get an interview. You do need the ability to communicate clearly both in writing and orally, people skills, and the know-how to run spreadsheet, word-processing, and desktop design software, too.

characteristics: People who advance in marketing are well organized, practical, creative, enthusiastic, and supportive of their colleagues' efforts.

Drew Chapman *is a marketing coordinator at a reference book publisher in New York City.*

How did you get the job?

Do you want the long story or the short one? In short, Drew answered an ad for his current job. He spoke well in the interview; he pointed out that he knew how to use Excel, Word-Perfect, and PageMaker. He emphasized the practical knowledge he gained from a job as a proofreader for a religious publisher and the insights he gleaned at a summer publishing program. And he noted the organizational skills he had developed as a practicing attorney. Which brings us to the long story.

"When I was in college, I wrote well and argued well, so my professors and some of my friends encouraged me to go into the law," Drew explains. "I went to law school and passed the bar in 1991. But once I started practicing I realized that I didn't like being the bully, I didn't want to be a bad guy all the time. So I quit."

That, of course, set Drew to thinking about what he did like doing. "I liked being around books and I liked working on something that mattered to people," he says. He made a few cold calls to small publishing companies in and around the midsize city he was living in, asking if they needed help. A religious publisher hired him as a freelance proofreader. This whetted his appetite for the book business, so, on the advice of a few colleagues, he enrolled in a summer course in publishing at Rice University. "I learned about options for working in the business that I had never considered," Drew says. "It gave me the idea that I might enjoy marketing as much as I thought I'd like the editorial side of the business." After completing the course, he picked up and moved to New York City. "I decided that my chances of getting a job in publishing were best in New York." And just two weeks after arriving, he answered that ad.

What do you do all day?

Drew's job shifts from preparing financial reports one day to designing ads for magazines the next to providing facts and figures to the telephone sales-people the day after that. "We produce reference books for very specific uses," he says. "So I think the most crucial part of our job is to develop ideas for prospects. These are big and expensive dictionaries usually bought by companies in the

> "SUMMER PUBLISHING PROGRAMS HELP YOU TO MAKE CONTACTS. THE LECTURERS ARE NOT NECESSARILY GOING TO GIVE YOU A JOB, BUT THEY'LL ALMOST ALL PUT YOU IN TOUCH WITH PEOPLE WHO MIGHT HIRE YOU."

field. Our job is to figure out what's the most effective way of reaching them—direct-mail solicitation, trade magazine advertisements, etc.—and then to design the direct mail package or the ad."

Though Drew is an assistant, he is involved with nearly every aspect of his department's func-tioning. "Of course, there's some drudge work to be done, but that's true of any entry-level job," he says. "I also get to design ads, contribute my ideas to the strategy sessions, and my boss lets me manage my assignments in my own way. That's worth a lot to me."

Where do you see this job leading you?

When Drew took the job, he thought of it as a way to get his foot in the door of a publishing company, all the while keeping his eye on editorial. Now he's not so sure. "It's too early to tell where I'm going," he says after a year with his current employer. "I still think this is a good way to prove to an editor that I'm committed to and understand the publishing business. But I wouldn't rule out staying in marketing at this point and working my way up to manager of my own line."

12. Book Packager

description: A book packager isn't exactly a publisher, though it's close. Book packagers perform some of the functions of editors, marketers, production managers, and agents, but are not just any of those either. The editors at book packaging companies develop ideas for books, write proposals for the marketing people at the company to sell to publishers, find and assign writers to do the books, edit the manuscripts, and often contract printers and other vendors to produce finished books. Editors at book packagers must coax writers to meet deadlines set by the publishers, and must complete their own work on time and to the satisfaction of editors at publishing companies.

salary: Entry-level editors for book packagers start out earning about what comparable editors at other publishing companies do: between $20,000 and $25,000 a year. Editors who are not involved in marketing peak at $40,000 to $60,000—maybe more in the media capitals.

prospects: Book packaging is a relatively recent wrinkle on the publishing business, so no one can say for certain what its long-term place in the industry is. However, as book publishing's risks and demands continue to escalate, it does seem likely that publishing companies will increase their reliance on packagers to take on projects publishers are not staffed or experienced in managing.

qualifications: Start with sharp writing and editing skills, toss in marketing sense, and top with a flourish for developing and sustaining relationships with writers and editors, and you have the recipe for a book packaging editor.

characteristics: If you can manage multiple projects at one time, paying attention to the details along the way, can learn new tasks quickly, and have broad-based knowledge, you'll be well suited to this kind of work. And it helps to have a sense of what's of interest to editors and readers.

Jason Sutherland *is an editor at a book packager in Seattle.*

How did you get the job?

Jason says he "strolled" into his job by answering a newspaper ad and interviewing well. Along with his thin veneer of savoir faire, he brought a journalism degree and experience as an editor of medical reference books and as a writer for a Seattle music newspaper. "The tech book publisher is where I learned how to smoke cigars and bark orders at the underlings, as well as to see large book projects through from start to finish," Jason says. "At the newspaper I learned how to work hard for little pay, and to produce quickly."

Jason believes those experiences and skills—and his obvious irreverence—are nearly ideal preparation for working as an editor in book packaging. "You have to be able to write well and quickly," he explains. "But the big job is guiding books through every phase of their creation and production."

What do you do all day?

When Jason is in an industrious mode, he arrives at his office at around 8 a.m. (fueled, of course, by a certain hot, dark brown, caffeinated beverage) and checks in on each of the more than a dozen books he's overseeing to determine where they are in their development from "embryonic state to post-collegiate child."

"At any time, on any given day," Jason says, "I am developing book ideas for our weekly staff meetings, writing two- to ten-page proposals, searching for authors to write the books, calling authors to be sure they're on schedule to meet their deadlines, editing the manuscripts, proofing book galleys, working with our art department on fitting copy to layouts, and answering the questions of editors at book publishers."

> "IF YOU WANT TO BE INVOLVED WITH BIG-CITY PUBLISHING COMPANIES BUT DON'T WANT TO LIVE THERE, BOOK PACKAGING IS IDEAL. WE WORK CLOSELY WITH MANY MAJOR NEW YORK PUBLISHING HOUSES, YET OUR COMPANY IS ON THE OTHER COAST."

That seems like a full roster of responsibilities, with or without coffee, but the nature of book packaging requires even more. "We take on the projects that traditional publishers are afraid of because they involve industries they are not familiar with," Jason says. "We did a book about beer brewing, for instance, and I had to arrange to get the components—the various tubes and ingredients—that were to be included with the book."

Jason went one further with a book about pitching baseballs for kids. He wrote the book, edited it, quarreled with the art department, and dealt with the company that provided the plastic ball that came with each book. "My daily tasks are quite varied," he deadpans.

Where do you see this job leading you?

Jason is typically blunt about his plans. "I plan to stay here and learn everything I can about the book packaging business. There's tremendous potential for growth, as publishers are seeming to use more outside help," he explains. "This job is an excellent way for me to establish contacts with writers, illustrators, editors, and publishers. I'm happy where I am."

13. Book Reviewer

description: Before you spend your hard-earned money on a new book, you want to know if it's worth reading. You can rely on the opinions of friends and neighbors, you can read the best-sellers list to see what's popular, or you can read a review in a newspaper or magazine. Book reviewers, quite simply, read and write about new books of all kinds. Those on staff at a publication are often responsible for book review sections, choosing the books to be reviewed, assigning the work to freelance writers, and editing the reviews as well as writing reviews themselves.

salary: Staff book reviewers earn salaries equivalent to other staff reporters and editors—usually $20,000 to $25,000 a year to start. Freelance critics usually are paid anywhere from $50 to $200 per review, and more if they are well-known writers reviewing books for national magazines.

prospects: Almost every major newspaper has a book section, but the full-time staff is rarely more than a person or two. Likewise, few magazines have more than one reviewer on staff; many rely entirely on freelancers. But lots of publications need freelance reviewers, especially those with specialized knowledge—such as expertise in children's literature, mystery novels, or science fiction.

qualifications: All you need is insight into books—an understanding of what makes those that are strong succeed and those that are weak fail—and the ability to explain that in clear, compelling language. Taking advanced courses in literature in college is probably the best preparation.

characteristics: Love reading books and discussing them? Then you'll enjoy reviewing them. If you can read at a pace that meets deadlines, then you'll be comfortable in this job. Few people, however, support themselves solely by freelance reviewing.

Anne Watts Morris *is the book editor at a daily newspaper in the Southwest.*

How did you get the job?

Anne, who has a bachelor's and master's degree in English and a master's in journalism, began reviewing plays and books while working as a copy editor at a newspaper that hired her after graduation. "The features editor needed someone to do reviews and I volunteered," she says. Anne continued to review books for the paper after she stopped working full-time when she got married, and when she returned to the workforce as an English teacher she kept up her reviewing.

When she moved to her current hometown, she contacted the features editor of the local newspaper and solicited freelance book review assignments. "Then I proposed a series of articles based on interviews with local authors, which the editor liked," Anne says. "When the editors decided to expand the paper's book coverage, they asked me if I would take on responsibility for the section full-time and I agreed."

What do you do all day?

Thousands of new books are published every year in a vast array of genres, so Anne must devote time each week to evaluating their merits and their potential appeal to her readers. "It's a job just determining which books are even worth reviewing," she says. "We try to cover a variety of books, but we have only limited space to fill—the section comes out every Sunday. Each section has two main reviews and three or four smaller ones."

Once she's decided which books deserve reviewing, Anne contacts prominent local authors to review certain books, assigns others to writers with interest or expertise in the book's field, and reviews some herself. "I review books that interest me and I try to assign reviews to people who have a perspective on the book," she explains. "For example, our best mystery reviewer is a housewife who reads them voraciously. And we run children's book reviews written by local kids."

In addition to editing all the reviews, Anne also interviews authors for profiles and she writes a regular column that reports book news and tells about events like book signings or readings. She also attends trade shows a couple of times a year to learn about what's coming up.

"I feel like most of my time in the office is spent managing the process—calling reviewers on the phone, making sure that they have what they need, that they meet the deadlines, and taking care of the details of putting the section together each week," she says. "I don't really have the time to sit around and read books. That I do at home."

Where do you see this job leading you?

"I haven't been cured" is Anne's simple answer to this question. She has written reviews on a freelance basis for a magazine and she'd like to do more of that, but most likely she'll keep doing what she's been doing at the newspaper.

> **"FOLLOW YOUR INTEREST. I NEVER REALLY WANTED TO BE A GENERAL ASSIGNMENT REPORTER, SO I TRIED TO GET INVOLVED IN WHAT DID INTEREST ME WHEN THE OPPORTUNITY AROSE. IF YOU HAVE AN INTEREST, PURSUE IT."**

14. Cartoonist

description: Good comic strips are funny observations about people and events conveyed by simple drawings and a few choice words. While the cartoonists who create the comics vary greatly in their artistic abilities—from the crudest to the best trained— all of them search continuously for relevant topics, and they must write succinctly and poignantly. Some cartoonists produce panels about specific news issues— these are known as "editorial cartoons" and are found in both newspapers and magazines. Other cartoonists create comic strips that regularly appear in newspaper feature pages. Cartoonists can be part of a newspaper's staff, but more commonly they're freelancers whose work appears in many papers.

salary: A staff cartoonist will be paid along the same scale as a reporter: about $20,000 a year to start. Freelancers earn based on the number of papers (or magazines) that buy the comic: the greater the publication's circulation, the more it must pay to run the comic.

prospects: This is a competitive field to break into. There are already so many established popular comic strips and many people are attracted to the glamour of the job. But the syndicates that sell comics to most major newspapers are always looking for new material—if you believe in your sense of humor and talent, submit your work, because it will be seriously considered and you can get a break.

qualifications: There's no training or preparation for this kind of work. You need nothing more than the ideas to create funny comics and enough ideas to keep producing them, and the ability to say a lot with a few words or pictures. You need very basic drawing skills and the capacity to think and convey ideas visually.

characteristics: Successful cartoonists need faith in their point of view and the self-confidence to keep sharing it with others. Oh yes, and a sense of humor, too.

Jimmy Johnson *is the creator of a comic strip that appears seven days a week in more than 200 newspapers across the United States.*

How did you get the job?

Jimmy Johnson has newspaper ink on his hands. Maybe not literally, but Jimmy's worked at newspapers steadily since he earned a bachelor's degree in journalism. "I found out early that I had an aptitude for expressing myself well," he says, "and I couldn't do math worth a shoot."

At weekly and daily papers, Jimmy served as a general assignment reporter—covering crime, politics, business, whatever—and as a sports and feature writer. "I've read that Hemingway said, 'Newspapers are boot camps for writers,'" Jimmy says. "And I agree. The discipline of producing every day, of getting information across in the most economical fashion, of maintaining your interest in what seems repetitive to everyone else—that's invaluable to any kind of writer."

Working at a newspaper gave Jimmy one other insight. "I learned about syndication," he explains. "So when I came up with the idea to create a comic strip, I knew exactly where to take it."

> "SYNDICATED COMICS IS ONE OF THE FEW WRITING-RELATED BUSINESSES IN WHICH YOU CAN SEND IN WORK 'OVER THE TRANSOM'—SUBMIT IT UNSOLICITED AND WITHOUT AN AGENT—AND IT WILL BE SERIOUSLY CONSIDERED."

Though Jimmy knew where to submit his work, it was far from immediately accepted. "I first proposed a strip with talking dogs, which I sent to several syndicates—and they all wrote back that while they liked the humor, they did not want talking animals," he says. "Then I sent another round of 12 strips about a group of people. And I got another round of rejections.

"But in that round was a personal note," he continues. "And the note said that the editor didn't care for the whole strip, but he liked the married couple in it. He wanted to know if I could do a strip on just that couple. Then we began a honing-in process on what the syndicate wanted."

In the 10 years since Jimmy and the editor agreed on the focus of the strip, the syndicate has sold it to more than 200 newspapers of all sizes throughout the United States.

What do you do all day?

"I think of my work as more of a writing pursuit than a drawing or graphic one," Jimmy says. "I spend a lot of my time thinking about the great and small truths, and how to express them in a very brief story that's funny.

"I read a lot of humorists' essays—by James Thurber, Roy Blount, that sort of thing—for inspiration."

Once he has an idea, Jimmy creates his strip by hand, with pen and ink. "I'm not a great drawer, but I think I've gotten better since I started doing the strip," he confesses. "I've always believed that a good idea can carry a weak drawing better than a good drawing can carry a weak idea."

Once a week, Jimmy puts six strips (for Monday through Saturday editions) through an electronic scanner and transmits them by modem to the syndicate's office. On another day he'll transmit a strip for the Sunday paper. He works a month ahead to allow time for revisions, though he can recall only a few occasions when he's been asked for changes.

"I try to pay close attention to the details," he says. "My spelling and punctuation are flawless."

Where do you see this job leading you?

Of course, for a successful comic strip there can be coffee mugs, greeting cards, toys, animated television specials, books. But Jimmy's aspirations are more qualitative than commercial. "Lots of comic features are launched and last just a short time," he says. "The ones that I admire are those that stay true to themselves and just keep going forever—'Peanuts,' 'Family Circle,' 'Garfield,' and others. That's an amazing accomplishment."

15. Catalog Copywriter

description: A successful catalog copywriter treads the line between advertising and magazine feature writing—the goal is to sell a product, but the approach is to create a mood. And a catalog writer must accomplish both goals in just three or four lines. Catalog writers and designers work very closely together, so it can be an attractive field for people who handle both words and images well. The deadlines for catalogs are rigid and frequent, often demanding long hours from the production team. The level of creativity in catalogs has dramatically improved in recent years, and many newcomers are responsible for that.

salary: As a catalog writer, you'll start at a salary slightly higher than staff writers at magazines and newspapers: $24,000 is about average to start. If your catalogs perform well, you can earn up to $50,000 or more.

prospects: Just open up your mailbox on any day and you're likely to find not just one but three or four catalogs. Direct-mail shopping has become very popular with consumers in today's time-limited world, and many companies eager to serve them have sprung up both in big cities and in rural areas across the country. If you have the skills and the qualifications, you'll have little trouble finding work in catalog copywriting.

qualifications: You must be able to write concise, lively copy that conveys the irresistible benefits of owning the product you're selling. You won't need a degree in a particular area—though one in marketing is especially welcome—but a well-rounded education will give you a broad frame of reference that will make your copy grab the attention of the target market.

characteristics: Be upbeat, quick, and thick-skinned, and you'll enjoy writing catalog copy. You must be upbeat, because you'll have to make your readers enthusiastic about what you're selling. Quickness is a necessity because deadlines are tight, and last-minute changes in design require on-demand text changes. And you'll need a thick skin to endure the editing of merchandise buyers, customer service specialists, and lots of other colleagues who are not professional writers.

Nan Gage *is a senior copywriter for a catalog company in the Northwest.*

How did you get the job?

Nan Gage's route to senior copywriter was something less than direct. After graduating high school, she worked at several restaurants and was a part-owner of one. "My experiences as a restaurant owner taught me a lot about the economics of running any business, which I think is useful in any job," she says. "And I learned that I had an ability to make people feel comfortable and put them at ease. That's an important element in my writing now."

When Nan was 26 years old, she enrolled at her home state's university and earned her degree in geography with a minor focus on writing. She had no intention of becoming a geographer, she notes, but she valued the diversity of the topic: "It encompassed studies of culture, history, politics, and the physi-cal landscape." She also had a course in Latin, which she considered useless at the time. "I've since discovered that knowing Latin really strengthens your understanding of words."

Though Nan's primary interest was in travel writing, she first took a job at a medical school writing patent brochures and medical reports, and then worked as a writer for a computer software company. "Writing about computers was terribly boring to me," she recalls, "but I did learn a lot about computers."

She learned enough about desktop publishing systems to land herself a job with her current employer. "The company was just deciding to make the transition from design and pasteup by hand to doing it by computer when I heard about an opening for a writer from a friend who works as an artist here," she says. "When I interviewed, I emphasized my familiarity with computers. And I think that's what clinched it for me."

What do you do all day?

The creation of a catalog involves three distinct stages, and Nan Gage is working on a catalog in each of those stages all the time. "First, we brainstorm themes for the catalog and work on ideas to carry it all the way through. Next, the photos are shot and the copy is written. And then the designers assemble it all and we go through a process of refinement," she explains. "So, for example, while we're putting the finishing touches on the fall catalog, we're writing copy

> **"IF THE PRODUCTS ARE GOOD BUT THEY DON'T SELL THE WAY THE BUYERS THINK THEY SHOULD, THE CREATIVES—THE WRITERS AND DESIGNERS—ARE MADE RESPONSIBLE."**

for the winter catalog and developing the concept for the spring catalog."

Nan attends a lot of meetings with buyers, inventory managers, and marketing specialists to generate ideas for the catalog. And she spends a lot of time with the designers working to tailor text to match the images and layout. But her favorite part of the day is the writing. "I love sitting down with a product in my hand and imagining what I'd do with it and where I'd go with it," she says. "And then I search for the fewest right words to convey that to our readers."

Where do you see this job leading you?

"I am really lucky, because I love what I do and I think it uses my talents very well," Nan says. "I do like working with art and color, too, so I might like at some point to move up to the job of creative director." Nan might consider running her own advertising agency someday, too.

16. CD-ROM Editor

description: CD-ROMs are a growing market, and CD-ROM editing is a rapidly evolving craft. Editors might work with software engineers to develop the form and content of CD-ROMs, including the text, sound, video, navigation, databases, help files, illustrations, animation, photography, 3-D models, and user interface. A producer oversees a team that includes programmers, animators, database designers, and other production people. He or she manages the entire project from conception to completion to distribution to the retailers. Everyone wants to get in on the ground floor of something new and exciting, unless, of course, it turns out to be just a fad.

salary: CD-ROM publishing is so cutting edge that lots of people want to do it, but few have skills and experience in the field. A person with training in multimedia software and strong ideas about content can start out at $40,000. An experienced producer can command a salary from $60,000 to $90,000.

prospects: Again, lots of people see the future in CD-ROMs and many publishers are just starting to invest in it. So if you are experienced in developing software content, you can write your own ticket for now. It may be a tough market to enter for someone with training in print media and easier for people who've worked in broadcasting, television, movies, and other electronic media.

qualifications: An education in the multimedia department at one of the few colleges that offer that kind of training makes you a shoo-in, but a background in computers, advertising, or broadcasting will help you land a job, too. A strong visual sense will distinguish you from candidates whose expertise lies solely in text.

characteristics: The ability to work as part of a team is critical in multimedia publishing. You must work with a whole menagerie of professionals to get the job done. You'll also have to adapt easily to change—the craft has hardly matured yet—and be able to manage projects in various stages of completion.

Dianne Jacob *is editor-in-chief of a West Coast company that specializes in 3-D activity and reference software for personal computers.*

How did you get the job?

Initially, Dianne Jacob didn't want her job. She first met the CEO of the company she works for at an industry trade show—she was the editor of a trade magazine with a degree (from Cal State Northridge) and background in journalism; he was a former employee of Time-Life Books with an idea but no product or staff. He began to court her to join his new company, but Dianne was reluctant. "I'm no techno-nerd, and I thought CD-ROM books were a fad," she admits. "But over the next two years he stayed in touch with me. When he asked me to copyedit one of his CDs two years later, I agreed to try it. By then he had one product shipping and another ready to go out the door, and a real editorial staff."

Dianne signed on as editor-in-chief after she tried competitors' CDs and couldn't get them to work, but marveled at the ease of using her company's product. "I spent two weeks playing with a bunch of different CDs and was totally frustrated by them," she says. "When I could use ours, I knew he was on to something." She did set one stipulation before taking the position. "I want to always remain a skeptical consumer," she states unequivocally. "I will not become a technology groupie. And I don't want to work on products that are for them."

What do you do all day?

Assembling a CD-ROM is a massive collaborative effort. "Each product is assigned to a team that includes an editor, graphic designer, product marketing manager, and software engineer," Dianne explains. "The editor has primary responsibility for the content."

The development department works on several CDs at any one time, each at a different stage. "On any given day, an editor will assign and edit writers for the text, hire voice talent for narration, and generate ideas for databases to add to a CD in progress," Dianne says. "CDs at the end of their production cycle are tested for bugs, proofread, and fact-checked by editors, too."

Of course, before any CD leaves Dianne's office, she makes sure that even someone who isn't a techno-nerd can use it. "The average person . . . has to be able to use it before it's ready to be shipped."

Where do you see this job leading you?

In a cutting-edge field like CD-ROM editing, looking ahead amounts to seeing the end of

> "PEOPLE WITH JUST WRITING EXPERIENCE ARE NOT GETTING JOBS IN MULTIMEDIA ANYMORE; YOU NEED GRAPHIC DESIGN AND EVEN VIDEO EXPERIENCE."

the week. "I'm just trying to keep up with this work," she says. "All I want to do is to better define what a CD-ROM is as distinct from a book and then create great CDs. Later, this job could lead to becoming a producer at another software company or becoming the liaison at a large publisher who works with a developer to make a CD-ROM."

17. Children's Book Author

description: A sizable portion of most bookstores is devoted to children's books, and schools purchase millions of books every year for both instructional and leisure reading. The authors of the majority of these books are neither famous writers nor educators, but people who understand the ability and interests of young readers and who can compose engaging material for that audience. Many children's authors produce series of books. Most generate their own ideas; some established authors receive assignments from publishers. Almost all work from their own homes and on self-determined schedules. Though all are credited for their work, only a select few authors become well known outside the publishing industry.

salary: For a first book, you may be paid an advance of $3,500 to $8,000 for a picture book—which you will split with the illustrator. Books for older children pay slightly more. And for those authors whose characters become very popular, the earning potential is virtually unlimited.

prospects: Hundreds of new titles are published each year, and publishers are always looking for more. If you have a salable idea, you'll find a buyer. If you have a steady stream of ideas, you can earn a living.

qualifications: You can read a few books or take a course to learn about marketing your work, but the only real qualifications for being a children's book author are the abilities to create ideas and write for kids.

characteristics: Authors must motivate themselves, be disciplined about deadlines, and be persistent in marketing their ideas.

Stephen Mooser *lives in the Northeast and is the author of 50 to 60 books for young readers.*

How did you get started?

Stephen earned a degree in film from the University of California at Los Angeles, but had little luck in breaking into the movie industry. So he went back to the school to study journalism, and that helped him land a job as a staff editor at a magazine, "but the magazine went out of business almost right after I started working there," Stephen says. That turned out to be his break into writing for children.

"To pay the bills, I took a job at an educational publisher writing reading programs for schools," he says. "In a few years, I had written 250 books for these programs and learned a whole lot about children's reading habits."

With that experience, Stephen was able to start selling his own book ideas—a process he now knows very well. "One of the nice things about the children's book market is that generally you don't need an agent to sell your work to publishers," he says. "If you have a nonfiction idea that's unique, you should describe it in a one-page query letter and send that to a publisher. If you want to sell a picture book, you should send the whole manuscript. For a novel, send a couple of chapters and an outline of the story." Stephen has written a few nonfiction and picture books, but most of his work has been what are called "chapter books."

"Chapter books," he explains, "are like novels for kids between second- and sixth-grade reading levels. The books tend to be 60 to 70 pages long and are broken into 10 to 15 chapters, so they're easy to read."

Stephen continues to create his own ideas for these books, but he does occasionally get calls from editors with ideas for books they'd like him to write. "I recently had a call from an editor who had a title—*Disaster Room 101*—that he wanted me to write a book about," Stephen says. "You see, many of the series books I write are sold through book clubs and the kids have little more than a title and cover art to pick from. So titles are very important."

> **"IF YOU CAN FIND A JOB WRITING ABOUT ANYTHING, TAKE IT AND USE IT AS AN OPPORTUNITY TO WORK ON YOUR SKILLS. THEN USE YOUR SPARE TIME TO DEVELOP BOOKS FOR CHILDREN."**

What do you do all day?

Stephen believes he should approach working at home as if he reported to an office. "I think it's critical that I stick to a disciplined routine for writing," he says. "This is my job, and if I don't do it diligently I'll be working down at the hardware store." For Stephen that routine means writing from 8:30 to 11:30 a.m. every day, playing basketball for an hour, and then getting back to his desk for an equal amount of time in the afternoon.

With that regimen, Stephen is able to turn out a new 60- to 80-page book in a month to six weeks. These days he is contributing books to two ongoing series: Creepy Creature Club and All-Star Meatballs. Stephen has also written some reading programs and the script for a show at Sea World.

Where do you see this job leading you?

In this case, back to the beginning. Stephen is planning a move to Los Angeles, where he and a writing partner (who is an independent film producer) will be working on scripts for family films.

18. Circulation Manager

description: A magazine's circulation department seeks out new readers, entices existing readers to renew their subscriptions, and manages the billing and fulfillment of the orders. The people in the circulation department must have strong word skills for devising and executing ideas for direct-mail packages that will appeal to the magazine's target audience; they must also have facility with numbers to analyze data on responses to those packages, to direct billing and fulfillment, and to control a budget that is critical to the publication's success. At most magazines, the circulation assistants contribute to both of those functions.

salary: The good news is that circulation people tend to make slightly more money than the editorial staff of a magazine. At large publishing companies in big cities, circulation assistants start at $20,000 to $25,000. Circulation managers earn $60,000 to $70,000, even more in some cases, at large companies.

prospects: As magazines compete against all the new (and old) electronic media for readers' allegiance, they need more compelling yet cost-efficient strategies for attracting new subscribers. So people with that uncommon combination of creative marketing ideas and sound numbers skills are in great demand.

qualifications: Training or experience in marketing will catch the attention of circulation managers looking to hire, but people with degrees in communications, journalism, or English will find opportunities, too. Basic computer skills—especially with spreadsheet programs—are critical.

characteristics: You have to like words and numbers, creativity and administration, your colleagues and your customers, and intense deadlines and waiting for results, to enjoy circulation.

Anne Haas *is a circulation assistant at a major publishing company in New York City.*

How did you get the job?

You hear a lot about how networking, making contacts, is the key to finding a good job. Here's proof. Anne had a bachelor's degree in English from Indiana University and some experience working in retail, but she really wanted to get into publishing. So she enrolled in the Rice University Publishing Program the summer after she graduated. "I learned a lot in the program's simulation about aspects of publishing that I had no clue about," Anne says. "And I got interested in circulation after listening to [the circulation manager of the magazine publisher where she now works]." Of course, Anne didn't just listen—she asked a lot of relevant questions and made a definite impression on the speaker.

"When I decided to move to New York to be where the publishing action is, I sent her a letter and resume," Anne says. "I had an interview right away and

> **"IF YOU MEET SOMEONE WHO CAN HELP YOU, BE SURE YOU MAKE A MEMORABLE IMPRESSION. AND DON'T HESITATE TO CALL THE PERSON WHEN YOU NEED THAT HELP."**

was hired within a week of moving to the city." Did that circulation manager really remember Anne? "She knew exactly who I was and told me that she remembered all the questions I asked."

Having a good contact and an eager approach to getting the job were certainly instrumental in getting an interview, but to get the job Anne had to demonstrate her ability to use Lotus 1-2-3 and WordPerfect and had to pass a basic math test. "To tell the truth, I had never used Lotus before I took the test," she admits. "But I practiced on a different spreadsheet program that a friend had, so I understood enough of the basics to prove I could learn the particulars of Lotus quickly."

What do you do all day?

Anne plays a role in all the functions of the circulation department. "I help write and proofread our direct-mail packages and renewal letters. I am on the phone to our fulfillment company in Colorado almost every day, helping them to solve customer problems. And I write lots of memos summarizing our reports," she explains. "I do analysis of our renewals and billing and I track the response rates to our direct-mail packages. I also do cost-summary reports analyzing how much the direct-mail packages cost per thousand and keep an inventory of the packages, to make sure we have what we need for each mailing."

That's a lot of different duties. Which of those does Anne like best? "Well, I guess I enjoy the creative work the most—coming up with ideas for the packages," she answers. "But I also like being able to see the results very directly.

"This may sound funny, but I think renewals and billing are fun, too," she adds. "I'm learning a lot about the business side of publishing and it's real interesting to me."

Where do you see this job leading you?

"Deeper into the magazine business" is Anne's confident response to that question. "I'd always thought that I wanted to work on the editorial side of publishing and I figured that circulation was a good way to get into a publishing company, then I'd move over when I saw an opportunity," Anne says. "Now I'm not so sure. I'm still intrigued by editorial, but I think that the marketing skills I'm picking up here will be useful anywhere I want to go. At this point, I'm fairly certain that I want to stay in the fast-paced world of magazine publishing rather than in books."

19. Columnist, Newspaper

description: Reporters cover the who, what, when, and where of news events in straightforward style; columnists write their impressions and opinions of people and current events in a more personal, essaylike style. While reporters receive their assignments from the newspaper's editors, columnists typically generate their own ideas. These days, columnists are rarely required to work in the office. A columnist's work may appear in the paper once a week or every day, but more commonly on a regular schedule of two, three, or four times a week. Columnists also enjoy a certain level of recognition among the paper's readers and are often syndicated, which means their column appears in many papers.

salary: Columnist is almost never an entry-level job—most are experienced as reporters before they become columnists—so the pay is slightly better than a reporter's: typically about $25,000 to $35,000 a year for a daily paper in a midsize market. Syndicating the column to other papers is pure gravy: 50 percent of what syndicates get for columns (which varies depending on the circulation of the paper picking up the column) goes to the columnists for work they've already done.

prospects: These are coveted jobs at most newspapers, so competition is fierce for the opportunities. You're more likely to get a shot at a paper in a smaller market.

qualifications: Usually you need experience as a newspaper reporter to get a chance to write a column—you certainly must have a reporter's ability to dig for information. Excellent writing skills and a distinctive point of view are critical to doing the job well. And you need a bottomless well of ideas for topics to write about if you want to keep the job.

characteristics: Curious, perceptive people who are self-motivated and capable of finding new ways of looking at the news will succeed as columnists.

Rheta Grimsley-Johnson *is a columnist for a major newspaper in the Southeast— her column also appears in 63 other daily newspapers.*

How did you get the job?

Rheta earned her stripes as a reporter from the ground up. After graduating with a journalism degree from a liberal arts college in the South, she went to work for a wire service and a few small-town daily newspapers. Then Rheta took a "bureau" job at a newspaper in Memphis. "A bureau job is the lowest-ranking job, paying the lowest salary at the paper," she explains. "Basically, you're assigned to a bureau out in the boonies and you provide all the paper's coverage from that area—crime, school board meetings, features, everything."

Despite the less than glamorous assignment, Rheta made the most of it, using it as an opportunity to practice her craft and hone her skills. "I learned how to find information— things like how to get a document at the courthouse," she says. "And I got to write every day. That's the best training for becoming a writer."

One day, Rheta's editor announced that he was looking for op-ed pieces (newspaper talk for opinion articles) from the staff. "I immediately sat down and wrote two of them—one of which was accepted," Rheta says. "That one was a very personal story about my father being let go from a job he'd had for 30 years; I got more mail on that story than for any I've written since.

"Anyway, based on that, the editor offered me the chance to write a column every week," she says. "Of course, that was in addition to my regular work." Still, Rheta eagerly accepted the opportunity and within a few years was able to relinquish her duties as a reporter and focus solely on the column. A few years after that, she was offered the chance to write the column for one of the South's most prestigious newspapers. Its popularity with the readers caught the attention of syndicators, who now market it to other papers.

What do you do all day?

Rheta picks up her mail and phone messages once a week or so at the office, but spends most of her time out searching for ideas for the column she writes four times a week. "I think that everybody has about 20 strong opinions," she says. "Columnists look for stories that express those in different ways.

"Covering breaking news is dangerous for a columnist; you can get caught with an opinion before the facts are all in," she continues. "But I do write

> **"IF YOU BELIEVE YOU WRITE WELL ENOUGH TO BE A COLUMNIST, START AT A SMALLER NEWSPAPER, BECAUSE YOU'LL COVER A BROADER RANGE OF TOPICS AS A REPORTER AND YOU'RE MORE LIKELY TO GET A CHANCE TO WRITE THE COLUMN THAN YOU WOULD AT A BIG-CITY PAPER."**

about the news. I try to give it perspective, for example, by talking to someone who's affected by a news event but who wouldn't normally be considered a newsmaker."

One inhibition that Rheta works to overcome is the sense of distance a reporter keeps from the stories. "As a reporter, you're trained to be as invisible to the story as you can be," she explains. "But as a columnist, you have to write about yourself and not feel silly about it."

Rheta has also learned not to be afraid of repetition. "Every year on Thanksgiving I've done a list of things I am thankful for," she says. "The one year that I didn't, I got a lot of letters from regular readers asking why I didn't do it."

That mail means a great deal to Rheta. "I get about 100 letters a week," she says. "And though I fall behind, I try to answer all of it. After all, reaching out to the readers, to other people, is why you do this."

Where do you see this job leading you?

Old columnists never die, they just collect their columns in books. Those that leave the column tend to go on to writing other books. "I'd never want another newspaper job," Rheta says. "I'm not ready to leave the column, but someday I might like to try my hand at fiction."

20. Contributing Editor, Magazine

description: Not quite staff editors, but more than just freelancers, contributing editors are a regular presence in a magazine. Despite the name, contributing editors are more often writers than strictly editors. Contributors are expected to bring ideas to a magazine's issue plans, as well as accept story assignments. Often they're responsible for coverage of a particular region, industry, or specialty that's of interest to the magazine's audience but that isn't covered by a staff writer. Contributing editors don't have office space or benefits, but they have a reliable (though usually modest) income and have the freedom to freelance for non-competing publishers.

salary: Many contributing editors are paid less than $10,000 a year, though some get more than $50,000. The median for trade magazines is not far from $10,000; for consumer magazines, it's closer to $20,000.

prospects: These may be the most coveted freelance jobs: you get to keep your own schedule, but you can expect to get paid at regular intervals. So these are tough gigs to arrange—but not impossible, particularly if you have in-depth knowledge of a subject within a magazine's scope.

qualifications: You must write very well, have plenty of pertinent ideas, be dependable and self-directed, and bring distinct value to the magazine. You usually have to prove all of that before you get the job.

characteristics: You're working outside the office, but must remain integral to the operation. To do so requires an attention to the details so that your work is in sync with the rest of the magazine. And good phone manners help, too.

Barbara Pleasant *lives in the Deep South, but she is a contributor to a magazine based in the Northeast.*

How did you get the job?

Barbara made the big step up from freelancer to contributor nine years and two editors ago. Before that, she'd earned a master's degree in social work, burned out in that field, and then taken a job as a legal assistant for 30 hours a week to allow her more time to spend on freelance writing. She began sending queries and accepting assignments from a consumer gardening magazine. When the regional editor in Barbara's part of the country became unreliable, she was offered the job.

"I had written some articles for the magazine already," she says. "But this was a monthly report. It was a great big deal for me. I still remember when the editor called—it was a Sunday morning in the middle of a snowstorm."

Though the magazine's editor-in-chief has changed twice since she became a contributor, Barbara has remained a consistent part of the team; in fact, she's now been with the magazine longer than any current staff editor.

"I decided early on that I had to both do a good job and be easy to work with," she says. "And I believe I must be even more dependable than the staff. I've never missed a deadline in nine years—I may have renegotiated some as they got close, but I have never reached one and not turned in the story."

Barbara is also compiling a monthly calendar for a statewide magazine. "It doesn't pay very much, but it's reliable and that's worth something," she says. "I read in a book that a professional writer should earn at least $30 an hour, less their expenses—I apply that to any job I'm considering."

What do you do all day?

Barbara's job hasn't remained static: the monthly regional report she was hired for was dropped, but she has been writing another monthly column, as well as six to nine feature articles a year, submitting ideas to the magazine's issue-planning meetings, and providing information and contacts from her region to staff writers.

The kinds of articles Barbara writes include lots of research, so she's a regular at her local libraries. She reads scientific studies, interviews both experts and laypeople on the phone, and reflects on her own experiences. With those tools, she carves out 2,000- to 4,000-word articles at least every other month.

"I approach writing like a craft—like weaving or building furniture—you work at it and you'll get results," Barbara says. She approaches the job of being a contributing editor like a sensible merchant. "I spend every other Friday taking care of my business," she explains. "I pay bills, keep up on my taxes, call in accounts unpaid, all of that stuff."

Where do you see this job leading you?

"Having a specialty can get you work, but it also can leave you pigeonholed," Barbara says. "I'd

> **"IT TAKES A CERTAIN PERSONALITY TO WORK 1,000 MILES AWAY FROM EVERYONE ELSE ON THE STAFF. YOU DON'T HAVE SOMEONE TO BOUNCE IDEAS OFF OF REGULARLY."**

like to break out of writing just about gardening and get into food and travel—and I could do it if I put all my energy into it, but I'd have to give up six months of income to get in." Barbara is submitting ideas to food magazines, as well as writing books about gardening.

"Once you have this lifestyle, you don't want to give it up," she says. "The idea of getting dressed and perky for someone else at 9 a.m. is now disgusting to me."

21. Cookbook Author

description: Compiling cookbooks is unlike writing any other kind of nonfiction book because the author must have at least some skill in the subject—cooking—and at best an expertise at it. Many are also knowledgeable about nutrition. A cookbook author must create recipes or collect them from other sources, and then typically tests and refines the recipes before they go into print. Some authors work with famous chefs (or other celebrities), and a few become well known themselves.

salary: A first-time (unknown) author typically is paid an advance ranging from $3,000 to $10,000, depending on the book's size and its sales potential. Authors with proven track records earn advances of $20,000 to $40,000 per book. When the books earn back their advances, the authors generally receive royalties on subsequent sales.

prospects: Scores of new cookbooks are published every year—they are by far the most frequently published type of book. If you have the skills to write the book, and a good idea for an angle on the book, you'll be able to find a publisher for it.

qualifications: You must be able to create or identify enticing original recipes; make those recipes (or hire someone who can) and amend them until they are right; and write clear and concise instructions, and engaging introductory text. You must also know about food safety, because cookbook publishers typically require the authors to assume liability for any harm that comes to readers who eat food prepared as recommended in the book.

characteristics: This is not a field you just get into because you need a job and think you can do it: you must love food and cooking, and be able to think about it creatively every day. And you must work systematically so that you can accurately pass along what you learn to the readers.

Linda West Eckhardt *is an accomplished cookbook writer living in the Northwest.*

How did you get the job?

Linda studied home economics and food science in college, but she was a fifth-grade teacher living in the country when a day of duck hunting with her husband set her on the course of a new career. "I'd always had a knack for writing when I was in school, but I never thought about doing it professionally until I was telling a friend, who is a writer and editor, about my experience duck hunting with my husband. My friend suggested I write down my story and send it to *Field & Stream* magazine," Linda explains. "So I took her advice and wrote the story, and I included two recipes for cooking the duck that we got. *Field & Stream* bought the story.

"After that story was published, I got serious about writing and went to graduate school to learn more about it," she continues. "Then I went to the local newspaper and proposed that I write a regular recipe col-

umn, which I am still doing today" (though it is now syndicated to more than 100 newspapers around the country).

The newspaper column led to a monthly magazine column, and that led to books published by the same company that produces the magazine. This progression from newspaper to magazine to book helped Linda overcome one of the biggest obstacles for beginning book writers in any genre. "To get a book published, you usually need to get an agent, but to get an agent you need a publisher to be interested in your work," she explains. "A newspaper or

> **"LOOK FOR OPPORTUNITIES TO ESTABLISH YOURSELF WITH ANY KIND OF WRITING IN YOUR FIELD—INCLUDING NEWSPAPERS, MAGAZINES, PROMOTIONAL BROCHURES, AND BOOKLETS THAT COME WITH PRODUCTS."**

magazine column is a good way to prove your marketability, but, if you don't have that, the best chance you have to get an agent is to find an editor who will make an offer on your manuscript, and then take that offer to an agent.

"Be sure to work with an agent who knows cookbooks," Linda adds. "Agents who specialize in cookbooks have contacts with the right editors at publishing companies, and know who publishes what types of books—all the inside stuff."

What do you do all day?

Linda's days are divided into writing and cooking. "I write in the morning, because that's when I can concentrate best," she says. "I spend the afternoons and evenings working in the kitchen on the recipes. Of course, the nice thing about writing cookbooks is that your work can be dinner."

As the deadline for a book approaches, Linda works 8- to 10-hour days—often seven days

a week. But even when there's no book deadline looming, Linda finds herself thinking about and working on recipes for her columns and books. "In a sense, our social life revolves around my work. When we travel, I go to markets and restaurants, and collect ideas," she says. "And many of our friends are in the food business in one way or another, so new ideas always come up when we're together."

Where do you see this job leading you?

Though Linda has written novels (one has been optioned for the movies) and short stories, she remains committed to writing her columns and cookbooks. "Right now I'm working with my 32-year-old daughter on a book about entertaining," Linda says. "It's a lot of fun for us to work together, even though she lives on the East Coast and I live on the West Coast."

22. Copy Editor, Newspaper

description: The last people to read newspaper articles before they go into print are the copy editors. They edit each story so that every sentence is clear. They correct the grammar, spelling, and style, trim stories to fit their allotted space, and write headlines. And they do it fast and without a mistake. Copy editors are anonymous outside a newspaper's office—there are no bylines and rarely a masthead mention for anyone but the copy chief—but copy editors have the trust and usually the respect of the paper's top editors. Because most daily newspapers today are published in the morning, copy editors typically work in the late afternoon and evening, after the reporters have written the day's stories.

salary: Copy editors at weekly or small-city daily newspapers start at $250 to $400 a week. At a daily in a midsize city, copy editors earn $500 to $600 a week; more experienced ones make $700, $800, up to $1,000 in the biggest cities.

prospects: Every newspaper has a crew of copy editors, and they move up and around in the newspaper business to better their pay and level of responsibility. Many copy editors also go to other departments within the newspaper. So copy-editing positions are often available to qualified people.

qualifications: Many newspapers give a test to candidates for copy-editing jobs; those tests pose questions about grammar, Associated Press style, and libel law, and provide challenges in editing and headline-writing skills. Experience is the essential qualification for advancement to bigger cities.

characteristics: Good copy editors can speed through stories without missing a turn, even in the worst conditions. And they have the creativity to write snappy, relevant headlines—on demand.

Mike Les *is the copy desk chief at a daily newspaper in the West.*

How did you get the job?

Mike started out as a newspaper reporter after graduating from Michigan State University with a journalism degree. Actually, he started as an intern at Michigan's *Lansing State Journal* while a student at MSU, and during his internship he worked as a reporter and served a stint on the copy desk. "You learn so much about how a newspaper is put together and you see a much broader variety of stories—20 to 30 stories a day—at the copy desk," Mike says. "And I was drawn right away to the people who populated the copy desk: real professionals who had command of their jobs and the respect of their colleagues."

Mike accepted a job with the paper as a reporter, but soon decided he wanted to be a full-time copy editor. So he moved to Santa Maria, California, where he gained experience on the copy desk of the local newspaper. The standard career path in newspapers is to grow from small cities to larger ones, and, two years later, Mike sought and won a job with his current employer, a newspaper in a medium-size city. Experience and dedication eventually earned him the job of copy desk chief.

What do you do all day?

Could you read a front-page newspaper article, purge it of any inaccuracies and inconsistencies of clarity, grammar, spelling, and style, and give it a punchy but informative headline within 20 minutes? Mike Les and his colleagues can, and they do it like clockwork from the time they arrive at the paper's office around 3 p.m. until the presses start rolling at 2 a.m. for the next morning's edition. Mike would like more than 20 minutes to copyedit the articles, and sometimes he can take up to 30 minutes with a story. "A copy editor will work on 20 to 30 stories a day," he says. "You can't spend more than a half hour or so on any piece."

> **"I'LL GIVE SOMEONE WHO DOES WELL ON OUR TEST A SHOT AT PART-TIME OR FREELANCE WITH FAR LESS QUALIFICATIONS OR EXPERIENCE THAN I NORMALLY EXPECT FOR FULL-TIMERS."**

Some of the copy editors who work with Mike are assigned to certain editions of the paper—ones filled with news devoted to the city's various zones. The others work on stories in all of the paper's departments—news, features, travel, etc.—except sports. "The sports department usually has its own copy desk," Mike says.

He believes that good headline writing may be the most difficult task to master. "I heard it said once that headlines are 'cruel poetry.' They must be economical enough to fit the limited space, but evocative enough to invite the reader into the story," he says. "It's a skill learned through practice. The inexperienced copy editors on our staff start out on a steady diet of writing heads for obituaries, community events, the stuff in the back of the paper. You have to prove yourself before you write one for the front page."

Where do you see this job leading you?

One newspaper job always seems to lead to another newspaper job. Yet Mike Les is content where he is right now. He is happy at the copy desk and likes the city where he works, but he won't dismiss the idea that he'll someday move up to a major metropolitan newspaper.

For other people, Mike points out that "there are so many skills involved in copy editing that it really lends itself to moving to different departments within the newspaper: assignment desk, design, layout, and production. And at the copy desk you prove yourself a deadline maker and a person who cares about accuracy and quality. That makes you a strong candidate to go to the other departments."

23. Corporate Magazine Editor

description: Large companies publish magazines (or newsletters) to disseminate news and other information to their employees, retirees, investors, customers, and other interested parties. The editors of these publications gather the news, develop ideas for feature stories, write and edit the articles, work with graphic designers on the layout, and coordinate the printing—not unlike editors of commercial and trade magazines. What is unique to corporate magazines is the close relationship between the company's management and the editors—management relies on the magazine to convey its messages, highlight its achievements, and generally depict the company in a positive light.

salary: Writers and editors in corporate communications start with yearly salaries around $25,000 to $30,000, slightly more or less depending on the size of the company and its location. Experienced editors earn $45,000 to $55,000, or more.

prospects: As more companies expand across the country and the world, the need for internal communications—and therefore the demand for corporate editors—increases as well. There are entry-level jobs in corporate communications to be found wherever large companies are based. You most likely won't be offered the editorship of the company magazine without any previous experience, but you can be a contributor and work your way up to it in fairly short order.

qualifications: Most companies seek corporate communications specialists with proven writing ability—training or experience in journalism, mass communications, marketing, and advertising are most common. Knowledge of (but not expertise in) business language and practices, along with the particular industry of the company, will enhance your application.

characteristics: If you're organized, persuasive, flexible, enthusiastic, and like people, you'll do well as a corporate magazine editor. It also helps to believe in the company's mission.

Susan Terpay *is the manager of internal communications for a transportation company in the Southeast and is the editor of its corporate magazine.*

How did you get the job?

Susan headed straight for the news business after earning her degree in communications (with an emphasis in journalism) from James Madison University in Harrisonburg, Virginia. She first worked as a radio newscaster at a small radio station, and six months later became a health and education reporter for the city's daily newspaper. "From the radio job, I learned the meaning of the word 'deadline' and how to write fast," she recalls. "From the newspaper job, I learned how to interview people and tell their story in simple language while striving to make the story moving and memorable."

She heard about a job opening in her current employer's public relations department from a friend at the company. "The company was looking for a generalist who could handle

> **"EVEN IF STUDENT INTERNSHIPS ADD A SEMESTER OR A YEAR TO YOUR EDUCATION, THEY WILL SWING DOORS OPEN."**

various job assignments," Susan says. "I suppose my varied background was my strongest credential for the job." She was hired as an assistant editor for the corporate newspaper, which was distributed to about 70,000 active and retired employees. Three years later she was named editor of the newspaper, then became manager of internal communications. In that position, she developed and launched a new magazine for the company.

What do you do all day?

Planning, writing, and editing a 16- to 20-page monthly magazine for the company's employees takes up most of Susan's time. She travels to various locations within the company's 20-state service region to report news and dig up feature story ideas. She assigns one full-time writer and an intern to the articles she doesn't write herself, and she assigns and directs photographers, too. In short, she sees her job as working "with all departments within the company to promote the vision and mission of the company."

Susan never forgets the distinction between the public news media and a corporate publication. "There is no freedom of the press for a corporate magazine. You have been hired to promote the company by spotlighting its achievements, reporting (some of) its setbacks,

and highlighting its people," she says. "You often will be told what to write about . . . and sometimes how to write it."

In Susan's spare time, she also writes press releases.

Where do you see this job leading you?

Developing one new medium for her company is not enough for Susan. She hopes to expand its internal communications beyond the monthly magazine to include an "electronic newsletter and other new communications tools using computers, the Internet, fax machines, and the telephone."

Later on, she'd like to be a travel writer for a magazine, where she'll write what and how she wants.

24. Database Editor

description: Information may be the most valuable commodity in the economy, but its true worth is linked directly to how manageable and accessible it is. Database editors compile information from newspapers, magazines, books, annual reports, newsletters, and other publications, then index and organize it so that their subscribers can find it and put it to use in their businesses. Database editing is computer-based work, but the critical part of the job is understanding users' interests and developing a vocabulary that will lead the users to the information they've paid for. The work involves both collaboration and solitary effort.

salary: Database editors just starting out will earn from $20,000 to $25,000 a year; experienced ones get $30,000 to $40,000, and salaries can exceed that in large cities or with bigger companies.

prospects: The world is just beginning to understand the value of databases beyond the common applications in libraries and direct-mail businesses. Lots of jobs are open for people with strong word and computer skills—especially in the nation's technology centers such as California's Silicon Valley, Boston's Route 128 Corridor, and Jacksonville, Florida.

qualifications: A diverse education in the humanities and some training in library science are a strong foundation for a database editor. In-depth knowledge in certain fields—sciences, law, business, or medicine, for example—will enhance your application. Familiarity with computers (though not expertise) is essential.

characteristics: Detail-oriented, curious, logical people make the best, most satisfied database editors. You have to like working alone, too.

Margot Diltz *is the manager of database quality assurance for a large information service on the West Coast.*

How did you get the job?

Margot has been managing information for her entire career. After earning her bachelor's degree in the humanities at a small college, she pursued a master's degree in library science at the University of California at Berkeley. With that education, Margot found jobs in both the archives and reference departments at several university libraries and overseas in international business libraries. She came to her position with her current employer by answering a newspaper advertisement; she's reasonably confident that her "commitment to her profession and her varied experiences" distinguished her from the other candidates.

The job requires a lot of contrasting interests and skills. Besides a strong grasp of language and the computer skills, Margot says you must also be aware of the world around you. "You have to be interested in current events to do this work well," she says.

> **"EDITING CONTROLLED VOCABULARY IS ONLY ONE OF THE JOBS IN DATABASE MANAGEMENT. INDEXING AND WRITING ABSTRACTS ARE THE OTHER KEY FUNCTIONS IN OUR FIELD."**

What do you do all day?

Margot spends her days studying words—the words that indexers will attach to articles and that the subscribers to her company's database will use to track down those articles. "We create what's called 'controlled vocabulary,'" she explains. "Indexers choose very particular terms—that controlled vocabulary—to define the articles our subscribers are looking for; we continually review those terms to be sure they are up-to-date.

"We continually comb through the terms, one topic at a time, and upgrade them," she goes on. "For example, we recently worked on real estate vocabulary. We reviewed all the trade magazines and professional journals in the real estate business to learn about current issues and trends, then developed new vocabulary to reflect them." With up-to-date terms, people researching real estate issues will be able to find the latest information in the database on the topic.

"Our work is a bit like washing the windows at the Empire State Building—by the time you finish doing the ones on the top floor, it's time to do the ones on the bottom floor again. By the time we finish with every other topic, it'll be time to update real estate again."

Where do you see this job leading you?

Margot has no immediate plans to work anywhere else. That may be because, as she says, "This industry is evolving so fast that I think the jobs I'll be doing in the future haven't been invented yet."

25. Dictionary Editor

description: Who says what words mean? We all do, but it's the dictionary editor's job to document the usage of words and write definitions and examples that represent the current standard for each word. These editors regularly update the dictionaries to reflect changes they've apprehended. They often work on different types of dictionaries—college, children's, medical, etc.—as well as on other language reference books. Computers have brought some changes to the craft of dictionary editing in recent years, but it remains painstaking work largely performed by meticulous people.

salary: Entry-level dictionary editors earn about $20,000, and the highest-paid ones rarely make much more than $50,000. An editor-in-chief may earn more because of management and administrative responsibilities.

prospects: Only a handful of companies publish dictionaries using more than a few full-time editors; many publishers use temporary editors during especially busy periods. Permanent positions are therefore difficult to get, but you can earn a full-time opportunity with determination and strong performance in temporary work.

qualifications: A broad education and the ability to write precisely and concisely are essential to working in lexicography. In-depth knowledge of the sciences or other technical fields will make your candidacy more attractive.

characteristics: Dictionary editing is a collaborative effort, but you'll be working alone most of the time. To succeed, you'll need to read fast, be well organized, and have a streak of perfectionism, too. And you have to care about words.

Steve Perrault *is a senior editor at a reference book publisher in the Northeast.*

How did you get the job?

Steve didn't target his education to lead him straight into lexicography, but you could see it heading that way. "I was determined to learn what I wanted to learn," says the University of Massachusetts graduate. "I majored in literature because I wanted to understand life and to learn how to think critically." Steve began applying to his current employer soon after college. His first interview with the company didn't result in an offer, but when another position opened up several months later, he applied again, and this time was hired.

"As the person who now hires people for our staff, I know that I am impressed by people who show continuing interest in working here," Steve says. "That kind of commitment suggests an individual who will probably enjoy the work and want to stick with it." Steve also believes that a strong writing sample (which is required of all applicants) was critical to his getting the job; he's sure it's important for people he now considers for positions.

What do you do all day?

"The authority of the dictionary rests solely in how well it represents how words are actually used," Steve says. "We spend our time trying to determine how each word is used." Editors do that by spending time each day reading current magazines, newspapers, and books, marking in them examples of new vocabulary and new uses of

existing words. "These citations, as we call them, are ultimately printed out onto three-by-five cards and filed," Steve explains. "We gather about 150,000 to 200,000 citations each year, and we have about 1.5 million when we revise our college dictionary every 10 years."

> **"I LIKE A PERSON WHO'S A BIT OF A PERFECTIONIST: THIS IS NOT WORK FOR SOMEONE WHO'S CARELESS."**

When the dictionary is revised—or a new edition is compiled—the editors progress through the alphabet, each of them reviewing a small sequence of entries at a time. The editors consider the citations for those entries and then write or revise definitions to reflect how the words are used. An editor will spend a year or two on each dictionary. "I worked for two years on a medical dictionary and was totally immersed in medical terminology," Steve says. "After that I spent two years working on a usage dictionary in which I researched and wrote essays on how words are used.

"I like the general dictionaries best because there's so much variety," he adds. "One afternoon I may be working on a word dealing with architecture, the next I may be studying a term of literary criticism."

Where do you see this job leading you?

After 15 years working for his current employer, Steve has no doubt he's found his home. "A lot of people spend their careers here," he says. "I'll be happy to spend the rest of mine here if they'll have me."

59

26. Educational Software Editor

description: Editors—professionals with ideas and images—create the content, research and organize the information to be presented, and suggest graphics for computer programs aimed at teaching and entertaining children. Software editors collaborate with (and/or serve as) the package designers, marketing staff, and documentation writers for the programs. Typically, the editor manages the whole project and is responsible for meeting its deadlines. The editor may also solicit opinions from professional teachers and focus groups of children about the software during its development.

salary: An educational software editor with experience either as a teacher or as an editor of learning books may earn as little as $25,000 or as much as $50,000 to $60,000, depending upon how much experience the individual has in teaching, editing, and computer software.

prospects: In 1985, computer users could choose from 37 different educational programs. By 1994, that total had risen to 409, and it appeared to be doubling in 1995. With strong ideas and a fundamental understanding of educational software, you'll have many options in various regions of the country.

qualifications: Most software publishers require editors of educational programs to have some experience in a classroom or editing textbooks, as well as good verbal skills and a working knowledge of computers.

characteristics: An organized person will be able to juggle the many facets of the software editor's job. An imaginative one will generate captivating ideas for using the medium of computers to teach children while entertaining them.

Kathy Cole *is a senior editor in the software division of a children's book publisher in the Great Lakes region.*

How did you get the job?

Teaching philosophy has been important to Kathy since she was an elementary education major at Oakland University in Rochester, Michigan, in the late 1970s. "I believe very strongly in the value of child-centered learning, that children develop in distinctive stages and that they learn best by doing some-

> "I BELONG TO THE SOCIETY FOR TECHNOLOGY IN EDUCATION SO THAT I CAN KEEP UP WITH TEACHERS IN ALL PARTS OF THE COUNTRY WHO ARE USING COMPUTERS IN THEIR CLASSROOMS, AND HEAR WHAT WORKS FOR THEIR STUDENTS."

thing rather than listening," she explains. "And I've considered every job in the context of that philosophy."

She applied her beliefs to kindergarten students in both Michigan and Wisconsin, and discovered along the way that children are engaged by working with computers. "I saw that two- to six-year-old students could load programs and work them," Kathy says, "and I saw that they liked to work with computers and that they learned from them."

After five years in a kindergarten in Wisconsin, she answered an ad for an opening at the publishing company where she now works. "There was just one editor in the education department when I came here," Kathy recalls, "and she was editing workbooks." Shortly after Kathy was hired, the company launched its line of educational software; the marriage between a venerable children's book publishing company and a deeply committed former kindergarten teacher with an appreciation for computers in the learning process was consummated.

What do you do all day?

"Juggling" is how Kathy Cole describes her daily functions. "We have programs in every stage of development, so my day usually involves brainstorming ideas for new software with the marketing department, consulting with teachers and researchers on ideas in development, talking on the phone with the programmers we contract to write the software, writing and editing workbooks that accompany the software, and meeting with package designers to help them understand what the software will do so they can sell it on the box," she says. Typically, a program will take nine months from conception to reach store shelves, and Kathy marks each stage of development herself. "The editor is the project manager and has to keep everything moving forward."

When she's not just catching her breath, Kathy finds time to visit teachers and kids at local schools to try out new software

with them. "You've got to stay fresh, and you can't become isolated from the real users of your programs."

Where do you see this job leading you?

Kathy sees a bright future for educational software and hopes only to produce better, more useful programs for kids. "We are just starting to develop CD-ROMs that I think will help kids learn without them knowing that they are being taught," she says. "As home computers become more robust, we will be able to develop even more exciting software. I have no ambitions other than to do what I do better and better."

27. Electronic-Game Designer

description: Electronic games today have more in common with movies than they do with games of the past. Game designers devise plots and write scripts that invent all the possible outcomes of any play session. Then, in collaboration with directors, computer programmers, and graphic artists, the game designers execute the scripts and create the games. They are also responsible for quality assurance—making sure the games work as they are intended to. Designers are usually credited for their work, and the very best of them can earn lucrative royalties on their games. While the game business seems like lots of fun—and it is—the deadlines can be demanding and rigid.

salary: Entry-level game designers earn around $25,000 a year; more experienced ones make up to $40,000. Those royalties can bring in more than $100,000, but they are for designers who have created the widely popular games.

prospects: Each succeeding generation of technology allows for more sophisticated games and increases the demand for designers with ideas that suit the technology and the skills to execute them. The jobs tend to be in those high-tech corridors where software companies cluster.

qualifications: You need two different types of attributes: the imagination to create and write dramatically, and some computer programming skills. Ideas for graphics, though not necessarily the ability to execute them, will help.

characteristics: You have to love and understand electronic games to enjoy and succeed at working on them all day. Collaborative team players who are self-directed are best suited to the job.

Andrew P. Morris *is a designer at an electronic games company in Texas.*

How did you get the job?

Andrew earned an English degree at the University of Texas and had been aiming for a career in journalism. "I had done well in creative writing courses and enjoyed them," he recalls, "but my mother didn't think that was very practical. So she directed me toward journalism, a real profession in her mind.

"But the day before graduation, I realized that I hated journalism. So I thought I'd work for an advertising agency. I got an offer from an ad agency in another city—one that I didn't want to move to—and I was hesitant to take it."

While Andrew was deciding whether to take the advertising job, a few of his friends, and then his girlfriend, got jobs as computer programmers at the company he now works for.

Virtually on his way out of town, he stopped into the company's office for an interview. "That was a fairly common practice for our company at that time," he says. Andrew brought to the interview his personal passion for games. "I think I impressed the guy who interviewed me with my understanding and analysis of games," Andrew says. "And he hired me on the spot. It was that simple."

What do you do all day?

Andrew takes game ideas given to him by the company's producers and directors and writes a script establishing the game's plot lines, dialogue, and reactions to the player's actions. Once a producer approves of the script, Andrew meets with the director assigned to manage the project, the programmers who will code the game, and the artists who give its images life.

"During the game's production, I choreograph the scenes," he explains, "then the artists create the background and props for it. When they're done, I'll manipulate the programmer's code to move the props around in the scene as the game proceeds."

For 12 to 24 months at a time, Andrew works on all phases of a single game. "We are under constant deadline pressure," he says. "That's because it's impossible to come up with a realistic schedule—the tools needed to execute our ideas are being developed as we're trying to implement them."

Those deadlines can mean long hours for the whole team. "If you don't love games and creating them, you will burn out in this job," Andrew says. "You may never want to see a game again after spending that much time with them."

Where do you see this job leading you?

Andrew, who still seems to love games after three and a half years designing them, sees two opportunities before him: producer or director. A producer oversees several game projects and all their details, from budgeting and marketing to personnel and quality assurance. Directors coordinate the efforts of the technical and creative staffs, one game at a time. "Right now I'm leaning toward directing," Andrew says. "It's more hands-on than producing. I like making games—I'd resist anything that involved more paperwork and less playing."

> "DESIGN GAMES—PAID OR NOT. IF YOU WANT TO BE THOUGHT OF AS A DESIGNER, JUST START DOING IT, AND THEN YOU'LL BE ONE."

28. Encyclopedia Editor

description: An encyclopedia is not static—it's a living, evolving document of our collected knowledge. Encyclopedia editors work continuously to update the information already in the volumes and to seek out new material deserving of inclusion in them. Like editors of other kinds of publications, these editors assign authors to write the articles, set guidelines and deadlines, and refine the manuscripts. Encyclopedia editors are relatively anonymous and are paid as modestly as others in the publishing industry. They tend to be people who relish the pursuit of knowledge and the sharing of it.

salary: An entry-level encyclopedia fact-checker earns about $17,000 to $20,000 a year, an editor-in-chief closer to $60,000 a year.

prospects: Dozens of companies publish general or special-interest encyclopedias—you can probably name a few off the top of your head. The editorial staffs tend to be relatively small and stable, but if you're determined to work in reference publishing and willing to start with the most fundamental work, you can break in. Most encyclopedia publishers are based in large cities.

qualifications: A broad-based education that includes reading in many subjects and detailed knowledge in one or two is your best preparation. Many of the candidates you'll be competing against have graduate degrees.

characteristics: Well-organized people attentive to detail and insistent about accuracy will succeed as encyclopedia editors.

Robert McHenry *is editor-in-chief of an encyclopedia published by a company based in the Midwest.*

How did you get the job?

Bob didn't prepare for a job. Rather, he pursued an education—starting with a bachelor's degree in English literature from Northwestern University, then a master's in English from the University of Michigan.

"In the 1960s, we tended to think all courses were irrelevant, but fortunately they were required," Bob jokes, adding that "all the courses that made me read the best that has been written and to think hard about what I read were good preparation for this job, as they would be for many."

So where did Bob go with his education? Straight to the state employment service. "A kindly gentleman there looked at my application form, noted my utter lack of any useful experience, and told me that the encyclopedia publisher was looking for proofreaders," Bob says. "That sounded like a good place for me to start.

"I passed the proofreading test easily," he adds. "I don't know if that's a knack."

Bob worked his way through the editorial ranks, moving first to production editor (what most publishers call a copy editor), where he learned to fact-check, fit the copy into its designated space, and check page proofs and the film that's sent to the printer. "I gradually learned what the whole enterprise is about," Bob says, "and most importantly what the standards are.

"Most of our editors have begun as copy editors or researchers, in trainee positions that, with learning and practice and mastery, lead to more advanced rankings."

What do you do all day?

Each editor on the encyclopedia's staff is responsible for the articles in one or several particular subject areas. The editors work with academic advisers to review every major article regularly and to ensure that the supporting shorter articles remain relevant. "Events that may provoke revision at some level are monitored through newspapers and journals, so that deaths, elections, discoveries, revolutions, and so forth are properly accounted for in our text," Bob explains.

> **"TAKE THE HARD COURSES, MAKE YOURSELF WORK AND THINK; THEN COME SEE ME."**

When the advisers and the editor determine that a revision is needed, the editor creates an outline for the article and assigns it to an author with in-depth knowledge of the field. The editor guides each author in producing an article that is for a general audience, then edits the article, seeking "to clarify obscure points and answer queries prompted by the manuscript," Bob says.

And how does Bob fit into this process? "My particular job," he says, "is to see that this all happens in an organized way."

Where do you see this job leading you?

Bob is where nearly every encyclopedia editor would like to be: editor-in-chief of a venerable institution. "This job has already led me further than I expected," he says. "At this point I just want to do it well. I have about 20 predecessors who set a very high standard."

29. Extension Service Publications Writer

description: Land grant universities—public colleges established by state governments—are required by their charters to gather and disseminate information useful to farmers, small businesses, and the general public. The cooperative extension service—the organization set up by the schools to fulfill that mandate—employs writers and editors to produce bulletins and other publications that contain information about agriculture, commerce, home economics, and lots of other topics. These writers and editors are not usually experts in those fields; rather, they work with professors and researchers to compile the information. Working for extension service publications departments is an excellent entry into academic writing.

salary: At a large university in a metropolitan area, this job typically pays a starting salary of $20,000 to $25,000 a year; it pays slightly less in less-populated regions.

prospects: Even a large school may have just a handful of writers working for its extension service, but the competition for these unique jobs is not all that fierce. And because they are often entry-level jobs, positions open up as people gain experience and move up to higher levels.

qualifications: You must be able to distill complex research into information people can use in their work and homes, and you must be able to translate academic terminology into language understandable by your audience. Expertise in the subjects addressed by the research isn't necessary, but working knowledge of them will boost your candidacy for a job.

characteristics: If you enjoy being in an academic environment, working alone and collaborating, and managing a lot of details, you're suited for this kind of work.

Karen Polyak *is a publications writer for the extension service of a large university on the East Coast.*

- -

How did you get the job?

After earning a degree in English writing from Penn State University, Karen moved to New York City "without a plan or a prospect," she says. But quickly enough she responded to an advertisement in *The New York Times* for a job at the New York Botanical Garden—and was hired onto the staff of its *Garden* magazine.

"That was a great experience," Karen recalls. "The woman I worked for was an excellent teacher and supervisor. We had a relatively small staff, so I got to do everything from assigning and editing articles to correcting color separations.

"Just two and a half years later, my boss left and she recommended me for her job. So I ran the magazine for one and a half years," Karen continues. "I guess you could say I was in the right place at the right time."

That good fortune expired, however, when the botanical garden ceased publishing the magazine. Karen was out of work for six months before she found a job as a copy editor at Rockefeller University Press and then as an art buyer at Oxford University Press. "At Oxford, I commissioned illustrations for the company's English as a Second Language book division," Karen says. "That was quite a different experience for me, and, I have to say, not one I enjoyed a great deal."

Karen left New York for personal reasons and began responding to ads in the newspaper in the area where she now lives. In short order, her background in scientific journalism in general and experience in horticulture secured her the job she has now.

What do you do all day?

Karen says simply that she "produces publications for the College of Agriculture and Natural Resources" at the university where she works. "About 50 percent of the publications I work on relate to agriculture," she says. "The rest deal with the environment, business, and other topics."

> "IT'S POSSIBLE TO GO THROUGH 16 YEARS OF SCHOOL AND HAVE ABSOLUTELY NO SENSE OF THE POLITICS THAT ARE PART OF MOST WORKING ENVIRONMENTS. WHEN YOU GET A JOB, BE AS POLITICALLY ASTUTE AS YOU CAN."

As in her first job, Karen oversees the entire production process of the publications for which she's responsible. "I receive manuscripts from authors, who are usually cooperative extension agents who have master's degrees in their field, but who are not professional writers. I edit—rewrite when necessary—their manuscripts," she says. "Then I proofread them, design and lay them out on a Macintosh computer, and output film that we send to the printer.

"It can be very rewarding to be responsible for everything," she adds. "But it's exhausting to be the last stop on the train all the time, too."

Karen spends about 10 to 15 percent of her time writing articles herself. She also is sometimes asked to compose press releases, posters, cards, and lobbying letters. "We have a new dean of our college," she says, "and he's big on public relations. We're the writers on the staff, so we're called on to write whatever he wants us to."

Where do you see this job leading you?

You can be sure that Karen is headed up and out from this job. "I think I could freelance as a writer and copy editor and do fairly well at it, but I don't think that's for me," she says. "I think I need to develop a specialty—I believe you can only move up in publishing if you're focused on one particular area."

Karen points out that other extension service writers go to other academic departments or they move over to university public relations.

30. Feature Writer, Newspaper

description: While general assignment reporters deal with the grim side of the news, feature writers delve into the more positive side of life in the paper's coverage area. The articles produced by feature writers tend to be longer than most news stories and require more time to compile—though feature writers live under regular deadline pressure, too. Some feature writers cover specific topics, such as the arts, food, travel, personalities; others handle assignments of all types. Feature writers typically have a few years' experience as a reporter before moving out of the news department and into other sections of the newspaper.

salary: Feature writer is not an entry-level job, but with just a couple of years of experience as a reporter, a new feature writer will earn about $25,000 at a daily newspaper in a midsize city—slightly more in bigger cities, less in smaller ones.

prospects: Feature writer is one of the most sought-after jobs at a newspaper. But newspapers are very transient places to work—people come and go, especially from smaller cities to larger ones, and experienced feature writers often move up to editorships or to magazine feature writing. So positions open frequently enough for dedicated reporters to get those jobs as feature writers.

qualifications: Feature writers have experience as a reporter (or at least training in journalism), above-average writing (as opposed to news-gathering) skills, and lots of strong ideas on how to bring the human element into the newspaper's coverage. Your application may be enhanced if you have in-depth knowledge and keen interest in one or two of the topics (i.e., fashion, architecture, music) regularly addressed in the paper's feature section. A journalism degree is usually very helpful, though not always required.

characteristics: Most of all, feature writers need to like working with people and to have the kind of personality that engenders trust in strangers. Successful feature writers are also highly self-motivated, often seeking out stories on their own rather than accepting assignments. They must have a strong writing style and a clear voice.

June Naylor Rodriguez *is a feature writer at a daily newspaper in Texas.*

- -

How did you get the job?

June has had only one job that mattered to her—the one she has now. "When I finished college, I didn't think I could get a job as a writer, so I went into advertising sales briefly, but I hated it," says June, who has a bachelor's degree in journalism from Texas Christian University. "Then I went to work for a public relations agency, but I hated that, too."

So finally, June, the daughter of a well-known local high school football coach, decided she wanted to be a newspaper reporter. "I called the sports editor at the newspaper, told him who I was, and asked if he had any assignments for a freelance reporter," she recalls. "He asked me to go to a girls' soccer game that day." June went to that soccer game, wrote about it for the sports section, and hasn't stopped writing for the paper since. "I called the news editor every day for six months to ask if he had any events he wanted

covered," she says. "He sent me to city council meetings out in the little Podunk towns that no one else wanted to go to. They were really great fun; I remember at one an argument broke out when one council member accused the mayor of stealing his pig."

> **"KNOW WHAT THE PAPER IS DOING— IF TUESDAY'S FOCUS IS HEALTH AND WEDNESDAY'S IS FOOD, SUGGEST APPROPRIATE IDEAS."**

With her persistence and her rare enthusiasm for every assignment—big or small, pig or no—June earned herself an opportunity to fill an opening on the full-time staff. When the paper's news editor moved to the features department a couple of years later, June followed him.

What do you do all day?

June's work now focuses on three major areas: restaurant reviews, her fitness column, and people profiles. "I do one or two dining-out reviews a week, which appear in the paper on Wednesdays and Fridays," she explains. Every other month, June and her two colleagues each submit a list of 10 eateries they believe worthy of review to the feature editors, who then decide which are to be reviewed and by which writer. Then June visits her assigned restaurants anonymously and writes about them. "We are also responsible for turning in a photo assignment so that a photographer is sent out to take a picture of the place."

The Tuesday fitness column is June's own idea. "I knew that a lot of people in this area were interested in fitness, so I suggested a regular column on it for our Life page," she says. "I do stories about local exercise experts, nutrition pieces, reviews of workout videos— almost anything associated with

fitness." June also answers calls and letters from readers who want more specific information than the column may provide.

Finally, June frequently writes long profiles of local personalities. "I'd say I spend 20 to 25 hours each week writing and rewriting," she says. "Most of the rest is spent interviewing people."

Where do you see this job leading you?

June is acutely aware of the difference between an editor and a writer. "Editors are tied to their desks, except when they go to meetings," she says. "I like to go out and meet people, and cultivate my ideas. And I truly like to write.

"Lots of writers can't wait to move up to editor," she goes on. "But all I want to do is come up with more ideas for things I can write."

31. Fiction Editor

description: Fiction editors decide which novels and short-story collections will be published each season and oversee their progress from purchase to printing. They read manuscripts and talk to agents, educate their company's marketing and promotion departments, and help make art and design choices. Fiction editors enjoy the power and glamour of determining what the public will get to read, but they must get the most notoriously complicated people in book publishing—fiction writers—to meet rigorous deadlines. Traditionally, most of these jobs are in New York City, though there are fiction publishers in other big cities and at universities.

salary: Editorial assistants, the entry-level positions in a publisher's fiction department, start out earning between $18,000 and $23,000 a year, depending on the company. Experienced fiction editors with a track record of picking winners can earn $60,000 or even more.

prospects: In spite of the low pay, the competition for entry-level jobs in fiction is fierce—even more so outside of New York City. But good editorial assistants move up to be assistant editors every year, and those entry-level jobs are open again. With determination and patience, you'll get one.

qualifications: You must be well educated in literature (either in college or self-taught) with a developed sense of personal taste. You need to write clearly and succinctly, and to be highly organized.

characteristics: People who are passionate about books and compassionate toward writers, and who can manage many projects at once, will succeed as fiction editors.

Mark James *is an assistant editor at a large publishing company in New York City.*

How did you get the job?

Mark enrolled in a summer publishing workshop after graduating from Miami University of Ohio with a bachelor's degree in English literature and classical history. "Everyone in both book and magazine publishing who came to speak to us during the month I was in the program said the same thing: 'Make an impression on people in the business and then follow up with them,'" Mark says. "And that's just what I did."

After the course was finished, Mark decided that he wanted to work in the editorial department of a book publisher. So he packed up and headed to New York City. "When I got to New York, I called everybody I had met at the course and asked if they had an entry-level job," he says. "When I talked to a book publisher who had spoken at the course, he offered to call someone in his editorial department for me." Within a month of arriving in the big city, Mark was working as an editorial assistant in the fiction department of one of the best-known publishers.

"Then my boss, who has been a bit of a mentor to me, got offered a job at another publishing company, which she accepted," Mark says. "She asked me to come with her and move up to an assistant editor. Of course, for such an opportunity, I took her offer."

What do you do all day?

Does keeping tabs on 30 to 50 books in various stages of progress sound like a full day? On any given day, Mark will read proposals, chapters, and completed manuscripts, then recommend that his company acquire the best, most marketable of these. He checks in with authors under contract to be sure their work is proceeding on schedule and he devotes a lot of his energy to getting the sales and promotions departments of his company excited about the books they will be selling.

"We have a sales conference every four months, and we spend a lot of time before it writing catalog copy and making sure that every book will meet its deadline," Mark says. "And we have to keep that enthusiasm up. We are selecting books three years in advance, so we're always pumping up the company's interest in those upcoming books."

Mark stresses that entry-level jobs involve a fair amount of administrative work along with the more fulfilling tasks of reading and talking to authors. "Because there's so many books in progress at once, you need to keep well-organized files on each one," he explains. "It's the easiest thing to slack off and mess up, but it's in those responsibilities that you prove yourself."

> "PUBLISHING SEEMS LIKE A CLOSED INDUSTRY, BUT ONCE YOU'RE IN—NO MATTER WHAT YOU DO—THE DOORS TO OTHER OPPORTUNITIES OPEN UP TO YOU."

Where do you see this job leading you?

Mark aimed for an editorial job in fiction publishing and struck a bull's-eye. Now he'd like to continue to move up, gaining experience and judgment along the way. "Once thing I've learned is that you can't just walk into an upper-level job," he says. "You build up to it step by step. That's what I'm doing now."

32. Freelance Editor and Proofreader

description: Many companies supplement their staffs during busy periods with freelance editors and proofreaders. Some freelance jobs may be standing ones—say, a certain number of days a week at a company—while in other cases freelancers are called in when needed. Freelance editors often take the work to their homes, but can be called upon to work in the clients' offices. Freelancers control their own schedules, yet must be flexible enough to adapt to their clients' needs. They tend to be paid on an hourly basis, though they sometimes are paid a flat fee for completing the assigned job. Developing a steady clientele is perhaps the most significant challenge for succeeding as a freelancer.

salary: A standard fee schedule for freelance editing and proofreading might go like this: $15–25 an hour for proofing, $15–30 for copy-editing, and $25–40 for line editing. Smaller markets will pay significantly less, however. Your yearly income will be based on how much work you can find and are willing to do.

prospects: The amount of work you can find as a freelancer is limited only by how aggressive and creative you are in seeking out opportunities. While publishers have obvious needs for editing and proofreading services, many other companies also rely on outside help to put a professional polish on brochures, sales flyers, newsletters, and other printed materials.

qualifications: To work steadily as a freelancer, you must be versatile in both skills and knowledge, with the ability to do everything from wholesale rewriting to proofing with a fine-tooth comb. Familiarity with business and technical topics—and their unique vocabularies—will broaden your opportunities. The best avenue for securing jobs is through references—establish a network of satisfied clients, and ask them if prospective clients may call them to discuss your work.

characteristics: Freelancers who earn repeat business—the key to succeeding financially—are adaptable to varied working conditions, work well both alone and in a group (usually with people they don't know), and can handle the pressure of ever-present deadlines.

Gayle Putman *is a freelance editor and proofreader in the suburbs of a large city on the East Coast.*

How do you get jobs?

Before deciding to strike out on her own as a freelancer, Gayle worked for several corporations as a script- and copywriter. "I wrote scripts for video presentations that were shown at sales meetings, new product introductions, and the like," she says, "and I wrote advertising and marketing copy.

"I enjoyed the work as a rule. And I was already doing some freelance writing in my spare time," she continues. "But I didn't like my boss's inability to delegate work or the subject matter I was writing about at my last full-time job, so I decided to be my own boss."

Since Gayle already had some contacts, she was up and running right away—writing copy for a couple of advertising agencies and newsletters immediately. But she didn't rest on that foundation. "I joined the International Association of Business Communicators and got a copy of its directory," she explains. "I looked for prospects in there and sent a half sheet of

paper with just a few paragraphs to each of them. I got a lot of responses without even calling to follow up."

Nowadays, Gayle gets a lot of referrals to all sorts of businesses. And with that broad experience, she has developed a sense of where the desirable work can be found. "The work may not be as interesting at most corporations as it is at book or magazine publishers, but it is somewhat easier to get into corporations," she says. "And corporate work pays

> "IF YOU DECIDE TO FREELANCE, YOU HAVE TO BE READY TO PAY ATTENTION TO THE BUSINESS OF FREELANCING: PURSUING NEW CLIENTS, MANAGING YOUR TIME, AND MAKING SURE YOU SEND OUT YOUR INVOICES AND GET PAID PROMPTLY."

better—the people don't blink an eye at the fee schedule, while many publishers try to negotiate you down. And in my experience, ad agencies have interesting work," she adds, "but they tend to pay very slowly."

What do you do all day?

Three to four days a week you'll find Gayle in the offices of several companies, editing and proofing their mailers, brochures, and other communications. "Corporations like this need to see you working in their offices because of tight turnaround time," she says. "Which is OK by me because it offsets the isolation that you live with most of the time when you freelance."

The bulk of the rest of Gayle's time is spent on jobs for various magazines and newsletters produced by publishers, corporations, and even the U.S. government. "Most of the time I'm either copy-editing or proofreading," she says. "And I do some of it in the office and some at home."

Home is where you're sure to find Gayle after school hours

every day. "I have two children, so I try to be finished for the day in the late afternoon, no matter what I'm doing," she explains. "I don't mind working at home on the weekends or, even better, early in the morning to get a job done. But I want time with my family, and as a freelancer, I can have it—that's the beauty of freelancing."

Where do you see this job leading you?

Gayle has been considering an offer to work as a full-time editor for the publishing company where she's been freelancing. "Now that my children are older and going to school, I am enticed by regular full-time pay and benefits," she says. "But I love the freedom I have. And I'd like to do more writing—especially magazine writing.

"I'm torn at the moment," she concludes. "I don't know what I will do, but I do know I could be happy whichever way I go."

33. Fund-Raiser, Nonprofit Arts Organization

description: Nonprofit organizations rely on the goodwill, generosity, and tax breaks of corporations, foundations, and individuals for their financial support. Nonprofits employ fund-raisers, including grant writers, to research and compose grant proposals and other printed literature that will appeal to those entities for donations. Depending on the size of the organization they work for, fund-raisers may devote their time exclusively to corporate grants or they may be part of a broader effort that includes writing appeals to individuals, philanthropic foundations, and government agencies.

salary: A fund-raising associate just starting work for a nonprofit organization earns from about $18,000 to $22,000, slightly more in larger cities and at big institutions. At the top of the fund-raising scale—managing a "development" department—you can earn $50,000 to $80,000 a year, or more.

prospects: Nonprofit institutions cannot function without fund-raisers, but limited budgets mean limited staff. But a person dedicated to the nonprofit's field of activity—the arts, social change, the environment, etc.—can earn an opportunity.

qualifications: Researching and writing are two primary functions of a fund-raiser with writing responsibility, so a liberal arts education with an emphasis on composition is ideal preparation for the job. Courses or experience in marketing is useful, too.

characteristics: Good fund-raisers are people-oriented people—they collaborate with lots of different people in developing proposals and they have a personal style that ingratiates them with the decision makers who will consider the proposals.

Lizanne Hart *is director of member/donor communications for an art museum in a Northern city.*

How did you get the job?

Lizanne is a classic example of making the most of an internship. "I was an intern in visitor services at the museum during my junior and senior years in college, and by the time the internship was over I had done enough work in different positions that my abilities, my productivity, my commitment were clear to many people at the museum," Lizanne says. "I was a known quantity." So, after she graduated with a bachelor of arts in art history and history from a small liberal arts college nearby, she was offered a temporary job in the development office, which evolved into a new, permanent position as a prospect researcher and grant writer.

After getting the job, Lizanne continued to enroll in professional courses on grant writing and prospect research offered by a local arts manage-ment organization, and she has continually learned and accepted new duties in the depart-ment. "I've created a kind of odd hybrid job for myself by always looking for new ways to contribute to our fund-raising efforts," Lizanne explains. "Now I am responsible for developing a common thread that runs through all of our communications with our members, individual or corporate."

What do you do all day?

Fund-raising begins with research. "First, you have to prospect," Lizanne explains. "The fund-raiser spends a lot of time combing through trade journals, annual reports, corporate newsletters, the local press, searching for corporations, foundations, or individuals that might be receptive to your organization's appeal." She also works with many other staff people at the institution to better understand which programs to target for funding, and gathers statistics about the museum's use and public service, and the

> "TAKE THE TIME TO LEARN ABOUT ARTS ADMINISTRATION IF YOU WANT TO WORK IN THE ARTS—IT'S A LOT LIKE RUNNING A CORPORATION, BUT WITH SOME VERY CRITICAL DIFFERENCES."

history of the programs. "The more you know about the organization you need support for, the stronger your case will be in seeking funding for it," she says.

"Writing for fund-raising is a lot like writing research papers in college," she continues. "You make a case statement and then you build your case with facts and clear, logical thinking." Before any literature is printed, Lizanne consults with editors on staff at the museum to ensure that it is grammatically and stylistically sound.

When Lizanne first started at the museum, prospecting and grant writing took up all her time. Now she contributes to every communication with the museum's members. "I also write brochures, direct-mail packages, newsletters, even the signs for membership sales in the museum," she says. "My job is to oversee or contribute to every communication we have with our members."

Where do you see this job leading you?

Lizanne Hart loves the arts and she hopes to keep working in either the visual or performing arts. She's happy at the museum for the moment, but "managing a performing arts company seems appealing to me," she says. "From my job, someone could either move into managing a whole fund-raising effort, or go into marketing and communications."

34. Fund-Raiser, University

description: Colleges large and small rely on money that comes from sources beyond students' tuition and government subsidies. Grant and fund-raising proposal writers are experts at asking corporations, foundations, and individuals to give money for nothing more in return than seeing the money well spent—the writers' talent is to persuade donors that the money is just that. Grant and proposal writers typically work in the college's development department—raising funds from former students and philanthropic foundations—or for particular departments that qualify for support for their research. Large universities may have several proposal writers on staff; at a small college, there's typically only one.

salary: At state-supported schools, proposal writers start at about $25,000 per year. An experienced writer at a private institution may earn about $45,000.

prospects: Grant writers can secure their own paychecks with successful fund-raising strategies. So, of course, those who can raise their own salary and bring in more money will always be able to find a job.

qualifications: You don't need to study proposal writing—though there are courses—but you do need to be able to write enthusiastically, persuasively, and concisely. A broad-based liberal arts education is a good foundation to start with, though training or experience in marketing will help, too.

characteristics: Upbeat, versatile, well-organized people with thick skins—to protect them from rejection and the editing of untrained editors (who occupy other jobs)—thrive as proposal writers.

Dara Kloss *is the assistant director of research and proposal coordinator at the Office of Alumni and Development at a public land grant university in the South.*

How did you get the job?

This is a tale of how a job got someone. Dara—who has a bachelor's degree in journalism from the university where she now works—set out to work in newspaper journalism. "I was the reporter and the photographer for a small-town weekly newspaper," she recalls. "After a year of low pay and long hours, I went to work in [the university's] horticulture department, where I assisted the faculty in preparing grant proposals, edited research papers, wrote and edited several newsletters."

A year or so later, Dara accepted the job of technical writer/editor for the chemical engineering department. In those first two jobs, she "learned how to grunt it out and produce quality work when I didn't feel like it," she explains. "Sometimes it's hard to get real enthusiastic about potting soil amendments or asphalt aggregate adsorption—but you

must." During her tenure in the engineering department, Dara worked with several university-wide committees that were putting together proposals. "Through that exposure and having had some big-dollar proposals funded, I earned the reputation as a good proposal writer," she says. "When the writing position opened in Alumni and Development, the woman responsible for hiring the new writer called me and asked me to interview.

"What set me apart from the other candidates," she goes on, "was my track record and experience—especially my versatility.

> **"VOLUNTEER TO HELP FACULTY AT YOUR SCHOOL WITH THEIR GRANT PROPOSALS. ALSO, MANY COLLEGE DEVELOPMENT OFFICES HIRE STUDENT ASSISTANTS."**

My portfolio has everything from newspaper clippings and brochures to research proposals and video I produced," she says. "And because [the school where she is employed] is a strong research university, my technical writing skills were an added bonus."

What do you do all day?

A university may seem like a quiet, low-key place to work, but it sure isn't that for the proposal-writing staff. "Last year I wrote approximately 50 grant proposals," Dara says. She composes appeals for funding for specific projects or for the school's general fund. She also researches potential donors, generates ideas for successfully appealing to them, and writes letters, case statements, and brochures in support of the fund-raising efforts.

Dara is fortunate enough to have an assistant who "helps

with cover letters, funding agreements, and a lot of other miscellaneous things that writers in small shops end up doing themselves," she says. That leaves her with some time left to keep the alumni office's development officers informed about the potential donors her research turns up.

Where do you see this job leading you?

"I would like to move into a fund-raising position that deals more with establishing relationships between the university and foundations and corporations," Dara says, and it's apparent how that kind of challenge would suit someone who has from the start enjoyed success raising money. Proposal and grant writers often climb through the ranks of development departments to top positions.

35. Greeting Card Editor

description: Have you stood at the rack in the local gift shop, overwhelmed by the variety of cards for every occasion and sentiment? Who do we have to thank/blame for that? Greeting card editors, whose job is to compile a line of cards that express a broad range of emotions for holidays, birthdays, and everyday occurrences. An editor at a large company may manage a particular line of cards—sympathy expressions, for example—while at smaller companies the editors usually contribute to the full gamut of cards. Editors work with graphic designers, freelance and staff writers, and marketing experts to meet their customers' needs.

salary: Entry-level editors earn about $20,000 at small to midsize companies, more at larger ones. Experienced editors work on more important lines of cards (say, Christmas rather than Saint Patrick's Day) and can earn $50,000 to $60,000 a year at larger companies.

prospects: It seems that greeting card companies are continually inventing new occasions that require card-buying, creating a demand for more card writers and editors. But there are just a few large companies, several that are midsize, and a bunch of small ones. Positions at those companies are highly sought-after.

qualifications: There's no degree offered in greeting-card editing anywhere, but training and experience in advertising and marketing will prepare you for developing the kinds of ideas and copy used in greeting cards. A strong visual sense will help, as will knowledge of poetic forms and conversational prose.

characteristics: To assemble a line of cards, editors must be able to set aside their own voices and manners of expression and consider all of the ways that individuals would like to express themselves.

Julienne Gehrer *is a senior editor at a large greeting card company in the Midwest.*

- -

How did you get the job?

Julienne has always felt challenged by writing and editing concise copy targeted at very specific audiences. With her degree in journalism/advertising from the University of Kansas, she landed a job at a major department store chain's Midwest division, where she wrote advertising and catalog copy. "Ad copy focuses very directly on consumer needs," she explains. "That's just what greeting cards do." Julienne took that experience to the greeting card company's advertising department, and for four years turned out scripts for radio ads, as well as copy for merchandising brochures and print advertisements.

"After working in advertising for a number of years, I decided I wanted to work with more sincere, more people-to-people expressions," Julienne says. "So

I tried what we call an 'internal portfolio,' which is a set of exercises on writing and editing cards. That goes through an in-house screening process, and if the creative directors believe you have promise, you will be offered an opportunity with one line of cards.

"I guess I showed promise," she laughs, "because here I am."

What do you do all day?

Julienne's primary responsibility is Mother's Day. That's right, for most of the year she generates ideas (and solicits them from in-house staff writers, writers under contract with the company, and freelancers) that say, in as many different ways as possible, that the senders appreciate their mothers, grandmothers, wives, aunts, sisters, and virtually any other female relation. "As society evolves and people's relationships become more complicated, the more help people need in finding a message that expresses the right nuance of their feeling," Julienne says. "For example, what do you say to the mother of your ex-husband whom you are

> **"YOU CAN LEARN SELLING LOGIC AND OTHER TACTICS THAT WILL HELP YOU MAKE YOUR LINE OF CARDS SUCCESSFUL."**
>
> - - - - - - - - - -

still close to? She's not your mother or even your mother-in-law anymore. Most people would stumble over that one, so we've developed several Mother's Day cards that express that closeness without mentioning a specific relationship."

Card ideas typically begin with the words and then are assigned to one of the two designers on Julienne's team, who finds the right illustrations or photographs to accompany them. She has input on each package, working as a creative team with her line designer. "Unless the tone of the image conflicts with that of the visual, I don't need to say much about the art," she says.

Julienne meets with the company's marketing staff and studies results of focus groups to ensure that she's always answering consumers' needs. "During the week or two that customers are buying our line of cards, I spend a day at a retail store listening to them talk about what they want, watching what they buy, and learning about what else they want," she says. "We want to provide a portfolio of expressions that meet as many needs as we reasonably can."

Where do you see this job leading you?

Julienne has been working her way up to editing ever larger lines of cards. And she has no goal other than to continue to do that. "I wouldn't want to be in a position that would take me away from what I wanted to do here in the first place," she says, "which is to be involved in those people-to-people expressions."

36. Greeting Card Writer, Freelance

description: You dream up ideas for cards for all occasions and reasons, write the lines down, perhaps suggest a graphic, mail the ideas to editors at greeting card companies, and they buy some of them. Maybe you get to know the editors and they call you with specific assignments. You work when you want, on what you want, when the inspiration strikes you. You get paid for each card you sell.

salary: Greeting card companies pay, on average, $150 to $175 for each card they buy from freelancers. Some smaller companies pay somewhat less; bigger companies and those that have given you an assignment may pay you slightly more. You'll be doing very well if you sell one in every 10 ideas you submit.

prospects: More companies produce more greeting cards for more occasions than ever before, and only a few of them have writers on staff. That makes for a lot of opportunities for freelance card writers. This kind of self-directed work demands persistence and diligence: you have to motivate yourself to produce a lot of ideas regularly and to keep sending them out in the face of frequent rejection.

qualifications: The ability to write cleverly, vividly, and concisely is foremost among a freelance greeting card writer's skills—no training is necessary. You must also be able to view common situations imaginatively, and it helps if you can visualize the card. Good phone skills will help you build relationships with editors.

characteristics: Self-motivated, persistent, and thick-skinned writers will succeed at selling freelance greeting card ideas. You need those qualities to produce and sell enough cards to earn a livable wage. That thick skin will come in handy when you receive the many rejections; you must ignore the rejections and continue to send out ideas.

Donna LaSota *is a freelance greeting card writer living in the Northeast.*

How did you get the job?

Donna LaSota takes a very practical view of her work as a freelance card writer. "I have skill that I can sell and that's what I do," she says. "I'm in it for the money." Before Donna started writing greeting cards, she had written some short stories that she was unable to sell. So, in response to an advertisement she read in *Writer's Digest,* she decided to submit some card ideas to United Greeting Card Co. "I got $25 for that first card," Donna recalls, "and I still remember how excited I was to sell that very first one." In the 18 years since Donna broke in, she's sold cards to almost every major greeting card company. And she's forged such a solid relationship with the editors at one company that she'll get calls with assignments several times a year.

What do you do all day?

"Freelance is my ideal way to work," Donna says. "I'm my own boss—I can work when I want, where I want (even by my pool), as much as I want." Still, Donna makes it a habit to sit down for a predetermined period of time and devise ideas every working day. "The only way to make a living selling greeting card ideas is to be dedicated to it," she emphasizes. "If you only write down ideas when they hit you on the head, you won't produce enough to keep the sales coming." After Donna has a list of ideas she's satisfied enough with to submit, she types each card's lines on a separate index card. "I'm no artist, so I don't even attempt the graphics," she says, "but if I have an idea for an image, I'll describe it on the card."

Donna's careful to submit the ideas to only one company at a time. "It will only cause you problems if you send the same ideas to different companies simultaneously," she says. "What will you do if two companies want the same card?"

Now that she's established relationships with certain companies, Donna will often ask the editors for needs lists. "The editors in this business seem to be almost universally nice people who will talk to you on the phone and help you. They like freelancers and encourage them to submit." And most companies, she reports, pay promptly on acceptance of your idea.

Where do you see this job leading you?

"I'm very fortunate that I do something I love—make people laugh—for the kind of money I can live on," Donna LaSota says. "All I'd like to do is keep selling my card ideas." She adds that she'd like to see card writers credited on the backs of cards as the illustrators often are.

> **"BEFORE YOU SUBMIT IDEAS, LOOK AT THE COMPANY'S LINE SO YOU KNOW WHAT KINDS OF CARDS THEY DO. IF YOU CALL MOST COMPANIES AND SAY THAT YOU'RE A FREELANCE CARD WRITER, THEY'LL SEND YOU A SAMPLE KIT TO HELP YOU FIGURE THAT OUT."**

37. Indexer

description: How do readers quickly find information in a book without reading the entire text? They look it up in the index. And who compiles the index? An indexer who carefully reads the entire text and identifies the topics of greatest interest to other readers, then organizes those topics in a logical format.

The indexer may play an unglamorous (and often uncredited) part in the production of a nonfiction book, but it is a role of critical importance to any book buyer. And the work of indexing can be a very instructive introduction into book publishing.

salary: Indexing is usually an entry-level job that pays an entry-level salary of about $20,000 a year—give or take a couple of grand for people working in regions of the country that have a higher or lower than average cost of living. Indexers working on highly technical books—such as reference books for medical professionals—may earn slightly more because those books demand that an indexer have specialized knowledge. A supervisor of indexers will earn $25,000 to $30,000 a year.

prospects: Nonfiction books are one of the strongest segments of the publishing market and thousands of new titles land on bookstore shelves every year. That creates a fairly high demand for indexers. Moreover, because indexing is an entry-level job, positions frequently open up as people move up into other jobs in publishing companies.

qualifications: A broad-based education will help you work with books on diverse topics and allow you to understand the interests of differing readers. A productive indexer must be able to read quickly but thoroughly. And, since most publishers now use widely available computer software to perform the process of compiling the index, you should be at least comfortable with, if not adept at, using computers.

characteristics: Though the indexer works with editors, proofreaders, and designers on the final product, indexing is essentially solitary work. But that doesn't mean you'll be left totally alone. You'll feel steady pressure to meet deadlines. And because the index is one of the last elements of the book to be completed, the pressure can be acute. If you'd enjoy reading by yourself virtually all day, can work quickly and efficiently, and have a head for organization, you can be a successful indexer.

Rebecca Mayfield *is an indexer for a computer book publisher in a large Midwestern city.*

How did you get the job?

Rebecca worked on her bachelor of arts degree in journalism and history from Indiana University with her eye on the book publishing business. "I've always loved to read, and working on books is what I've wanted to do since I first started planning my career," she says.

When she graduated, she applied at a few book publishing companies, but received no offers. So she bided her time with freelance assignments from the publications office of a nearby university, writing brochures for prospective students and guidebooks for new students.

But she kept submitting her resume and published clippings to book companies, and when a friend at her alma mater told her about a specific opening there, she finally won an interview.

"Patience and persistence really paid off," she recalls. "I kept checking in for two months after I took the indexing test, and I finally got a second interview and the job."

What do you do all day?

Read, read, read. With just four or five days to spend getting to know a book inside and out, Rebecca must devote almost all of her eight hours each day to absorbing the book and understanding its readers. "You have to learn what's important to the

> **"BE PATIENT AND PERSISTENT; THE JOBS ARE OUT THERE, BUT SOMETIMES YOU HAVE TO WAIT UNTIL YOURS OPENS UP."**

readers of the book, so that you can organize the index according to what they will want to know most," she explains.

As Rebecca reads, she codes those sections she believes readers will refer to with keywords. "This is where your memory and organizational skills are essential," she says. "You must be consistent, logical, and pre-

cise so that the readers can find exactly what they are looking for right where they expect to find it." She directs PageMaker, the desktop publishing software used by her company, to assemble the index using those keywords.

Where do you see this job leading you?

Now that Rebecca has won a place in book publishing, she has no intentions of leaving soon. After just a couple of years in the business, she's not sure exactly where she'll end up. But of this she is sure: "I want to learn everything I can about publishing, and I know that I'm getting a good dose of that right now." She does, however, fancy the title of editorial director.

38. Interpreter

description: In the ever-expanding global economy, public agencies and businesses require foreign language specialists to interpret during transactions and to help with training of international employees. Many multinational corporations have interpreters on staff, while smaller companies hire agencies that provide interpreters when their need for the service arises.

Interpreting, you should realize, is distinct from translation (see page 198) in that the former is done while the parties involved wait for you, and without the benefit of deliberation and the ability to consult reference books; the latter is done with a document and is more solitary and generally more precise work. And an interpreter's days will be as long as the client's—the job is finished when the people are done talking to each other.

salary: Agencies pay interpreters from $20 to $40 an hour, depending on the language (the less common, the higher the pay) and the level of technical vocabulary required. A corporate interpreter is likely to start between $25,000 and $35,000 a year, again depending on the language and technical knowledge.

prospects: If you speak an Asian (particularly Southeast Asian), Middle Eastern, or Eastern European language fluently, you're a hot property. People who speak Western European tongues are still in demand, but less so, except, perhaps, for Spanish, which is useful to businesses working in Latin America.

qualifications: You need nothing more nor less than near-native fluency in the language you want to interpret and an understanding of the cultures in which the language is spoken. Knowledge of engineering, legal, and medical terminology increases your value and, of course, your earning potential.

characteristics: Reliable interpreters think well on their feet, genuinely like other people, and are sympathetic to foreigners' perspectives.

Evangelia Vassiliadis *is the managing director of a translation agency in Texas.*

How did you get the job?

Evangelia got her current job by creating it for herself. "I was educated in both Greece and the United States, and I settled in the U.S. while I was working as an interpreter for the Greek consulate here," she explains. "I noticed that the consulate was getting daily requests for an interpreter from companies that wanted to do business in Greece. I thought that if the Greek consulate handled that many requests, the other consulates must be getting at least that many. So I realized that there was this great demand for interpreters that wasn't being filled—and I decided to start my own business to meet that demand."

Just five years later, Evangelia has a regular crew of about 80, almost all of them graduate students. She prefers interpreters who come from the ethnic background of the language

> "LEARN TECHNICAL VOCABULARIES— THE MORE TECHNICAL, THE MORE IN DEMAND YOU WILL BE."

they will interpret. "A first- or second-generation American is still close enough to their heritage to understand the culture," she explains. "I wouldn't exclude someone just because they learned the language and culture entirely in school—it's just rarer to find someone who's studied enough to be on a par with a native or near-native speaker."

When she was launching the business, Evangelia canvassed local companies, offering her services and seeking opportunities to bid on their jobs. But no longer. "If you do a good job for someone once, they want you back every time they need an interpreter," she says. "We're almost all repeat business these days."

What do you do all day?

An interpreter spends all day with the client—in business meetings, training sessions, or court, at doctor's appointments, or anyplace else the client would like to go. "Many of our clients are oil and gas companies," Evangelia says, "so our interpreters spend a lot of time in classrooms with engineers from foreign subsidiaries, helping them to understand what's being taught.

"Also, because the city where we live has a major medical center, we are often hired by visiting physicians and patients," she continues. "That's why we place a premium on technical knowledge in those two areas. In other places, the particular demands might be slightly different."

When the visitors' work is done, they frequently want to

get in a bit of fun. "Interpreters can become, in a sense, the clients' friends here in the U.S.," Evangelia says. "The interpreter might spend 14 hours on a weekend day showing the client around the area. That's a lucrative and fairly easy day for an interpreter."

Where do you see this job leading you?

An appointment book full of repeat business is fine, Evangelia says, but she'd like to expand her business into other regions—perhaps even franchise it—and she'd like to get more translation work. "I've done some translation myself and I think we could provide that service to publishing companies interested in international editions," she says. The interpreters on her staff often go on to teach foreign languages, to work as consultants for companies interested in expanding into international markets, and to hold positions with multinational corporations.

39. Librarian, Legal

description: Many multi-partner law firms rely on staff librarians to manage the comings and goings of the inventory of law books shared by the firm's partners and associates. More importantly, the librarians also guide inexperienced clerks and time-is-money attorneys through the ever increasing array of information sources, both printed and electronic. Law librarians understand (and have often studied extensively) legal language and can be called upon to research specific issues for the firm's lawyers. This is a support job with a lot of pressure and demands for speed and accuracy, but little of the glamour and compensation that lawyers typically enjoy.

salary: Inexperienced librarians earn around $20,000 at a medium-size firm. People with legal expertise start at a higher salary, as will librarians at the largest firms in big cities.

prospects: Only larger firms need (or can afford) librarians, but this is a relatively new field with lots of opportunities for people with skills in law, library science, and words. The availability of information, which the legal profession relies on, is multiplying exponentially, increasing the demand for people who can manage and find info.

qualifications: The best candidates for this job have some training in library science, a facility with computers, the ability to write clearly and concisely, and a working knowledge of legal language and issues. Experience in working for the government or in a court is priceless.

characteristics: Law librarians must be self-motivated, must work quickly but accurately and prioritize requests from various attorneys, and must enjoy long hours spent tracking fine details. This is cooperative work, not solitary effort in a quiet library.

Denise Uzee *is the librarian at a law firm in the Deep South.*

How did you get the job?

Denise took her undergraduate degree (bachelor of arts in English) to law school, but left after a year. "I enjoyed doing the research for our assignments, but I hated everything else about law school," she says without equivocation. So she left and went to graduate school in her state's capital to earn her master's degree in library science. That background won Denise a job as a research librarian for the state legislature, where for nine years she provided support for senators and members of the assembly who were writing bills to be introduced and voted upon by the legislature. "I learned all about the legislative process," she explains. "Things they don't teach you in law school."

Of course, government jobs don't pay very well, and Denise's level of mastery of the law and library was bound to command a higher salary in the private sector. Sure enough, Denise answered a newspaper ad and was hired by her current employer because of her experience in regulatory work as well as her graduate degree. "I'm the first person at this firm to be a full-time librarian," she says. "I know that my familiarity with the law and the legislative process helped the partners feel like they were getting more than just someone who could file the books."

What do you do all day?

Managing the traffic flow of books in and out of the library is Denise's most obvious responsibility. "No one knew who had what books before I came here," she laughs. "The attorneys were wasting a lot of time just looking for the books they needed." But book monitor is not the most valuable part of Denise's work. "The clerks here do most of the background research and casework for the attorneys," she explains. "I help them find the resources they need—be it here in our library, in the state's libraries, the local law schools, or on computer networks like LEXUS/NEXUS."

Because of her experience with the legislature, Denise is called upon to look into many questions about state regulations herself. "I still love to do research; it's like being a detective, only I don't do anything with what I find," she says. "I just write a memo to the attorney and explain what I learned." Discovering computers has been fulfilling for Denise, too. "I hadn't worked with them much before I came here, but I've really come to enjoy digging around in the networks for information," she says. "You learn a lot along the way."

Where do you see this job leading you?

Denise knows that with her skills and experience she'd fit in at any other library (especially one at a law school), but she enjoys working for a private firm. "My job has all the things I like about the practice of law," she says, "and very few of the things I don't like."

> **"KNOWING ABOUT THE PROCESS OF LAW WILL DISTINGUISH YOU FROM OTHER PEOPLE WITH JUST A BACKGROUND IN LIBRARIES."**

40. Librarian, Medical

description: Doctors, nurses, and other health-care providers cannot possibly stay abreast of all the accumulated knowledge or current research on the countless conditions that may afflict their patients. So they rely on medical librarians to help them find and use information that will aid them in caring for patients. Medical librarians also help laboratory scientists gather background material for their research. These specialized librarians have some knowledge of the disciplines they're researching and they are adept at using the latest information technology. Most of the people in this field have one or more postgraduate degrees.

salary: Entry-level salaries range from $20,000 to $35,000 per year in this field, depending on the region (higher in big cities) and the librarian's specialty.

prospects: The almost daily release of new health information virtually demands that medical schools, hospitals, pharmaceutical companies, and other institutions continue to expand their capacity to get that information to the people who need it. In short, people who prepare themselves to work in medical libraries will be able to find work.

qualifications: A bachelor of science degree in biology, chemistry, or a similar field is a sturdy foundation, to which you'll need to add a master's degree in library or information science, and perhaps another master's degree in the sciences. You must also be comfortable working with databases on computer.

characteristics: Detail-oriented people who enjoy digging for answers, who can manage several projects at one time, and who can read complex information and understand it make good medical librarians.

Elizabeth Cooley *is the biotechnology bibliographer at a medical school library in the Midwest.*

How did you get the job?

Libby (as she calls herself) began preparing for the job of medical librarian by pursuing the best education available to her. After earning a bachelor of arts from the University of Nebraska at Lincoln, she attended the University of Michigan, where she worked toward a master's degree in information and library studies. "When I arrived at Michigan, it was ranked the number one library program by the Association of Research Libraries directors," she says. "At the time, I didn't know I wanted to be a medical librarian and waited until the second term of my first year to specialize in it."

One of the most important lessons Libby learned while a student was that "you can never tell what will be useful later. Some of the required courses, such as cataloging, felt useless since I knew I would never be a cataloger or work in technical services. But when I was offered the job of assistant director of collection services at the University of Virginia, the collection services department was a division of the technical services department, and that cataloging course helped with many of my primary assignments."

While still working on her master's degree, Libby also served as a research assistant for a medical library professor. "It

> "TRY TO WORK IN AS MANY AREAS OF THE LIBRARY AS POSSIBLE, AS EARLY IN YOUR CAREER AS POSSIBLE. NOT ONLY WILL THIS GIVE YOU AN IDEA OF WHAT YOU WANT TO PURSUE, IT WILL ALSO GIVE YOU THE EXPERIENCE YOU NEED TO PURSUE IT."

was important for me to put theory (school) into practice (job) simultaneously," she says. "I also believe that this led me to acquire a position at a highly ranked medical library upon graduation, which opened up numerous opportunities within my everyday work and beyond."

What do you do all day?

As a bibliographer, Libby focuses on the content of the library's collection of books. She continually evaluates the collection, making sure that it is complete and useful to the faculty, researchers, and students who depend on the library.

"My primary focus is on our biotechnology and veterinary medicine collections," Libby says. "I'm also the bibliographer for genetics, cytology, molecular biology, zoology, human anatomy and physiology, microbiology, biochemistry, statistics, mathematics, computer science, and general medicine."

Another critical responsibility for a bibliographer in a medical library is coordinating borrowing, lending, and collection development with librarians at nearby institutions. "The National Medical Library has divided up the country into regions with the goal of building regional collections from which users from any institution in that region can borrow," Libby explains. "This is the most cost-effective way for each library to build its collection and make virtually anything a user wants available."

Libby is also the library's liaison to the school's veterinary medicine and biotechnology faculties and helps them evaluate instructional materials for the department's students.

Where do you see this job leading you?

After six years in several medical libraries, Libby has earned the rank of assistant professor and is involved in developing policy for all the bibliographers in the library. But she continues to aspire to more. "With the experience I have gained in the sciences and biotechnology, I am looking at other opportunities in health science libraries, general academic science, or special libraries (such as at a biotechnology company)," she says. "I do plan to return to higher education and obtain a second master's or a doctorate to become more marketable."

41. Librarian, Reference

description: Questions are the domain of reference librarians. Whether you're working on a research project, searching for a job, or trying to settle a bet about trivia, you can ask a reference librarian to guide you to the resources that will contain the answers to your questions. A reference librarian in a public library will deal with queries about a broad range of topics, in contrast to the more limited scope of references required of a librarian in a corporate, legal, or other specialized library. Librarians tend to work regular hours, though not necessarily 9 A.M. to 5 P.M., five days a week.

salary: A reference librarian with a master's degree in library science but no experience might earn about $16 to $18 per hour in a large city's public library; in a smaller city, the same person might earn $10 per hour. The more lucrative jobs in libraries are management positions.

prospects: Reference librarians know where to find information, a valuable skill in our economy, no doubt. But public libraries are funded by taxpayers' money, and in areas where funds are scarce or the citizens don't place a high priority on libraries, they can struggle to remain viable.

qualifications: A bachelor's degree in the humanities can be sufficient to get a job as a reference librarian, but libraries offering better-paying jobs are often able to choose from candidates with bachelor's or master's degrees in library science. At the very least, you ought to take a few undergraduate courses in library science if your goal is to be a librarian.

characteristics: More than any other type of librarian, reference librarians need to like working with people, to be a good listener, and to have a genuine interest in finding answers to people's questions. Good reference librarians tend to be naturally curious themselves.

Wendy Miller *is a reference librarian at a public library in the Southeast.*

- -

How did you get the job?

"Everything you learn in school is potentially useful in your work as a librarian," says Wendy, who studied history and preschool education at Earlham College in Richmond, Indiana, and political science at the London School of Economics before earning her master's degree in library science at the UCLA Graduate School of Library and Information Science. How did she finally choose librarianship as her career after that varied education? "I wanted to work in public service, to work around books, to earn a livable wage, and to have a skill that was transferable from one place to another," she explains. That transferability became especially important when for personal reasons she left her job in a public library in Los Angeles and moved to her current hometown. Her education and expe-

rience, plain and simple, were critical to her success in landing a job at the public library where she now works. Between the two libraries, she's spent three years as a reference librarian.

One thing Wendy has learned is the value of education. "More libraries are requiring master's degrees in library science, but if you don't want to do that, you should at least earn some credits from a library school," she says. "There are salary connections to education."

What do you do all day?

"In a busy hour, I might work with 10 to 15 people, helping them find answers to a whole range of questions," Wendy Miller says. "A busy day on the phone will be about 20 calls per hour."

Of course, librarians' educations and personal interests prepare them to handle some

topics more easily than others. "I feel stronger working on questions about philosophy, international relations, Russian history, cooking, and wine, and I don't feel very competent with questions about chemistry," Wendy admits, adding, "I think I was weak with business questions when I started, but I've gotten stronger with them."

While books remain the predominant resource in a library, they are certainly no longer the only one. "A good reference librarian has a fundamental working knowledge of all the sources of information in the library, and how the information is organized and where it is," Wendy says. "You are the most help to a person with a question when you can direct them to the most appropriate resource for their question."

Where do you see this job leading you?

Wendy Miller is one of the rare people who have found a job with which they are content. "Being a reference librarian fulfills all of my primary criteria for work," she says. "Moving into library management would remove me from working with people and books and into administrative work. And I'm not interested in that."

> **"I BELIEVE LIBRARIANSHIP IS AN APPRENTICESHIP JOB. YOU LEARN AN AWFUL LOT BY WORKING WITH EXCELLENT COLLEAGUES."**

42. Linguist

description: The study of language and its evolution, structure, and applications is the science known as linguistics. The scholars who specialize in this field are usually college professors, though some are clinical psychologists working with people who have difficulty communicating. And a few are employed by corporations and foundations—most notably high-technology companies that hire them to help in the development of "artificial intelligence." Linguists are guided more by their passion for knowledge than by the requirements of their employers. Linguists are not likely to become rich and famous, but they may make an important contribution to our understanding of ourselves and how we communicate with each other.

salary: Entry-level college teachers (assistant professors) start out earning $30,000 to $35,000 at a state university; more experienced professors earn $40,000 to $60,000, depending on the school— and publishing books brings in a little more money. Linguists working for corporations tend to be experienced and can earn more than $60,000.

prospects: Most major universities have linguistics experts in their English departments, yet few have more than one or two. But those positions are attainable for people devoted to the science. Industry jobs are rarer— they tend to go to the most imaginative scholars.

qualifications: You probably need a doctorate, and you certainly need a master's degree, to teach at a college. You must also have published research in the field and have ideas for further research to be a professor or work for a corporation.

characteristics: Only someone with a scholar's genuine love of language and insatiable curiosity about it will enjoy and succeed at being a linguist. You also have to persevere in the face of colleagues and department heads who may not see the value of devoting resources to this kind of study.

Natalie Maynor, Ph.D., *is an English professor at a state university in the South.*

How did you get the job?

Natalie has always been a teacher and scholar, but came to specialize in linguistics only relatively recently. She earned her bachelor of arts and master's degrees in literature and took no linguistics courses. A few years later—after working as an instructor at the college where she now is a professor—Natalie went back to school to work toward her doctorate. She took a class called Modern English that caught her attention.

A passion for linguistics ignited then, but Natalie didn't change her direction immediately. "Part of the reason I didn't consider switching might have been laziness. I knew that all the exams I had to pass to get my degree would be on literature," she says. "Or maybe it was just that literature was familiar."

She finished the coursework for her degree and was working on her dissertation when she found a paper she had written for that linguistics course and she sent it to *American Speech,* a linguistics journal, which published it. She was hooked by

that modest success and the following year gave herself over to the study of linguistics after attending seminars on dialectology, the discipline that catalogs and analyzes regional nuances in a spoken language.

As an assistant professor, Natalie pursued her "interest in linguistics, too naive to realize what that might cost me when my tenure came up for consideration. If my position here had been clearly designated as English Literature Professor, research and publications in linguistics would not have counted toward tenure and promotion," she recalls. "But fortunately, students in our department were demanding more linguistics courses and we had no full-fledged linguist. So I was able to change gradually from a literature professor to a linguistics professor."

What do you do all day?

Natalie teaches three classes each semester—both introductory and advanced studies of linguistics—and spends approximately 25 percent of her time on research leading to publication. She cherishes that research

> **"YOU SHOULD STUDY LINGUISTICS WITHIN A BROADER ENGLISH DEGREE, SINCE MANY TEACHING JOBS FOR LINGUISTS ARE IN ENGLISH DEPARTMENTS THAT MIGHT NOT HIRE SOMEONE WHO CAN'T TEACH OTHER ENGLISH COURSES ON THE FRESHMAN AND SOPHOMORE LEVEL."**

time, which she devotes to analyzing the different speech patterns among the various social strata in the American South. For example, she and a colleague interviewed and transcribed tapes of interviews with all sorts of people, then evaluated them to discern patterns of usage for the verb "to be." That work, which was published, revealed how language is used differently by blacks and whites, rich and poor, and urban and rural people.

"I've also done a small amount of work on the history of 'ain't' and am in the early stages of working on the use of 'y'all' and 'you-all,'" Natalie explains. "And I've combined work and hobby by writing a couple of papers on topics like the language of e-mail."

Natalie spends a good bit of her spare time with professional organizations. "I also run another e-mail list that began as a forum for discussion of the English language but has evolved into a discussion of anything the subscribers want to discuss—I consider that recreational rather than professional."

Where do you see this job leading you?

"I guess I have already arrived— I'm a full professor at a state university," Natalie says. "But right now I'm trying to decide whether to move in a different direction. It's not that I dislike what I'm doing now; it's just the 'we-only-go-around-once' idea. How will I know whether I would love or hate tech writing, for example, if I never try it? Can an English professor find a new life in the computer industry?"

43. Literary Agent

description: Agents represent authors to publishing companies, television producers, and movie studios. Agents evaluate manuscripts, solicit bids on them from editors and producers, and handle all the details of the negotiations. Agents must have an astute eye for literary talent, a sharp sense of marketing, an understanding of contracts, and the steely nerve of a deal maker. They also must engender trust with the authors they represent and with the editors and producers they sell to. Though agents can be instrumental to the process of buying and selling manuscripts, they are largely anonymous to the general public. Agents earn commissions based on the fee they negotiate for manuscripts.

salary: Entry-level assistants at literary agencies start at about $20,000 to $23,000 a year; people with experience in publishing or at a production company may start out earning a low salary plus commissions on manuscripts they sell.

prospects: Large literary agencies thrive in the media capitals, and opportunities for entry-level jobs frequently become available as experienced people move up to more responsible positions. The continued increase in the number of books published and movies and television programs produced virtually assures that literary agents will be increasingly vital to the process of connecting writers, editors, and producers. That should make more jobs available.

qualifications: The best preparation for this work combines training in literature, publishing, marketing, and business with insightful study of the media. A few years' experience in the media will strengthen your application.

characteristics: A happy, successful literary agent is encouraging to writers, collegial with editors and producers, and hard-nosed when negotiating.

A long-time agent whom we'll call Josephine *(not her real name) is a senior vice president at a literary agency on the East Coast.*

How did you get the job?

Josephine started on the path to her current job during her lunch hours when she was an assistant in the office of a busy agent. "In the first couple years I was working in an agency, I often ate a sandwich at my desk and read manuscripts and the letters to the authors from my boss," she recalls. "I was trying to understand his responses, what he liked and didn't like about the work, to see if I could learn how an agent looks at manuscripts."

Josephine has never stopped trying to learn, an attitude she considers critical to her success. "I think that just about everything I've ever learned about any topic has been useful in doing this job well," she says. "I believe you should never feel superior to your job—there's always something you can gain from taking it seriously and doing it well."

As direct and well planned as Josephine's career path may seem, she does wish she had taken one detour before arriving at her current position. "I think I would have had a better insight into this job if I had spent some time working for a publishing company," she says. "Anybody who's determined to be a literary agent would do well to work for a publisher first, especially in subsidiary rights."

What do you do all day?

Josephine can define her job fairly simply. "I evaluate and place with publishers the work of authors whom I represent," she explains. "I have a stable of authors I work with, but I am interested in new writers, too. I handle mostly general trade books, occasionally place magazine articles. I don't handle poetry, textbooks, or anything too specialized. And our agency has separate departments for dealing with television and film producers and foreign publishers."

OK, simple enough. Now how does that work get done? "I vet contracts, meet with authors and editors, talk to them on the telephone, and keep up correspondence," Josephine says. "That fills up my days. I take manuscripts home and read them at night."

> **"PUT YOUR LEARNING ABOUT YOUR JOB AHEAD OF YOUR PLANS FOR ADVANCEMENT."**

Josephine tries to stay informed about virtually everything. "You have to read the newspapers and the trade journals, listen to people who talk to you, pay attention to what's going on in the world," she says. "To be out of touch is to miss opportunities, to not see what will be of interest to editors and their readers. This is not a job to hide in."

Where do you see this job leading you?

"Most agents grow along with their clients," says Josephine, who began as a clerk and now represents some well-known authors. "People who leave agencies often go to work in editorial jobs, others go on to teach, while still others leave publishing altogether." Though Josephine has no plans to change her job, the teaching option is the one that appeals to her most.

44. Magazine Production Coordinator

description: Between the creative vision of editors and art directors, and the printed page stand the production staff, who attend to every detail of text and design in a magazine. While some production coordinators have strong word skills, and others are more visually oriented, all must keep a steady eye on the magazine's one immutable deadline, the date it must be shipped to the printer. Like anyone who works on a magazine, production coordinators are often asked to put in long hours when that deadline looms. The production staff enjoy little prestige or even recognition outside the magazine's office, but all successful publishers rely on a dependable, thorough team to get each issue out.

salary: Entry-level production staff can earn $20,000 to $25,000 a year, more in big cities and at larger circulation magazines.

prospects: Production has changed dramatically with the onset of desktop publishing—many jobs once done by hand are now managed electronically—but almost all major magazines, especially the weeklies and bimonthlies, still have large production/design departments. The continued vigor of the magazine publishing business is the key to prospects in this field, and nothing appears poised to undermine the industry.

qualifications: Production coordinators must have strong language, organizational, and technical skills, grounded in a diverse education and topped with a working knowledge of desktop publishing software. This can be an entry-level job, but your application will be more competitive if you have experience in any aspect of publishing, either as a student or as a freelancer.

characteristics: Detail-oriented people who like variety in their work and perform well under pressure enjoy magazine production. Your time will be split about equally between working with other people and working on your own.

Susan L. Backus *is an editorial production coordinator at a consumer magazine on the West Coast.*

How did you get the job?

Susan knew she wanted to get into magazine publishing after she graduated with a bachelor's degree in political science from a small college outside St. Louis. "I had an internship at a magazine while I was still in school that I liked a lot," she says. That experience helped lead her to seek an entry-level position in magazine publishing.

She answered an ad her current employer placed for an editorial assistant. "It was primarily a proofreading job, and I took it," Susan says, "and I guess I got the job because I had some experience, with my internship."

> "IN MAGAZINE PRODUCTION, YOU WILL SPEND A LOT OF LONG HOURS WITH THE OTHER PEOPLE ON THE STAFF, AND IT HELPS IF YOU LIKE THEM." ASK TO TALK TO DIFFERENT PEOPLE BEFORE YOU TAKE A JOB.

In the succeeding five years, Susan strengthened her position and expanded her responsibilities in the production department by learning QuarkXPress, the widely used desktop publishing program, and the other systems employed in the production department.

What do you do all day?

The magazine's production cycle dictates the tempo of Susan's days. After the designers have incorporated the writer's text files into Quark layouts, Susan and her colleagues "get the Quark files from the designers, and we go in and clean them up to make sure that things align properly, put in the most recently edited text, make sure the files conform to the publisher's design style, and make sure they will function well when the final low-resolution scans are put in.

"Then we print out a hard copy that is circulated to the story editor and then to the copy editors. After that, we input any corrections, print out a new copy that is proofread by freelancers, input that set of corrections, and put the copy on a disk to send to our prepress house." Final corrections are made, and then the film of the disk is sent to the printer, Susan says. Then the cycle begins again.

Where do you see this job leading you?

Susan set out to work in magazines and after more than five years doing just that, she's sure that's where she wants to stay. "I really enjoy the process of putting together a magazine," she says. Being a managing editor is where her aspirations lie. "Working in production is generally a totally different track than being an editor or a writer," she says. However, Susan notes, "The skills I have learned here—how to manage a magazine's production and coordinate the efforts of the various departments—are certainly transferable."

45. Magazine Staff Writer

description: Magazine writers produce both feature articles and regular columns, develop story ideas, often cover particular "beats" (or territories, either geographical or topical), and nowadays can be called upon to correspond with readers through online forums sponsored by the magazine. Magazine deadlines are less frequent than those at a daily newspaper, but they are no less rigid, and because the articles tend to be longer and demand more in-depth research, those deadlines can be at least as taxing. Some staff writers are required to work in the magazine's offices; others work in the field or from their homes.

salary: At nationally circulated consumer monthlies, staff writers start around $25,000 per year and can earn up to $50,000 or $60,000 at the senior level. At the weekly newsmagazines, staff writers may earn a bit more; at trade or regional magazines, the starting salary can be slightly less.

prospects: Staff writer is not an entry-level job at most consumer magazines, but editorial assistants and reporters often move up to the job. People switch jobs frequently in the magazine business, which means positions regularly open up.

qualifications: Strong writing skills and knowledge of the magazine's topic are the only absolute requirements. You'll need published work to demonstrate the former and must have persuasive verbal skills or experience to communicate the latter.

characteristics: Successful magazine writers are persistent in their pursuit of the story and self-motivated in their work habits. They're also determined enough to stand up for their story but flexible enough to accept editors' opinions.

Peter Bodo *is a senior writer for a sports magazine in the Northeast.*

How did you get the job?

Like many magazine writers, Peter started out working at newspapers—first as a general assignment reporter and later as a sportswriter. "Working on a newspaper is great discipline for any writer," he says. "You're compelled to write every day, day after day." Peter earned enough of a name for himself in the business to land a job on a brand-new nationally circulated newspaper based in New York City, but he became disillusioned by the paper's sensationalistic bent.

"I decided I wanted to write fiction—novels and short stories—so I left the newspaper," he recalls. "After a couple years without much success as a fiction writer, I needed to think about the future, about having some income." Through connections with former col-leagues, Peter found out that the magazine where he now works needed a regular contributor. And, he says, his writing skills, experience as a reporter, and knowledge of the sport won him the job. "If you have a modest talent and work hard, you'll find opportunities," he says. "If you add to that genuine enthusiasm, you're bound to get a job you like." Peter started out as contributing editor for the magazine, but five years ago took the more regular job of senior writer. "Now I'm more involved in planning stories and in the design of my articles."

What do you do all day?

Peter works at his home most of the time, but he's as productive as anyone who sits in an office every day. He writes a 3,500- to 4,000-word story for each monthly issue—typically they're interviews with personalities in the field and reports on events of interest to the readers,

> **"GET A JOB WRITING, ANY JOB WRITING, AND KEEP WRITING."**

with the occasional essay or lengthy interpretative article included in the mix—and a regular column, too.

"I come into the office a couple times a month for planning meetings with the editors," he says. "We discuss ideas for two issues down the road and come to an agreement on what I will do. At the meetings, I'll also give some suggestions for graphics for stories that are already written."

Peter also writes a column on the outdoors (wildlife, hunting, and the environment) for a major metropolitan newspaper a couple of times a month. "The paper and the magazine are owned by the same company," he says. "I used to work with the editor of the newspaper section the column appears in and he asked me to write it for him."

Where do you see this job leading you?

Having already tried his hand at fiction, Peter knows where he definitely doesn't want to go. "I don't write fiction anymore," he says. "But I still enjoy writing for the magazine and the newspaper, and I'll be happy to keep doing just that." Peter has recently written a book about the sport the magazine covers and he expects to produce more nonfiction books. "Writing is writing, whether it's for a magazine, newspaper, or book," he says. "But each one demands something a little different. That can keep the work fresh."

46. Market Research Editor

description: If information is the most valuable commodity for a business, then the people who collect and sell useful information provide an invaluable service to businesses. A market research editor searches for studies, surveys, and demographic analyses that will help companies in dynamic industries better understand their competitors and customers. The editor may buy reports already finished or, in some cases, contract original work. The pace of the deadlines in business-to-business publishing is no slower (and often faster) than it is in consumer publishing, but the pay is generally better. This kind of deep immersion in a particular industry prepares editors to move into positions with trade organizations or corporate communications.

salary: An entry-level editor at a business-to-business publisher may earn $23,000 a year to start, depending on the industry being served and the region where the publisher is based. Experienced editors make $30,000 to $50,000 a year.

prospects: The increasing volume and complexity of information available to business continues to fuel the demand for people who can find and sift through it. You'll find these kinds of publishers in most major cities and especially wherever high-tech companies cluster.

qualifications: A well-rounded education—best of all, with some business courses—and the ability to read and understand market research are essential. A patient, politic phone manner and strong organizational skills are almost as important.

characteristics: Resourceful people eager to learn and able to keep up a vigorous deadline pace will succeed in this kind of publishing.

Ashli Towler *is the editorial development manager at an East Coast business publisher.*

How did you get the job?

Ashli moved to a large Eastern city after earning her bachelor's degree in English from Vanderbilt University, then began searching for work. With persistence and networking, she landed a job as a directory editor for one of the country's largest business-to-business publishers.

"As a directory editor, I learned where to find information and how to organize it for a particular set of readers," Ashli says. "And I met a friend who later took a job at the company I now work for. When a position opened, she told me about it immediately. I initially resisted, wanting to make a change from directory publishing. But she sold me on the company and the position, and I submitted a resume and was invited in for an interview.

"I asked the woman who interviewed me to tell me how her job had changed since she came to the company and to describe a typical day in the office. What I heard told me the company allowed people freedom, most of all to create their own career paths," Ashli continues. "I had been ready to move away from directories and experience another side of publishing, but after the interview I was so sold on this company and the opportunities there that I took the job."

As it turns out, Ashli spent just a few months editing a directory at the new company. At that point, a position opened in her department that involved dealing with outside authors and consultants, something Ashli had gained some experience in during her directory editor post. "I was offered this new position," Ashli says, "and I've grown to really enjoy it."

What do you do all day?

With nearly 70 new reports to gather and prepare for publication each year, Ashli is almost always up against a deadline. "We publish in high-tech industries that are changing all the time, so our customers can't afford to wait for information to find them," she says. "We do about 10 mailings a month to them."

Ashli spends most of her time talking on the phone, negotiating prices and rights with authors of market research reports, assigning researchers to conduct original studies for her, and following up with authors who are working on research. "These are very bright people, and I've learned a lot from them: about the industries we publish in, about building and maintaining relationships, about diplomacy and negotiation," she says.

Ashli handles some administrative work for her department as well. "When we have more help, I'd like to hand off the paperwork—typing contracts, taking care of invoices, etc.—and spend more of my time focusing on new sources of information and expanding our customer base."

Where do you see this job leading you?

Ashli is definitely an "I'll see what's next" kind of person, but she's grown to love her work and her employer so much that for the moment she can think of no reason not to build her career with them.

"At one time, my dream was to be a fiction editor," Ashli says. "And I believe that the skills I've learned in this job will be equally useful in a fiction environment."

> "NEVER RULE OUT A JOB THAT DOESN'T SOUND EXACTLY LIKE WHAT YOU'RE LOOKING FOR. YOU CAN OFTEN GET INTO A COMPANY YOU LIKE AND THEN WORK YOUR WAY TO A JOB THAT YOU WILL WANT."

47. Medical Information Scientist

description: Pharmaceutical companies provide in-depth information about medical conditions and their remedies to doctors, nurses, and other health-care professionals. That information is gathered and prepared by specialists with training in the sciences and writing skills suited to the unique demands of the field. These medical information scientists create material for their companies' sales efforts and respond to direct queries from working medical professionals. The information specialists typically work in teams that include trained physicians. The hours and pay for this type of job are very attractive when compared to those in related fields—but this work requires a unique background.

salary: This is not an entry-level job, but qualified people getting started in this field earn $45,000 to $60,000 a year; entry-level researchers earn somewhat less.

prospects: The pharmaceutical industry continues to grow and new medical information is revealed nearly every day. Qualified people should have no trouble finding work at drug companies throughout the United States.

qualifications: The best preparation for this work will include in-depth study of biology or biochemistry, along with courses in business, technical communications or journalism, and information science. Experience as a researcher is essential to reach this level of job. You'll need to be comfortable using computer word-processing and database programs, too.

characteristics: If you work well as part of a team, if you don't crave recognition, if you can shift gears smoothly—speaking to a lay audience for one project, a technical group for another—and if you are resourceful in seeking out information, you'll thrive in this job.

Frances Princivalle Chadwick *is a medical information scientist for a large pharmaceutical company on the East Coast.*

How did you get this job?

Fran had set her hopes on working for this company when she left college with her bachelor's degree in biology, but she didn't have the experience necessary to get in. "So I took a job as a research associate at a local medical college, where I ran experiments for one of the doctors," Fran says. "I worked there for nine months after I graduated, proving that I was committed to the medical field."

When Fran heard about another opening at the pharmaceutical company, she applied again and this time landed a job as a staff biologist in the company's laboratories. "I worked in research for a couple years, and also in our manufacturing division," she says. "Then I moved over to our Medical Information Management Department, where I was an information researcher."

Within another year or so Fran not only proved herself capable of researching, but demonstrated a facility for writing, too. "If I had imagined that I could have a career as a medical writer, I would have taken more writing courses in school," she says, "and I think I might have taken business or marketing courses, too. That would really help me write for our marketing people."

What do you do all day?

Fran belongs to the company's team that specializes in "anti-infectives, of which we have three, and vaccines, of which we have many," she says. Fran, along with other members of her team, researches and writes "medical backgrounders" for the company's sales staff. "Each one has a disease section and a product section," she explains. "The first part tells all about the disease, its causes, and its symptoms. The second part gives the salesperson in-depth information about our product, its his-

tory, the research that supports it, how it works, and possible adverse reactions. We also define competitive products for the sales force.

"These backgrounders have to be written at a level that salespeople, who are not always trained in medicine, can understand and use in their presentations to doctors," Fran says.

The anti-infective and vaccine team also handles all questions about its products from health-care professionals—and

> "TRAINING IN INFORMATION SCIENCE MAY BE THE NEXT WAVE IN PREPARING FOR THIS JOB— LOTS OF PEOPLE HAVE THE BIOLOGY BACKGROUND AND MORE AND MORE MINOR IN BUSINESS. THAT EXPERTISE IN INFORMATION SCIENCE WILL REALLY SET YOU APART."

they are committed to doing it within 24 hours of the question.

Though Fran and her colleagues all have science training and knowledge and experience within their specialties, their work undergoes rigorous editing by experts. "Virtually everything we write must go through medical and legal review before it is sent out. With this type of information, that safeguard is absolutely critical," she says. "To give the information more credibility, the doctor on the team signs his or her name to everything that we produce."

Where do you see this job leading you?

"Lots of people from this field go into marketing; some go to other parts of the company," Fran says. "I never thought about doing this type of work and I'm still enjoying it. Maybe down the road I'd like to be a sales representative, or, even better, to be one of our health science associates who visit doctors' offices, hospitals, and clinics and teach about diseases and new products."

48. Medical Reference Book Editor

description: Pharmaceutical companies hire publishers to produce books and pamphlets that inform health-care professionals about the causes, symptoms, diagnoses, and treatments of particular conditions for which the company makes remedies. The editors of these publications select expert authors, guide them during the writing process, manage the manuscript's trip through production, and keep the project on schedule and within budget. These editors also propose ideas for books that the publisher's sales staff markets to the pharmaceutical companies. This is not publishing for an eager audience as we normally think of it, but it does provide useful information to its readership—and it often pays better than other types of publishing.

salary: An editorial assistant (an entry-level job that involves supporting all the functions of an editor) can start as high as $28,000 at a midsize company in a large city. In similar circumstances, editors earn $35,000 to $45,000 a year, depending on their experience and knowledge.

prospects: More pharmaceutical companies produce more drugs than ever before, which means an increased demand for people who can help them provide information to their customers. Most major medical publishers now have a division of "custom publishing" that focuses on producing books sponsored by pharmaceutical companies. People determined to find work in this field will find it.

qualifications: Strong communications skills—particularly oral—and a sense of organization are required to be a medical reference editor. Education in the life sciences will bolster your application.

characteristics: To work in this field, you must function well as part of a team, have a limited need for public credit for your work, and be attentive to budgets and deadlines.

Beth Adams *is a senior editor for a medical publisher on the East Coast.*

How did you get the job?

Beth's career path has led to a diversity of communication-oriented jobs. After graduating from Indiana University of Pennsylvania with a bachelor's degree in journalism, she went to work for an architectural firm, where she wrote marketing support materials—brochures, newsletters, press releases, and proposals. A couple of years later, she applied for and was awarded a staff position on a trade magazine for the natural foods industry. "I started out as an assistant editor—I even had to do some typesetting at the time," Beth says. "When I left six years later, I was the managing editor."

Her next stop was the development department of a local art museum. As manager of the annual giving program, "I came up with the concepts, wrote the copy, and worked with the designers on the production of direct-mail packages that solicited contributions from the general membership. There were three large-scale campaigns each year, along with several smaller solicitations, that took the form of a personalized letter," Beth explains. "I also was responsible for the writing and production of the development publications, which included two newsletters, special-project brochures, and print advertisements."

Hard times hit the museum, and Beth was forced to move on. So she answered a newspaper ad placed by her current employer. "My boss hired me, I think, because he saw on my resume that I knew how to take an idea and turn it into a finished printed product," she says. "And he saw that with my diverse experience, I was very adaptable, that I could fit my skills into whatever job I am doing.

"He spent a lot of time reviewing my writing samples and stressing the importance of hiring a strong writer," she adds, "which gave me the impression that I'd be doing more writing than I am. I thought we'd be producing more patient education than we have been, which I would have been involved in writing."

What do you do all day?

Well, not much writing. Most of Beth's time is spent on the phone with authors and clients and in meetings with the designers and production team. "I stay in touch with the authors while they're writing, to keep them focused and on schedule," she says. "During the writing stage, I also work with the author and a freelance illustrator to get any needed illustrations produced."

Beth oversees the projects through the production process, working closely with the production team (designers, production editors, and manufacturing staff), as well as the authors and clients, to be sure the projects meet all expectations within the set deadlines and budget. This production stage involves everything from selecting a cover design to reviewing final proofs.

The actual writing involved in Beth's job is for proposals. She will work with the sales staff to develop a proposal that outlines the content and estimated cost of producing a particular project. These proposals vary in their length and complexity, but will routinely include suggested authors, a proposed table of contents, a description of the project in relation to the client's audience/marketing goals, and production costs. Certain proposals may also involve contacting an author to write a sample chapter and then working with a designer to present it as page proofs within the body of the proposal.

Where do you see this job leading you?

That's a difficult question for Beth to answer—who could predict where this veteran of an architectural firm, health-food publisher, art museum, and medical/promotional publisher will go next? Yet Beth does know that she'd like to go back to working on material that's closer to her heart. "I don't think I want to stay in medical publishing for the long run," she admits. "I want to again work on projects in which I can be more actively involved in contributing to the content of the finished piece."

49. Medical Writer

description: Ever try reading a doctor's handwriting? Now imagine what it must be like to understand their unedited sentences. Professional medical writers help doctors turn research results into readable reports. Many hospitals, pharmaceutical companies, and medical schools employ full-time staff writers to work with their researchers; others hire on freelancers to help doctors complete specific reports. In some cases, the writers collaborate with the doctors in a give-and-take process. In other cases, the doctor turns over a draft, which the writer polishes for the doctor. Writers are rarely credited for their work, but they are responsible for accuracy nonetheless.

salary: Freelance writers may charge $20 to $25 an hour for rewriting, $30 or more for composing original drafts. Staff writers start at $20,000 to $35,000, depending on the type of employer: you'll make more at a pharmaceutical company than at a public teaching hospital. Experienced writers command much higher salaries.

prospects: You don't need to be a brain surgeon to know about the explosion of health care in the United States: there are more doctors, hospitals, drug companies, and researchers in this country than anywhere in the world, and it's a growing industry. And the consumer press is publishing more and more articles about health and medicine. Knowledgeable medical writers are in demand almost everywhere.

qualifications: Take strong word skills, both written and verbal (you must talk to the doctors), combined with training or knowledge in biology, chemistry, and other sciences, and you have the prescription for a medical writer.

characteristics: Doctors tend to be bright, driven, and notoriously (perhaps only slightly without cause) egotistical; writers who intend to work with them must be diplomatic and self-effacing, yet confident enough in their own area of expertise to stand by their judgment.

Joann Merriman *is a medical writer who now works for a biotechnology firm in New England.*

How did you get the job?

Joann's been writing professionally since she won the chance to contribute a weekly column about her high school to the daily newspaper in her hometown in New Jersey. Later, after earning an English degree at Agnes Scott College in Georgia, she took a job as an editorial secretary at Prentice Hall Publishing, then worked her way up to editing books and newsletters there. When motherhood propelled her into freelancing, she wrote articles for newspapers and newsletters, as well as advertising and fund-raising copy. "Writing is good training for being a writer, no matter what kind you are doing," she says. "I wanted to write all different kinds of material to see which kind I liked and which I was good at."

> **"I GOT JOBS WHEN I WAS FREELANCING BY ATTENDING MEDICAL CONFERENCES ON A PRESS PASS AND HANDING OUT MY CARD TO THE DOCTORS THERE."**

When her family situation allowed for it, Joann worked full-time in development and fund-raising for the Yale University Hospital. A few years after she moved on from that job, a friend at Yale met a doctor looking for help writing a chapter for a book on sports medicine. The friend recommended Joann for the job, and the doctor offered Joann the opportunity. "He gave me his data and I studied it, and I read a lot of medical books to get an idea about the style and tone used in them. Then I wrote a draft and gave it back to him," she recalls. "He rewrote it entirely, but I still think well of the experience because I discovered that I liked that kind of writing and that I was pretty good at it."

Joann took graduate-level courses in science communications at Boston University and got a job writing a column for a weekly newspaper on science and health. With those experiences and training, she won her current position.

What do you do all day?

Joann now works on reports that are submitted to the federal Food and Drug Administration for the purpose of documenting research on her employer's products. "I don't presume to interpret medical data; it's more like translating a foreign language," Joann explains. "First I work with the researchers to summarize their findings, and then I organize the information in a logical order. I also conduct a literature search using certain databases and assemble a bibliography of related articles. Then I write the report using the conventional language of the specific field, such as genetics or biochemistry."

The researchers involved have final approval of each report, and winning that can take three or four (or more) exchanges. "Scientists typically don't like this process, though they rely on it," Joann says. "So you have to be strong and tenacious but delicate in dealing with them."

Where do you see this job leading you?

"The work I've enjoyed most has been writing for a lay audience about complex scientific issues," Joann says. "If I found an opportunity to write about science and medicine for a newspaper or magazine, I'd jump at it. Otherwise, I'll be content working at biotech or pharmaceutical companies, because, frankly, they pay the best."

50. Newsletter Editor, Hospital

description: The editor of a hospital newsletter has a finger on the pulse of a large and diverse community. Keeping the medical staff, the support personnel, the patients, and the community-at-large informed about the hospital's current events, news, services, financial condition, and innovations requires the same journalistic skills as those employed by a newspaper editor and reporter. The newsletter editor also often writes the hospital's promotional materials and functions as its media relations specialist.

Newsletter editor may be one of the few jobs in a hospital with 9-to-5 hours, but because even the biggest hospitals don't have huge communications staffs, the days tend to be busy from morning to evening.

salary: You'll make from $25,000 to $40,000 a year as a newsletter editor at a public hospital in a medium-size city, depending on your level of prior experience. You may make more in private hospitals and bigger cities, less in smaller ones.

prospects: The health-care business is very competitive and hospitals—private and public—need to work hard to attract patients and skilled employees. Successful hospitals rely on communications specialists to help get the word out. That means work is available for people with word skills at the large hospitals in most cities in the U.S.

qualifications: Experience in print journalism or public relations is most likely to get noticed by a potential employer, but education in those areas will not be overlooked. Demonstrate excellent communications skills—both written and oral—in an interview and you'll tighten your grip on the job.

characteristics: Upbeat, self-directed, enthusiastic people who can earn the trust of both staff and management make successful communications specialists in a hospital.

Sandy Zec *is a marketing writer at a public hospital on the Gulf Coast.*

How did you get the job?

Though Sandy had been writing all her life, she had never relied on her writing for income until after she was married and her children were grown. At that time she went to the University of Missouri to earn her master's degree in journalism. Within two weeks of graduation she had secured a job as a reporter with a six-days-a-week afternoon newspaper in Hollywood, Florida. "I handled the paper's school and education beat," she recalls. Two years later, Sandy took a job at another newspaper—this time as the bureau in a rural region of the state. Not as the bureau chief, but as the entire bureau. "I was the only reporter there," Sandy explains. "I covered government, crime, business, everything that happened there.

"You learn a lot in that kind of situation," she says. "You learn how to deal with all kinds of people and how to win their trust. You learn, most importantly I think, how to write fast and accurately. "

Sandy learned enough to keep moving from bureau to bureau, until she won a spot at the paper's main assignment desk. "Then one day I looked around the newsroom and noticed that everybody was considerably younger than me," she says. "And that's when I realized that newspaper reporting is for the very young and energetic, who don't mind the demands, the hours, that go along with the work."

When she found an advertisement from a local hospital looking for a media relations person, she very carefully considered the idea of taking it. "I called all of my friends who had been newspaper reporters and were then in public relations, and I asked them if they had any regrets," Sandy says. "None did, so I went for it."

What do you do all day?

Sandy divides her time between writing and talking. "It's about 50-50," she says. Most of the time she's generating material for *The Wednesday Report,* the newsletter that circulates to the 3,600 employees of the hospital

> **"JOIN PROFESSIONAL ORGANIZATIONS— THEY'RE A GREAT PLACE TO MAKE CONTACTS AND TO LEARN ABOUT HOW OTHER PROFESSIONALS DO THEIR JOBS."**

where she works. "Actually, it's not substantially different than working on a newspaper," Sandy says. "A hospital the size of this one is a lot like a small community." The stories that Sandy covers include pieces about business, government, and people. "Some people mistakenly believe I write a lot about medical procedures," she says. "But that's actually pretty rare. I'm more likely to write about the board of trustees meeting or legislation before Congress that will affect health care."

This editor does stand firm on certain principles she learned as a newspaper reporter. "I seek out news, I don't wait for it to come to me," she says. "And I don't believe I should be a

mouthpiece for the hospital's management." Sandy relates the tale of how she convinced the hospital's management to counteract a nascent union movement among the staff by providing more in-depth information about the hospital's financial status to the employees through the newsletter. "I told them that if we don't tell the employees how it is, someone else will tell it the way they see it," she recalls. "And it worked— the employees developed trust and the union movement never caught on."

Where do you see this job leading you?

Sandy is so proud and fulfilled by her work that she'd like nothing more than to keep doing it better. "This job has all the elements I loved about newspaper journalism, but the stories and people are nicer and the hours are much better," she says. "All I want is to make the newsletter more valuable to the readers."

51. News Service Editor

description: Staff reporters can't efficiently cover every story newspaper editors want to include in each edition of their paper, so the editors use stories from other newspapers' reporters that they buy through national news services. The service's editors survey articles from their contributing newspapers, then retool them to suit the needs of the subscribers' papers. News service editors work on both hard news and feature stories, under steady (though not crushing) deadline pressure. They don't get bylines. Most work during the day, but nearly everyone has to take the overnight shift at some time in his or her career.

salary: An assistant editor (the base-level editorial job at a news service) will generally have five years' experience at newspapers and start out earning $35,000 to $40,000 a year. More seasoned editors earn up to $60,000 to $70,000, or even more.

prospects: The newspaper business is very transient, with people building their careers by moving from one publication to another. That means jobs are almost always opening up for qualified people. The several national news services provide material to a growing number of small-town newspapers.

qualifications: You already know you typically need five years' experience at a small to midsize daily before the news services will consider you. You must have an aptitude for swift editing and a sense for judging what stories will interest newspaper editors and their readers in all parts of the country.

characteristics: A quick thinker who can concentrate despite distractions and who doesn't require public recognition will be happy and successful as a news service editor.

Ray Walker *is the news editor at a service based in the East that serves 350 newspapers around the country.*

- -

How did you get the job?

Ray had decided to take his degree in journalism and become a newspaper reporter, but before he ever got that far he accepted a job as a clerk at a small newspaper in the Southeast. "I was assigned to the copy desk and the copy editor that I worked with there was a terrific teacher and a real inspiration," Ray says. "He was so inspiring that I've never done any reporting—I've always worked as an editor."

After 14 years working his way up through the editorial ranks of the newspaper, Ray received a call from a friend working at the news service that now employs him. "She called and asked if I wanted the job of assistant news editor for the service. I was ready for a change, and I took it."

> "WORKING AT A NEWSPAPER IS A PRICELESS EDUCATION FOR ANYONE WHO WANTS TO WORK AS A REPORTER, WRITER, OR EDITOR OF ANY KIND."

Ray was an assistant news editor for a couple of years, served as the service's sports editor for six years, then was promoted to news editor—a job he won based on his proven nose for news and his organizational skills.

What do you do all day?

Ray works the phone. Really works it. "The first half of my day is spent talking to the news editors of the 40 papers that provide stories to us, asking questions about what their reporters are working on," Ray explains. "I have telephone friends all over the country—people I've talked to nearly every day but have never seen. These editors fill me in on the stories their staff is working on, so that I can develop a budget—a selection of articles—that we'll be offering our subscribers."

The rest of Ray's day is spent assigning those stories to be edited by the five assistant news editors on his staff and making sure that the edited versions are proper, on time, and on their way to the service's 350 subscribing newspapers. "After our copy desk edits the story for grammar and style, our editors condense it, strip out any local references, and fully develop its broadest appeals," Ray says. "We can turn a story around in

five minutes, though we generally prefer more like 20 minutes when we can get it. We strive to get every story done by 10 p.m., with sports turning in the late scores from the West Coast by 2 a.m."

That quick turnaround time is no excuse, in Ray's opinion, for an editor to breeze through a story. "Reporters compile long lists of facts and quotes and try to put them together in an article," Ray says. "But good editors develop coherence in the stories, they recognize themes and bring them to the fore."

Where do you see this job leading you?

Ray could continue up the editorial ladder at the news service or he could go back to newspapers, as many news service editors do. But he'd rather go back to his alma mater and "be a flak for my university," he says. "I love the town itself and I have so many friends there."

52. Nonfiction Book Editor

description: Nonfiction books are written by one or two experts on the topic, but they reach their final form through the combined efforts of a team of publishing professionals. Project editors lead the group of designers, copy editors, illustrators, proofreaders, indexers, and production specialists assigned to each book. Project editors don't select the books—that's the work of acquisitions editors—but they guide the manuscript from the time it is submitted by the author until it is shipped to the printer. While the primary function of nonfiction editors is to manage book production, the job demands a firm grasp of the content and an unwavering attention to its language and style.

salary: An editorial assistant (the entry-level position) at a medium-size publisher in a large city—where most of the jobs are—will start at about $20,000 a year. Project editors with broader responsibilities make from $30,000 to $50,000, depending on their experience.

prospects: Nonfiction publishing is the fastest-growing segment of the book business and the expansion of electronic media does not appear to threaten that. So, although there isn't a lot of turnover in the field, it seems likely that opportunities will continue to be available for qualified people interested in book publishing.

qualifications: A bachelor's degree in the arts or sciences provides the kind of broad-based education that will be a solid foundation upon which an editor can build understanding of the book production process and knowledge of the books' contents. Further study of book publishing and graphic design will strengthen a candidate's application.

characteristics: Detail-oriented, collegial, decisive, flexible, and visually imaginative people able to work on several fronts at the same time will make happy, successful nonfiction book editors.

Randy Ladenheim-Gil *is a nonfiction editor at a major publishing house in New York City.*

How did you get the job?

Randy obtained her first job in publishing shortly after graduating college with a bachelor's degree in communications. Initially, she had been unsure of what to do after college—she was interested in film and television, as well as in books and magazines—and a promising ad in *The New York Times* led her to a small publishing house where she was hired as an editorial assistant. During the course of her year there, however, she saw her list of responsibilities, and her list of job titles, grow. In rapid succession, she became office manager, managing editor, trafficking manager, and the assistant to the chairman of the board. Her career in publishing was well on its way.

Randy's desire to further her education, however, caused a temporary exit from publishing as she pursued, and obtained, a master's degree in journalism from Boston University. When journalism opportunities were not always forthcoming or appealing, Randy returned to New York City, where she became a production editor at a midsize, independent house. "They made me swear that I had no interest in becoming an acquisitions editor, ever," she recalls with a laugh. But that is exactly what she ended up doing.

At her next job, and for the next nine years, she rose through the editorial ranks at William Morrow (beginning as an assistant editor and ending as a senior editor) where, among other duties, she ran the company's travel guide division. Corporate downsizing brought Randy to her next job, as an editor for a reference book publishing house. There she developed and acquired individual titles and series that were primarily geared to school and library markets. Dramatic changes in the corporate structure there brought Randy to her current job, as editor for the House of Collectibles, a nonfiction division of Random House's Ballantine Group.

What do you do all day?

Typically, Randy is engaged in the responsibilities that consume most editors' days: "I edit manuscripts, negotiate contracts, write jacket copy, attend meetings with other departments, and deal with authors and agents," she says. In addition, Randy manages the book program of the House of Collectibles, which involves overseeing each book through the publishing process. And though there are a lot of administrative tasks that fill her day, Randy says she is happiest when editing manuscripts. "That's what brought me to publishing in the first place," she says.

Where do you see this job leading you?

Randy is unsure of where she would like this job to take her, but notes that an editor can typically move to a position of senior editor or executive editor, or higher up into a management role. Or one can move into the worlds he or she edits—in Randy's case, to work for a company that is involved in the collectibles industry, like the Franklin Mint.

> **"YOU NEED A SENSE OF HUMOR TO KEEP A LEVEL HEAD AND A POSITIVE WORKING ENVIRONMENT THROUGH WHAT CAN BE VERY STRESSFUL DEADLINES."**

53. On-line Magazine Editor

description: Magazines aren't just on paper anymore. People with computers can now read current versions of many publications on computer networks and back issues are becoming available on CD-ROM. The editors of electronic publications attend to most of the same issues as do editors of paper magazines, and they have several other concerns. Content remains the focus for an on-line editor, not computer programming.

These publications are in the early stages of their evolution, so no one can say for certain in what form on-line magazines will exist in the future or what the editors will be doing exactly.

salary: The pay scale for this work (like so many other aspects of it) is just beginning to take shape. Entry-level editors can reasonably expect to earn $25,000 to $30,000 a year—depending on the publication. The top of the range has surely not yet been established.

prospects: This is a new field and most of the magazines publishing electronically are just getting their feet wet, with small staffs and limited commitment. Still, there are few editors who have the combination of skills necessary for the work. And the field is likely to continue to grow, creating more opportunities for entry-level people.

qualifications: You must have sharp researching, reporting, and editing skills. You also need an eye for images, a thorough understanding of how to use computers, and ideas for how to make use of the medium's unique capabilities in a way that enhances the magazine for the readers.

characteristics: Adaptability may be the single most important attribute for an editor of electronic publications. The field is changing so fast that what you know today may be of no importance tomorrow.

Basil Guinane *is the director of new media and information services for a news magazine published in Canada.*

- -

How did you get the job?

Basil says he was interested in journalism while a student at the University of Toronto, though he was a political science and history major. "I wrote for the school newspaper, but I was intending to go to law school," he says. "Then I got interested in electronic information management, and I went back to school to earn my master's in information science."

After working toward that degree, Basil took a job at a national newspaper's electronic information service. When the job of chief librarian for the magazine was advertised, Basil applied for and won the job. Almost immediately he began suggesting that the magazine develop electronic products.

"I proposed that we compile an archival CD-ROM, which was approved," Basil says. "And that has done well enough for us to continue to explore new media for the magazine."

> **"IT'S NOT JUST PUBLISHING COMPANIES THAT WILL NEED EDITORS COMFORTABLE WITH THE WORLD WIDE WEB—CONSUMER PRODUCTS COMPANIES ARE PUTTING UP HOME PAGES ON THE WEB AND WILL NEED PEOPLE WHO CAN PRODUCE THE CONTENT OF THOSE PAGES."**

And well enough for Basil to have the budget to hire a few new people for his staff. What's he looking for? "You must be a strong researcher, reporter, and editor," he says. "You also need design ideas, because the computer is such a visual medium.

"And you need to be comfortable on the Internet and the World Wide Web," he continues. "Though it seems to me that the software for getting on the Web is getting easier and easier; any reporter could learn it in a week or two of using it. Which makes that background in journalism—J-school or experience working for a daily newspaper—all that much more important to us."

What do you do all day?

Basil is the weekly magazine's chief librarian and manager of its copy and research departments, and he devotes a major portion of his time to the electronic media. "I check in regularly on our on-line edition to make sure the articles are accessible and that the questions asked in our discussion forums are promptly answered," he says. "I also line up special guests for the forums."

In addition to being available through a popular on-line service, the magazine is accessible through the Internet's Electronic Newsstand. "Each week we upload the latest issue's table of contents and the full text of one or two articles to the News-

stand," Basil says. "And we're continuously discussing ways to add value to the on-line version of the magazine." For some publications, that means including sound bites; for others the extras are special images.

The magazine also has contracts with eight different companies that have created databases or CD-ROMs using back issues of the magazine. "It wasn't hard to convince the magazine's publishers of the value of this," Basil says. "We've already compiled the information for our readers once; selling it to others to use is just gravy."

Where do you see this job leading you?

Basil laughs at this question. "Anyone who can answer this knows more than I do," he says. Basil expects that he will continue to develop new media where he now works—at least until the media is no longer new.

54. Packaging Copywriter

description: Before you buy a new product, you read the package to find out exactly what's inside. So, like advertising writers, with just a few carefully chosen words, packaging copywriters must capture the customers' attention, inform them, and stimulate their urge to buy. Packaging writers work with product engineers to create clear instructions for the merchandise, with the marketing department to place the product in the appropriate context, and with the company's legal counsel to ensure compliance with all the regulations and restrictions to which the product and its packaging are subject. Oh yes, and the words better be witty, clever, and memorable, too.

salary: Freelance packaging writers working in a big city charge $40 to $50 an hour. Staff writers make $35,000 to $45,000 a year working for a large company in a big city.

prospects: The three industries that most commonly keep packaging writers on staff are toys, food, and cosmetics. Where you find the largest companies in these industries, you may find opportunities. Beyond those areas, you're more likely to get packaging work on a freelance basis. Many advertising agencies provide this service to their customers.

qualifications: An education in advertising or marketing may get your resume read, but what you really need is the ability to write creative copy quickly and concisely. The more you know about trademark law and the other legal issues of packaging, the stronger your candidacy will be for any job.

characteristics: You have to play well with others, possess a bottomless font of ideas for saying many of the same things in different ways, and be able to take criticism from nonwriters to be a successful packaging writer.

Leslie Graham *is a packaging manager for a large toy company on the West Coast.*

How did you get the job?

Leslie graduated from the University of Notre Dame with a bachelor's degree in English (focused on creative writing), then went straight into advertising. She worked as a freelance advertising copywriter for several years before answering a newspaper ad for a copywriter at a medium-size toy company.

> "LEARN AS MUCH AS YOU CAN ABOUT TRADEMARK LEGAL. YOU CAN LEARN IT ON THE JOB, BUT IF YOU KNOW SOMETHING ABOUT IT ALREADY, YOU'RE ONE UP ON THE OTHER CANDIDATES."

While Leslie was working her way up to manager of the packaging department, the company was bought by a larger one and both eventually went out of business. So she targeted her current employer (a competitor of her former employer) purposefully, confident that she understood its business and could meet its needs.

"Once you understand product development and marketing, you can understand the people who will hire you and approve your work," Leslie says. "And that's often the difference between freelancers and staff—freelancers may have the ideas, but they don't know the process."

What do you do all day?

Leslie names new products every week, giving toys their identities and a story in which they come to life. "If you're working on a product that's an original creation of your compa-

ny, you get to name the whole product line and all the individuals in it, and invent a story for them," she explains. "But if it is a licensed product, then you typically only name the individuals and/or come up with a story for them.

"The names and stories are the context in which we sell the toys," Leslie says. "We get what's called the 'positioning' from marketing and then we sit with the toys and decide who they are and what they're doing. I never spend less than 4 hours on a name, and I've spent up to 80 hours on a single tag line."

Once she settles on an idea, Leslie works with her team of two graphic designers and a product engineer to style and fit her copy. Then the marketing department gets to approve her ideas for the names and stories, as well as the words on the package and the package as a whole. "Marketing has veto

power over our work," Leslie says. "It's a real challenge to get them to sign off on the names, stories, and promotional copy."

When marketing and engineering have given their approval, Leslie sits down with the legal and safety departments to get them to sign off on the copy. "I know this is critical stuff," she says, "but it seems that the more creative we get, the more restrictive they get."

Where do you see this job leading you?

Leslie is trying to work her way back to management. You see, many of the people she works with now were on her staff at her previous employer. "I didn't realize how unusual it was for a writer to be managing a packaging department," she explains. "At an ad agency, the copywriters become the managers. But in packaging, graphics rules."

55. Part-Time Editor

description: For more and more people, a reliable route to full-time income is through a few part-time jobs. You fill the needs of two or three publications that do not need a full-pay-and-benefits staffer, while you get steady checks that add up to a livable wage. You also enjoy the diversity of working on different kinds of subjects and with a variety of people. Of course, you pay for your own benefits, but your schedule is more flexible than that of a full-timer. And you enjoy a unique sort of security: if you have one job and it's eliminated, you have no income; in contrast, when one of three part-time jobs falls through, you have two others to carry you until you find other work.

salary: There's no standard pay scale for this kind of work, but it is safe to say that you can make $20,000 to $40,000 a year from three part-time editing and writing jobs.

prospects: Lots of associations, publications, and corporations in all parts of the country have some steady part-time work for writers and editors. You'll have to hustle to line up enough of them to pay your bills, but if you're determined and resourceful, you can do it.

qualifications: Beyond the essential high-caliber writing and editing skills, you need to manage your time well, be adroit at covering different kinds of subjects, and be very persuasive when selling yourself.

characteristics: It takes a truly reliable person to pull off this kind of arrangement: you must treat each job as if it were the only one that mattered. That means never letting one get in the way of doing the others as well as you can.

Trevor Smith *is the editor of an association's newsletter, a senior writer of a consumer magazine, and contributing editor to a trade magazine.*

How did you get the job?

Writer and editor is Trevor's second career. For more than 20 years he was a researcher in the physiology department of a major consumer products company's corporate laboratory—that's what his education in biology and chemistry prepared him to do. But when the company scaled back its research efforts in 1986, Trevor was forced to accept early retirement. Still relatively young, in need of income, and eager to explore a lifelong love of words, Trevor decided to become a freelance writer and editor.

"The first thing I did was sit down and figure out my financial situation," he says. "And I determined that if I could earn $24,000 a year within three years, I could make this work without having to search for a full-time job.

"Once that was settled, I decided to get involved in the writing community in my area, so I joined the independent writers group here," he contin-

> "TO WORK PART-TIME JOBS, YOU HAVE TO TAKE A HARD LOOK AT HOW MUCH YOU NEED TO SURVIVE, AND THEN SET REALISTIC GOALS FOR GETTING THERE."

ues. "I looked in that group's job bank and I saw an advertisement for a position editing an association's newsletter. I had sold only two articles to this point but I applied for the job, because I was involved in the community that the newsletter was addressed to.

"When the association's executive director interviewed me, she handed me a manuscript to edit, which I guess I did adequately, because within a few days she hired me."

A couple of years later, Trevor saw the first issue of a new fitness magazine. He noticed that it had just a small staff—one full-time editor—and that it could logically include articles about topics similar to the ones he was writ-

ing for the newsletter. "I sent the editor a letter explaining what I'd like to write for his magazine and within a few days he called to offer me an assignment for the next issue," Trevor says. "I have written for every issue in the six years since then."

Trevor also has arranged a third steady assignment—this one contributing monthly to a magazine for chemists.

"A freelancer lives from query to query," he says, "but I know what I can expect each month from my part-time jobs."

What do you do all day?

Trevor writes most of the association's eight-page monthly newsletter himself, though he does try to find association members to write at least a portion of each issue. "I write and edit the copy on my home computer," he explains, "then submit it on disk to the association's director for layout and design."

Before he writes for the fitness magazine, he phones his story ideas to the editor, who has been buying four of

Trevor's articles for each bimonthly issue. But for the chemists' magazine, Trevor just sends in his story each month without discussing the topic with the editor. "I know what the readers know and want to know very well," he says. "I was one of them during my first career."

Where do you see these jobs leading you?

"At the moment, my activities meet my needs very well," he says. "I've exceeded my income expectation. Of course, all of these jobs have open-ended month-to-month contracts that can be terminated by either party. But I'm confident that if I continue to meet the standard with each one, the arrangement will remain the same.

"I get a couple of calls a year from editors of more glamorous magazines asking me to write about the topics I'm known for, and I like to do those," he concludes, "but I'm not interested in moving away from the solid quality of what I do, into publications with more flash than substance."

56. Play Editor

description: Several large companies and some smaller ones publish and sell new and selected older plays to schools and community and children's theater groups, who put them on for their respective audiences.

The editors at these publishing companies evaluate unsolicited manuscripts, generate ideas for new plays and contract authors to write them, edit completed works, and assist customers searching for material suited to their needs. These editors tend to be involved in the theater, either professionally or as amateurs, where they learn about the interests of production companies and schools.

salary: An entry-level assistant editor at a theatrical publisher will start between $20,000 and $25,000 a year; more experienced editors earn in the $30,000 to $40,000 range.

prospects: There are just a few companies in the United States publishing most of the plays, and all of them have small staffs. But many of the people working in this field tend to find work in the theater, so opportunities do open up for determined job seekers.

qualifications: In-depth knowledge of plays and strong editing skills are the two key prerequisites for this kind of work. A basic understanding of the theater market will enhance your application.

characteristics: People dedicated to the art and craft of theater, and with lots of ideas for plays suitable to school groups, will enjoy being, and succeed as, a play editor.

John B. Welch *is the managing director and chief editor at a play publisher in New England.*

How did you get the job?

John has been involved with the theater in virtually every imaginable way. "I was a theater major in college and I produced several plays while still in school," he says. "I've worked as a professional actor and as an associate manager of an Equity [professional] theater for a while, too.

"When I graduated from college, I applied for a job with this publishing company and got a job as clerk—you know, typing, filing, filling orders," John continues. "I left and went back to working in theaters, but after a few years the general manager here, whom I kept in touch with, asked me to come back as chief editor for the company."

He believes that working with theater companies is the best way to prepare for the job. "There are so many little things to pay attention to when editing a play that it's almost impossible to be aware of if you haven't ever worked with a script under real conditions," John explains. "My experience has been that someone who comes right from college with just classroom study is going to have a hard time picking it up.

"But I want to add that any individual who is bright and who is committed to learning the process can acquire the knowledge to do it well," he concludes. "It just makes sense more quickly if you've had practical experience in the theater."

What do you do all day?

"We publish 20 to 25 new plays a year," John says. "Many of them are unsolicited submissions, which we first read and evaluate for both quality and marketability. If we accept a play, we may ask for revisions."

Those changes often have more to do with the logistics of putting on a play than with the writing itself. "The cues, for example, from the playwright to the actor in a script may not be grammatically correct, but they must be clear and feasible," John says. "And continuity issues are very important in play

> **"THIS IS A FIELD YOU HAVE TO LOVE AND BE COMMITTED TO. TO UNDERSTAND THE MARKETPLACE, YOU MUST SEE PLAYS, KEEP UP WITH WHAT'S CURRENT, AND REMEMBER WHAT WAS POPULAR."**

editing: if an actor is directed to exit in a scene, he can't suddenly reappear later in that scene without an entrance."

John's company also commissions plays that he believes will interest his customers. "We have a family of playwrights we work with to create very specific material for us," he says. "For example, there was a film called *Murder by Death* a few years ago, and we had some calls from customers asking for the play—only the movie was not based on a play. So we hired a writer to create a play with similar themes. We've since sold 125,000 copies of that manuscript, and I think it has been produced about 1,500 times.

"We're now looking for playwrights to create a Mark Twain–themed revue and a baseball-themed play—we've had requests from customers for both of these kinds of work."

When not developing new material, John and his staff are furnishing their customers with popular plays of the past. "We agent quite a number of what you'd think of as standards," he says. "*Our Town* alone could keep our cash flow steady."

Where do you see this job leading you?

John is as content in his job as he thinks he ought to be. "This job allows me to work in the theater, which I love," he says, "but it's more stable than any theater job. I wouldn't say I'd never go back to working in a theater, but I'd think long before I left this job."

57. Playwright

description: Far from the bright lights of Broadway, thousands of schools, civic organizations, and community theaters put on dramas, musicals, and comedies every year. And many of those productions begin with scripts written by dedicated, self-supporting, but relatively unknown playwrights. A few repertory companies may have staff writers, but most playwrights are freelance. Yet they don't always just write and hope someone will want to buy and produce their plays—many playwrights receive commissions to write for theater publishers, advocacy groups, and communities.

The pay is rarely lucrative and the work hardly glamorous, but if you love writing for the theater, with hustle and determination you can earn a living at it.

salary: You may be paid as little as $50 or as much as thousands for an original play. This is not an undertaking for anyone who needs a steady income. But after you become established you can earn enough to support yourself as a playwright.

prospects: There are three publishing companies that buy manuscripts from playwrights and sell them to schools. Many public service groups underwrite productions to help disseminate their message. Countless local theater groups seek out new plays to put on. The opportunities exist for playwrights—you must work hard to find them.

qualifications: To make a living writing this kind of play, you must be versatile and able to produce good-quality work within guidelines established by others. Oh yes, it helps to have talent and imagination.

characteristics: You have to be humble—people with lofty aspirations and an inflated sense of their work need not apply. It takes a person who is flexible and determined, and who loves writing plays above almost all else.

Dan Niedermyer *writes plays at his home on the East Coast, and sells and produces them throughout the United States and in Europe.*

How did you get the job?

You don't go to school to become a playwright, Dan says; you are one. Dan sold his first play when he was 16 and formed a theater production company when he was 18. "I decided in the beginning that I wasn't going to run away to New York or Los Angeles to do this," he says. "I wanted to do it my way—writing all kinds of plays for whomever wanted one."

He got started selling his plays to publishers that market them to schools. "At first, I wrote plays with my own ideas and sent them around to the publishers," Dan says. "After I sold a few, the publishers began to call me and say, for example, 'We'd like a hillbilly play with parts for 20 kids' or 'We need a musical comedy.'

"Just recently, I got a call from an editor at one of the big publishing companies and he gave me a title he liked— *Wanna Be's,*" Dan continues.

"He wanted me to write a play about young girls who want to be actresses—which I did."

Dan has broadened his experience and contact base by doing nonprofit work. "I've written plays for every charity under the sun," he says. "To keep working, you have to market yourself. And the more people who have seen your plays, the more opportunities you create for yourself."

He includes opportunities overseas as well. "I have worked with a production company in Sweden," Dan says. "Now I'm working on a commission from a small community there that wants a musical about a local hero who found gold in America in the 1800s."

What do you do all day?

Dan treats his work like a steady job. "I write for three or four hours nearly every day; I love sitting down at the word processor and just putting words on the screen," he says. "I also am constantly jotting down ideas or thoughts—I even scribble notes while I am driving."

Dan can create an original play for, say, a junior high theater group in a week or two. "That comes almost straight out of my imagination and onto the page," he says. Other kinds of work can take longer. "I was working on a play for the AIDS foundation that is to be put on in schools by professional performers," he explains. "For that I interviewed hundreds of kids and did all sorts of research. I worked on that play for almost two years."

When he's not writing plays, Dan produces, directs, and appears in them. "I wrote a play last year on Johnny Appleseed for a recycling organization in Texas," he says. "Then for two months I was traveling to elementary schools all over Texas to perform in it. We did it five days a week for eight weeks.

"Acting in plays really helps my writing," he adds. "It helps me to understand what works on stage."

> "IF YOU WANT TO WORK STEADILY IN THE THEATER, DO DINNER THEATER, SATURDAY MORNING CHILDREN'S PERFORMANCES, CHARITY EVENTS, SCHOOL ASSEMBLIES— WHATEVER OPPORTUNITY IS OFFERED, TAKE IT. AND IF YOU AREN'T OFFERED AN OPPORTUNITY, YOU FIND ONE."

Where do you see this job leading you?

"I have no illusions about being on the fast track to stardom," Dan says. "But I travel around the country and in Europe performing my own work, and sometimes when I am in a city somewhere in the U.S., I look in the paper and see that a high school is putting on a play that I wrote—it's very gratifying."

123

58. Press Secretary for a Public Official

description: Even people who talk for a living often employ professionals to talk for them. At least when those people are politicians, they do. A public official's press secretary manages the official's relations with the media, specifically fielding interview requests, arranging press conferences, and preparing the official for public appearances. Press secretaries must be (or at least appear to be) completely committed to the officials they represent, yet sustain friendly, positive relations with the reporters in the press corps who cover them. This is a high-visibility position that can lead to lots of opportunities; press secretaries need them because they can lose their jobs at every election.

salary: Press secretary is not an entry-level position; however, many elected officials have less experienced writers on staff who produce press releases and compose speeches. They generally start around $25,000 to $30,000 a year; more is possible in bigger cities and when working for more prominent officials. Press secretaries for midsize-city mayors make up to $60,000; those working for big-city mayors, representatives, and senators can earn six-figure salaries.

prospects: Only a limited number of positions as press secretary are available at any one time, but print or broadcast reporters with experience covering politics and government can dedicate themselves to a candidate and land the press secretary's job if the candidate is elected. Less experienced writers can find jobs as staff writers.

qualifications: Experienced journalists who write persuasively, who are able to speak knowledgeably and extemporaneously, and who build positive professional relationships can handle the job of press secretary. Strong organizational skills come in handy, too.

characteristics: Loyalty is paramount for a press secretary. Enthusiasm and stamina are important, as well as belief in public service.

Doreen Picozzi *is the press secretary for the mayor of a midsize city in New England.*

How did you get the job?

Doreen is not ashamed to admit that she started at the very bottom of the editorial ladder. "Two months after graduation, feeling dejected about the poor job opportunities available, and despite a foolish vow to avoid newspaper work, I picked up the telephone and called a local alternative newspaper. As fate would have it, the person who answered the phone was a former classmate in need of an assistant," she recalls. "It was part-time work that paid $15 a day; it was at the seat of an ancient typesetting machine and pasteup board." But she's proud to point out that her "sweetly aggressive nature and comprehensive education led to the publishing of my first article before my first week at the paper was complete."

In short order, Doreen became an associate editor of the paper, and then a reporter, editor, and columnist at a couple of other publications. She was the managing editor of a local paper and a freelance writer for a statewide publication when her current boss was elected mayor of her hometown. "I had the opportunity to get to know him throughout 11 years of covering politics and government for the newspapers and magazines, and he got to

> **"THERE ARE MANY GOOD WRITING POSITIONS IN GOVERNMENT FOR TALENTED AND DEDICATED PEOPLE WHO CAN CRAFT A GOOD SPEECH, GRANT, OR LETTER."**

know me," she says. "He offered me the position of press secretary, which I did not solicit. I believed in him and in the city and agreed to take on the responsibility."

What do you do all day?

Doreen manages every interaction the mayor has with the press. "We receive approximately five to 10 press calls daily," she begins. "We research and write responses to questions from the press." Doreen also plans press conferences: she persuades the press corps to attend, produces media materials to be passed out at the conference, arranges the site, and edits the speech to be delivered. She develops other opportunities for press coverage, too. And she briefs the mayor before appearances on local news shows, writes or edits all of the city's publications, and administers the press office staff.

One of the most critical tasks of the job is building a solid rapport with the press corps assigned to cover the mayor. "The ability to work with sometimes adversarial members of the media is key to success," Doreen explains. "I have to be able to respond spontaneously and knowledgeably to difficult inquiries about all the issues and initiatives of concern to the mayor's administration and his constituency."

Where do you see this job leading you?

Doreen knows exactly when her job will expire, unless the mayor wins again. In 1999, after the mayor's fifth term ends, she'll have to move on. "My plan is to remain in this position for the duration of the term; it's a matter of commitment," she says. "As a mother without a job, I would hope to create my own opportunities in publishing that will be compatible with my lifestyle."

59. Professional Writing Consultant

description: Corporations and small businesses, government agencies, and private groups of all sorts recognize the value of clear, effective communications, but many of them lack the resources to hire full-time staff writers and editors to help create top-quality documents. Those organizations often contract professional writing consultants to write and edit, and most importantly, to teach their business and technical people how to communicate better themselves. These consultants may have brief, temporary assignments or be contracted for ongoing services. Professional writing consultants must work continuously to generate business for themselves; however, they tend to have very flexible schedules.

salary: The kinds of clients you have and services they contract will dictate your income. You could earn $20,000 to $30,000 a year when you're just starting out, and double that once you're established.

prospects: Businesses and other organizations in all parts of the country hire professional writing consultants. If you work diligently at making contacts, you can build a client base for yourself.

qualifications: Strong business and technical writing skills are just the foundation. An engaging teaching style is equally critical. Your ability to market your services will determine how successful you are at making this your livelihood.

characteristics: You speak the language of business, you command the attention and respect of your clients, you are able to adapt your knowledge and expertise to the situation. You are suited to the work of a professional writing consultant.

Lee Clark Johns *is a professional writing consultant in the Southwest.*

- -

How do you get the jobs?

Lee was a college teacher—freshman English and advanced grammar—before she "let go of the safety net" and became a full-time consultant. While she was still teaching, she had consulted in her spare time with local corporations, particularly in the energy industry, and had developed a limited client base. But when she committed herself to making a living as a consultant, she needed to expand on that.

"I've found that advertising really doesn't work—networking does," she says. "You talk to your friends in organizations, you talk to clients you've already worked with, you attend conferences, and you follow up on every lead you get.

"Now some of my best friends are my clients," she adds. "And they send the referrals my way. That's what keeps the ball rolling."

If you want to get started and have no experience, Lee offers two pieces of practical advice:

1. "If you're still in college, find a professor at your school who's consulting and offer to help out."

2. "Join the Association of Professional Communications Consultants," says Lee, who is an active past president of the group. "The organization exists, in part, to help people get started in this business. We publish booklets, a code of ethics and statement of professional practice, and we host professional development workshops."

What do you do all day?

Lee works from her home, and meets some clients there. "Right now, I'm working with a guy who needs to draw up a proposal for a new business," she says.

"We met and discussed what he really wanted his proposal to say, and now we're working on saying it, in his words."

At other times, Lee travels to the clients' offices to present seminars for larger groups. "I teach bright, educated people—scientists with Ph.D.s in many cases—how to write clearly," she says. "This is different from college teaching; I don't lecture them; they won't stand for that. The seminars have to be more

> **"THIS WORK TAKES A SPECIAL COMBINATION OF SKILLS: YOU MUST BE ABLE TO WRITE WELL, TEACH BETTER, AND MOST OF ALL, UNDERSTAND YOUR CLIENTS' BUSINESSES."**

interactive, they have to break down the audience's anxieties about writing.

"So many technical people have become scared of writing because of what English teachers did to them in school," she adds. "Some of my time is spent just getting these people to relax and feel comfortable writing."

When Lee is successful at that, she finds the results immensely satisfying. "People like learning to write better. It's very liberating," she says. "I just love to see the look of delight on their faces when they finally can get down what they want to say."

Where do you see this job leading you?

Lee has built a thriving consulting business and she's not walking away from it anytime soon. But she does hope to "carve out more time to write myself," she says. "So many of the materials on the market—either books or computer programs—designed to help people learn to write better are either too academic or aimed at too young an audience. I'd like to create some material for people in business."

60. Public Affairs Specialist, Utility Company

description: Utility companies often don't have to line up customers to buy their products—many have them by default—but they often do need to generate public support for issues and initiatives of particular concern to them. Public affairs specialists at the utility help the company's management present its positions on those subjects and work to promote a positive image of the company as a corporate citizen. Those specialists also deal with the news media and guide management's communications with employees and shareholders. In some cases, these communications experts become integral elements in the corporate decision-making process at the highest levels.

salary: An entry-level public affairs specialist will earn around $25,000—maybe more at bigger companies or in more populated cities.

prospects: Utility companies recognize more than ever the value of effective communications with their communities, employees, and the investors, so they are devoting more of their budget to their public affairs departments—which, plain and simple, translates to more public affairs jobs.

qualifications: The ability to write and speak clearly and knowledgeably about technical topics is fundamental; skill in interacting with people is almost as important. Long-term success in this field will depend on how well you can think strategically about the company's decisions.

characteristics: The ideal public affairs specialist at a utility company is congenial yet businesslike, delicate but frank when addressing controversy, and eager to learn about the technical aspects of the business.

Roberta Bowman *is the general manager of communications and community relations for a large power company in the Southeast.*

How did you get the job?

Roberta was a political science and English major headed for law school when she found a job at a utility company. "I quickly discovered that this business has all the challenges and demands of the law," she says, "and I never considered going to law school after that."

She also quickly discovered what skills anyone who wants to work in the communications department of a utility company should develop. "Good writing and speaking skills are just not enough," Roberta says. "You need critical thinking skills, problem-solving skills, and the ability to synthesize ideas. And you need that basic academic skill—you have to know how to learn what you don't know."

Roberta believes that a great deal of opportunity will be available for young people who are familiar with information technology. "Many utilities are getting on the World Wide Web," she says. "So much of the current workforce doesn't know about computer networks

> **"JOIN THE DEBATE TEAM—IT'S AMAZING WHAT YOU LEARN BY HAVING TO DEFEND A POSITION THAT'S NOT YOUR OWN."**

and products. There will be an increasing need for people with all those skills I've already mentioned and facility with the new media."

What do you do all day?

Roberta categorizes her department's areas of responsibility three ways: media relations, employee communications, and strategic issues management. "The common theme is using words to influence opinions within and outside of the company," she explains.

The media-relations function involves fielding interview requests from reporters, pitch-

ing articles about the company to the press, and preparing staff people who will interact with the media. "We teach others in the company about the methodology of communications," Roberta says. "We try to get them to think about the message and the message giver."

Employee communications involves not only producing an internal newspaper, but, more critically, consulting for management on decisions affecting the employees.

What Roberta refers to as strategic issues management seems the most challenging part of her job. "We help management identify issues of concern to the company, then we determine the best ways to influence legislation and public opinion on them," she says. "We are a nuclear utility, which is a very sensitive topic for the public. So we have faced some significant public relations challenges because of that, and now we take a proactive approach to the issues."

Whenever the company sets out to generate a policy, it includes a member of Roberta's staff. "We have cross-functional

teams that include engineers, businesspeople, and communicators," she says. "We view ourselves as the spokespersons to management for our customers, as much as we speak for management to our customers."

Where do you see this job leading you?

Interestingly, Roberta is headed out of the communications department. "I'm very fortunate to work for a corporation that recognizes that critical thinking, problem-solving, and communications skills are valuable in many areas of our operations," Roberta says. "I'm just about to begin an 18-month rotation into other areas of the company."

Roberta adds that the people on her staff who are most successful make the effort to learn about the technical aspects of their business. "We have experts in nuclear thermodynamics walking around here," she says. "The more you know about what we do, the more valuable you are, the more opportunities you'll have."

61. Public Relations Specialist, Agency

description: As PR representative at an agency, you'll handle a broad range of clients rather than representing just one (as a PR rep in a corporate PR department would) and will direct a variety of promotions for the clients. That includes writing press releases about the clients' products or services, arranging for clients to appear on broadcast talk shows, staging events to bring their message to the public, and devising wildly creative strategies for attracting positive exposure for your clients. In an advertising agency, the PR staff works closely with the advertising team to develop an entire marketing strategy for each client. Eventually, you'll be called upon to participate in presentations aimed at attracting new clients for the agency.

salary: Entry-level public relations assistants earn about $20,000 a year, while more experienced representatives can make $50,000, or even lots more in the major cities. Once you start bringing clients to the agency, the sky's the limit on your earning potential.

prospects: In a media-saturated world, more and more companies are recognizing the necessity of positive public relations. Since only the biggest companies can afford full-time staff to handle their PR needs, more advertising agencies are seeing the value of on-staff PR professionals to offer a full range of services to their clients. The result: ever increasing opportunities in public relations for eager young professionals.

qualifications: Your acuity with words goes a long way in public relations—both written and verbal skills are paramount for getting the good word out about your clients. You'll also need a thorough understanding of the various media outlets and how they handle the leads you'll be providing them.

characteristics: Persistence short of pushiness, and being assertive but not annoying are essential qualities of successful public relations reps. If you have a feel for catching people's attention and the power to persuade them, PR is your ideal field. Oh, and it helps to give good phone.

Valerie Gleason *is the public relations director at an advertising agency in a midsize East Coast city.*

How did you get the job?

Valerie never thought twice about her interest in public relations. "My family jokes that all I ever wanted was a job in which I could be paid to talk on the telephone," she laughs. "I have to admit, it's not entirely untrue." After graduating with an associate's degree in fashion marketing from a business school in New York City, Valerie took a sales job at Barneys, a clothing store in Manhattan. In her spare time, she hung out at a club called Limelight. When the club planned to stage an AIDS benefit, Valerie volunteered to help with the promotion of the event. Her contribution was so valuable that the club's management offered to pay her to organize and promote an event every week.

With that experience and her background in sales, Valerie won a position in the corporate public relations department at Times-Mirror magazines in New York. She later joined the staff at Rodale Press in Pennsylvania as the publicist for *Bicycling, Backpacker,* and *Organic Gardening* magazines. "But even the variety of magazines wasn't diverse enough for me," she says. "All of the promotion we did was basically of the same type." That sent her in search of a position with an agency, leading her to her current job.

What do you do all day?

"I am constantly, almost every waking moment, dreaming up ways to get my clients exposure," Valerie confesses. "That's what's going on in the back of my mind, no matter what else I'm doing." The formal parts of her day include meeting with clients and the advertising reps at her agency, writing and editing press releases, planning

> **"DON'T HESITATE TO TELL YOUR SUPERVISORS ABOUT YOUR IDEAS. THIS IS NOT A BUSINESS FOR THE SHY AND RETIRING."**

events and promotions, and, of course, talking on the telephone to make contact with editors and producers as follow-ups to those press releases. Valerie also spends time each week calling potential clients and giving them presentations on how her agency can provide both public relations and advertising services.

Where do you see this job leading you?

"To my own agency," Valerie Gleason answers without hesitation. She believes that watching and learning from the experienced founders of her firm is providing her with the comprehensive education she needs to get her own agency started someday. (She's also working toward her bachelor's degree in English and marketing at the University of Delaware.) She counts every contact, every successful event, every promotion idea toward her goal. "Everything I do that works is another tool that I draw on for the clients we have now," she says, "and that I can put to use for clients in my own agency." This is a long-range goal—"I'm only in my 30s," she notes, "and I'm just beginning to see the big picture in this business"—but Valerie keeps that goal squarely in front of her throughout her day.

62. Public Relations Specialist, Corporate

description: A corporation's public relations staff develops ideas and strategies for presenting the firm's image positively to its community and customers. PR reps work with the media, coordinate special events and outreach programs, and are often called upon to write speeches and text for presentations. Unlike PR reps at an agency—who must seek new business for the agency to represent—corporate PR people handle one client and one client alone, so they develop a more in-depth understanding of the company's products and services, and its customers. Corporate PR reps sometimes serve as spokespeople for the company.

salary: Entry-level corporate PR staffers will start at about $25,000 in midsize cities, and that is slightly less than a comparably experienced agency rep will earn.

prospects: Most big companies and lots of smaller companies keep PR specialists on staff to manage their public images at all times. If you're qualified and determined, you'll find work in corporate PR in large- and medium-size cities.

qualifications: You must be persuasive in oral and written communications and understand the various media outlets to get a job as a corporate PR rep. Study or experience in marketing will strengthen your application.

characteristics: Corporate PR reps are invariably upbeat and enthusiastic, work well as part of a team, are gushing with ideas, and are capable of polite persistence. Successful ones can speak with equal confidence to engineers, editors, and entrepreneurs.

Rebecca Wilson *is public relations manager for a consumer products company in the Midwest.*

How did you get the job?

Rebecca took the unusual step of studying what she really wanted to learn in college, rather than what might look good on a resume. "I didn't want to treat college as a trade school—I wanted to learn how to think and reason," she recalls. "I was an English major with a focus on medieval studies. My father used to say, 'If anyone ever comes across a job opening for a medievalist, have them call collect.'"

That call never came, but Rebecca had no trouble finding a job—as a sixth- and seventh-grade English teacher. After a few years in the trenches of junior high school, Rebecca decided to skip a few classes ahead: she went back to school to earn her master's degree with the intention of becoming a professor. While in graduate school, Rebecca worked for a local temp agency, which placed her at the office where she now works. "My boss was the father of a student of mine," she recalls. "He offered me a full-time job with the company."

For the next few months, Rebecca worked on projects for many of her firm's departments, including research and development and production. "Finally, my boss said to me, 'You're a communicator, why don't you come to public relations and marketing?' I agreed."

What do you do all day?

Media and community relations are the two primary responsibilities that dominate Rebecca's days. On one hand, she works with reporters, editors, and other members of the press to get them information for coverage of the company and its products. "Because I've worked with all those other departments, I understand our products very well, and I can represent them sincerely and with credibility to the press," she says. "That seems critical to doing the job well to me."

In her other main function, Rebecca fields and considers requests from organizations,

> "I'VE HAD OFFERS TO GO WORK AT AGENCIES, BUT I'VE TURNED THEM DOWN BECAUSE I'M AFRAID I'LL HAVE TOO LITTLE TO SAY ABOUT WHICH CLIENTS I REPRESENT. TO BE A SUCCESSFUL PR PERSON, YOU HAVE TO BE KNOWLEDGEABLE AND SINCERE—AND IT COULD BE HARD FOR ME TO DO THAT FOR EVERY CLIENT AN AGENCY HAS."

community groups, and schools for sponsorship of events by her company. "We manufacture some products for children, so we consider every request carefully and weigh its ramifications," she stresses. "We try to be selective in who we will help out, to maintain our positive corporate image."

At a small company like the one where Rebecca works, employees wear many hats. In addition to her primary duties, she also helps the marketing department with some writing and desktop publishing.

"I like the warmth and friendliness of a small company, and the fact that I represent a company whose products and attitude as a corporate citizen are positive," Rebecca says. "That's very important to me."

Where do you see this job leading you?

"I'm very lucky because I have a job working for a good, responsible company I'm proud to represent," Rebecca says. If she were to leave this job? "Well, maybe 10 to 15 years down the road, I'd like to do what I'm doing for a college or university," she confesses. "I love the academic atmosphere, and this way I wouldn't have to become involved with battling for tenure and other campus politics."

63. Publisher's Sales Representative

description: Representatives are the intermediaries between publishers and the buyers at bookstores. Independent reps work for themselves, acting for small publishers that don't have staff reps and for larger companies in areas where it's not practical to have staff reps. Independent reps set their own schedules, spend a lot of time traveling to bookstores, and are paid strictly by commission; staff reps earn some salary as well as commissions, and tend to work much of the time in their company's office. While this is primarily a sales job, successful reps know the books they are representing and the readers that patronize the stores where they are selling.

salary: Staff reps start out earning around $25,000 (including commissions) and can make up to $45,000 (plus commissions). Independent ones—who almost always have some experience—can bring in $40,000, $50,000, even up to $100,000 in yearly commissions, depending on the popularity of the books they represent and the sales volume of the bookstores they serve.

prospects: Plenty of jobs as staff reps are accessible today, but getting started as an independent is more difficult. Reps are an integral part of the book publishing business now, but consolidation among publishers and the expansion of large bookstore chains are changing the industry dramatically. That makes the future less than clear.

qualifications: You can learn how to be a staff rep on the job, but you will need to bring to it a well-rounded education along with a passion for books and a basic understanding of book marketing. Independent reps almost always have some experience in the book business before they get started.

characteristics: A successful rep is well read, perceptive about buyers' and readers' preferences, enthusiastic and outgoing, persistent, and able to sell with subtlety. If you want to be an independent, you'd better like to travel regularly, too.

Nanci McCrackin *is an independent publisher's sales representative working out of her home in the Northeast.*

How did you get the job?

Nanci has worked the book business from several angles. She started out as a clerk in a bookstore, then moved up to book buyer. Later, she helped a friend open a bookstore, learning "the whole business, inside and out." After moving from the West Coast to the East, she spent 11 years working as a staff representative for two different New York publishers.

"A lot of reps I knew encouraged me to go out on my own and, frankly, I'd had enough of working in an office and doing the corporate thing," she says, "so I went to work for a group of independents. When I felt confident enough in my network of contacts, I left the group and went to work for myself."

> "IF YOU WANT TO BE INVOLVED IN BOOKSELLING IN ANY CAPACITY, SPEND SOME TIME WORKING IN A BOOKSTORE. IT'S THE MOST SOLID FOUNDATION YOU CAN BUILD ON."

Today, Nanci represents 11 small publishers to bookstores and wholesalers in six states. "For the first five years, I worked only with people I already knew—this is really 'an old friends network' kind of business," she explains. "My client and customer base has been growing slowly but steadily since then."

What do you do all day?

Twice a year, Nanci attends sales meetings with all of the publishers she represents. "The publishers' editors and marketing departments hold meetings in New York in December and May, and for two weeks the independent reps go from one meeting to the next with each of their clients," she explains. "The publishers give presentations on the books to be released in the upcoming spring or fall seasons. We sometimes see manuscripts, finished books, or just covers and descriptions for the books. And we get to ask questions."

With her head and her briefcase jammed with information about new books, Nanci hits the road for 10 weeks of visits to bookstores and museum shops (she represents publishers of art books that are sold in museums, too). "I'm not away from home for 10 straight weeks, but every week for that time period I'm on the road for several days," she says. During those visits, she sits down with book buyers and tells them about the titles she believes will interest the store's customers.

"It's not just selling; we really are performing an invaluable service for the buyers," she says.

"There are thousands of vendors in the book business. No buyer could just read catalogs and make informed choices. If the rep knows the store's customers and their buying habits, she can guide the buyer to the books on her list that will sell well.

"The truth is, hard selling doesn't work with book buyers," she says. "We provide information and direction more than anything else. The sales follow from that."

Where do you hope this job will lead you?

Nanci is sure it won't lead back to an office job. "I could never work for someone else again." Beyond that, she's not sure where her next move will be, "but I probably will stay in the book business. It's an industry people love and rarely leave."

64. Puzzle Editor

description: Puzzle editors don't worry about getting caught working on crosswords at the office, they worry about getting caught not working on them. These editors make up themes for puzzle books and magazines, assign them to writers, edit the instructions and clues, and work with the art department on the design and layout of all kinds of puzzles. And the editors do the puzzles, of course—but just to make sure they work. This seems like fun work and it is, but you can't help but wonder if puzzle editors read actuarial tables when the boss isn't looking.

salary: Entry-level jobs in the puzzle publishing business pay $21,000 to $24,000 a year, depending on the company and its location. You can earn more than that if you have more experience or take on more responsibility.

prospects: Lots of publishing companies produce lots of puzzle books, yet the work doesn't require a lot of people, so there aren't a lot of jobs. But puzzle editing is generally entry-level work, which means editors move up into management or on to other kinds of publishing. That leaves positions open for new people.

qualifications: No accredited postsecondary school in the United States offers coursework in puzzle editing, so puzzle publishers hire editors who can write crisply and concisely, and have a well-rounded education and broad knowledge on many topics. Basic computer skills are essential.

characteristics: A self-directed person who pays attention to details will enjoy the work of a puzzle editor. It helps to like solving puzzles.

Fran Danon *is editor-in-chief of a puzzle publisher in the Northeast.*

How did you get this job?

Fran's route to her current job was not what you'd call direct. Since earning her English degree from Syracuse University, she's sold real estate and written direct-mail advertisements for a number of companies. Fran considers both of those experiences valuable. Selling real estate "helped me develop the skills needed to work effectively with people. Working in the direct-mail field helped me realize the importance of the written word," she explains. "And I've done volunteer work, which enables me to work hard for little recompense."

A newspaper ad for a part-time administrator brought Fran to her current employer. For the next 12 years, she worked her way up through the ranks, until she was named editor-in-chief. "Honesty, maturity, and sincerity were probably the attributes that got me the job," Fran says.

What do you do all day?

Working on puzzles has a unique meaning in this context: puzzle editors spend their time on "data entry of puzzles, clueing to the level of difficulty of the particular magazine being edited," Fran explains, "and verifying the accuracy of every clue and answer."

Entry-level editors can expect to learn a lot about puzzle publishing after they're hired. "There are few jobs that will prepare one to edit puzzles," Fran says. "We offer on-the-job training." Before you've mastered the job, you'll know and understand all the puzzle formats, will be able to work the puzzle software your company uses, and will have accumulated a body of knowledge about many topics. "A sense of humor goes a long way," Fran says, "because getting every clue and answer exactly right is painstaking work."

Where do you see this job leading you?

Fran's already reached a top job in a field she enjoys, but most of the staff editors move on to other jobs in nonfiction publishing.

> TO SUCCEED IN
> PUZZLE PUBLISHING,
> FRAN SAYS,
> YOU MUST BE:
> * A PUZZLE LOVER
> * ENTHUSIASTIC
> * COMPUTER-
>   LITERATE
> * WELL-READ
> * A TRIVIA FAN
> * A TEAM PLAYER
> * A PERFECTIONIST

65. Radio Newscaster

description: We're a nation of commuters, so many of us get our daily dose of news from the radio. In brief bites of facts and little bits of sound, radio newscasters give us the day's events on the way to and from our jobs. Most radio newscasters are on the air in four-hour shifts. Morning drive-time newscasters generally get to work long before daybreak and are finished when the morning rush ends; afternoon newscasters get to work in the middle of the day and finish after almost everyone else is at home. Radio newscasters don't work alone: they rely on producers and reporters to help gather and write the news.

salary: Reporters (the entry-level radio news job) at a station in a medium-size city start at about $20,000 to $25,000; top reporters in big cities often command six-figure salaries.

prospects: Radio remains a strong presence in the news business and nothing appears to threaten it—not even the growth of other electronic media such as cable TV and computer networks. As reporters and newscasters move from smaller to larger markets, entry-level jobs open up for new reporters. But broadcasting is a competitive field; you'll need to work hard for an opportunity almost everywhere.

qualifications: A degree in journalism or a broad-based liberal arts education is a strong foundation, to which you should add training in the technology of radio. In-depth knowledge of politics, business, or science will boost your application.

characteristics: A solid speaking voice and captivating reading style are essential. The ability to think and react quickly is important, too. And you'd better like working on your own to some degree; once you're in the booth, no one is with you but the listeners.

Jerry Hudson *is the news director of an all-news-and-talk AM radio station in a midsize Midwestern city.*

How did you get the job?

Jerry took his degree in mass communications and history from the University of Denver straight into the Air Force, where he worked in the Radio and Television Service for four years. "The armed forces is a great place to get introductory experience in broadcasting," he says. "It's an often overlooked avenue, but that's too bad, because you can learn a lot while Uncle Sam picks up the tab for your room and board." When Jerry left the military, he began to work his way up the ladder in radio, working first as a reporter in small towns and then in larger ones throughout the West. "I have been at so many stations, I almost can't remember them all anymore,"

he says. "I left my job as news director at a station in Houston, frankly, because I was offered more money and better working conditions here.

"I think people in radio move around until they find a place they really like," Jerry adds, "and my family and I decided we prefer the quality of life in a medium-size city to that in a real big city like Houston."

What do you do all day?

Jerry's day begins at 4 A.M., when he arrives at the station and meets with his producer, who's been working to assemble the news that's come in over the wire service and news monitors overnight. At 5 A.M. Jerry is on the air, filling early morning listeners in on what's been happening. "You start out the day with stories prepared before you

go on," Jerry says. "But as often as not, your producer is bringing in new material while you're on the air. You've got to be able to deliver the news at that point without taking the time to write and rewrite the stories."

At 9 A.M. Jerry's shift on the air is over, but his day is not. "As the news director, I am responsible for all of our coverage," he explains. "I meet with our assignment editor and reporters to discuss the focus and direction of our coverage, and help them to develop angles

> "IT MAY SEEM
> OBVIOUS, BUT
> PRACTICE READING
> ALOUD IN A CLEAR,
> UNACCENTED
> VOICE. TOO MANY
> PEOPLE NEVER
> BOTHER TO
> DO THAT."

on national stories that bring them home to our audience."

Jerry leaves the station at noon, but the next day's reports are already being compiled. "Our reporters do most of their work when my day is over."

Where do you see this job leading you?

Jerry isn't planning on going anywhere. "The management at this station has been very generous to me so far and gives me every indication that they will be so again. And we like living here. So I could stay here indefinitely," he says. "But that is subject to change at a moment's notice. You get offers, you consider them. If the Chicago Cubs called me today to offer me the play-by-play job, I'm gone and I'm not even calling in to the station."

66. Rare Book Finder

description: When you can't get a book you want at the local store—whether it's from a small publisher, or it's rare or out of print—you can turn to professional book locators who rely on a network of unique resources to hunt it down. Rare book finders often work out of used-book stores, but they field requests from customers all over the country and conduct nationwide searches for books. Many specialize in particular types of books or subjects. Book locators generally set their own work schedules and they get paid when they find books.

salary: In this job, you earn when you succeed in finding what the customer wants. If you devote full-time effort to the job and are fairly successful at locating books, you'll have no trouble making $10 an hour on average and you could make double that if you develop a clientele with a taste for more lucrative rarities and collector's editions and the ability to find them.

prospects: You will create your own opportunities in this field. You won't have much trouble finding a used-book store to work in—they're especially abundant in college towns and arts communities—and there you'll meet customers interested in hard-to-find books.

qualifications: To support yourself as a rare book finder, you'll need to think like a detective, negotiate like a Hollywood agent, and maintain an accountant's view of your bottom line. To do all that, you'll have to study the book business inside and out.

characteristics: Persistent, resourceful people who like books and who can develop beneficial relationships over the telephone will enjoy this work.

Kubet Luchperhand *is owner of a rare book–location firm in the Great Lakes region.*

How did you get the job?

Anthropology had been Kubie's field—specifically, teaching it to college students. "That's right, I am a recovering academic," Kubie confesses. "I left my job when I no longer had zeal for it and decided to get involved in the book business. I started a small publishing company. Then I opened a used-book store to support the publishing company, and I got into the business of searching for hard-to-find books to help support the bookstore."

Before long, the selection of books in Kubie's store and his success in finding ones that weren't in his collection established him in the field. "I have 70,000 to 80,000 books in stock at my store," he says. "I have a very strong African history department, a lot of Asian history, too, and a great selection of women's studies books. And I think it's safe to say that I have more Latin American novels than you've ever seen—there's 300 of them here.

"I know every book that's in my store," Kubie adds. "Because nothing is in here that I didn't put here."

While those well-stocked shelves attract customers within a five- to six-hour drive to the store, it is Kubie's success at finding rare books that brings in customers from all over North America. Advertisements offering his services to readers of *Harper's* and *The Atlantic* magazines and *The Washington Post*—among other publications—help those customers find him.

What do you do all day?

Every customer who wants Kubie to search for a rare book must put up $5 before Kubie goes to work. "The $5 immediately separates the serious customer from the not-so-serious," he says, "and it helps to pay for the advertising we rely on to get the word out that we are looking for a particular book."

> **"IF YOU WANT TO GET INTO BOOK SEARCHING, GET A JOB AS A QUOTER IN A WELL-STOCKED USED-BOOK STORE AND LEARN THE TERMS AND HOW TO PRICE."**

That advertising appears in specialty journals read by "quoters," who are the people who comb through estate sales, auctions, and other used-book stores looking for hard-to-find books. When they find what a searcher has advertised for, the quoters send three-by-five-inch cards to the searcher, noting the book's condition and quoting a price.

"A book's condition is described by the terms 'good,' 'fine,' and 'very good.' A 'good' book is good no matter how old it is. Its defects must be described in the quote," Kubie explains. "A book that's 'fine' is essentially as new. A 'very good' book has its dust jacket intact and its binding barely broken in.

"There are about 1,200 quoters out there and you get to know who is reliable and who is not," he adds. "This is a business that relies on trust—in many cases the book and the check cross in the mail—so building relationships with quoters is essential."

Where do you see this job leading you?

"There are companies that search for books strictly as a business. They have 15 people working the phones all day long," Kubie says. "But for many of us, we are in this because we love books and want to help our customers."

Don't expect that Kubie will leave this second career anytime soon.

67. Reading Specialist, Elementary School

description: The current trend toward "back to basics" in education has renewed the focus of school districts across the country on the critical skill of reading. In response, many districts have hired specialists who design schoolwide reading programs and help tailor individual courses for students with particular challenges to literacy. These reading specialists typically have classroom experience, but they are not assigned to one specific class. Reading specialists devote time to studying the latest developments in understanding the process of how people learn to read. They generally work the same hours as teachers do and are paid along the same scale.

salary: Entry-level pay for first-year elementary teachers ranges from $17,000 to $21,000 a year, depending on the region and school district as well as the teacher's subject specialties and level of education. By the time teachers have the experience and education to be reading specialists, they can earn from $25,000 to $60,000 a year, again depending on the region and school district.

prospects: Entry-level elementary school teaching positions can be found by qualified people in almost every part of the country, though they are more available in regions like the South and West where population is growing rapidly. Specialists are competing for fewer jobs, but since this is an increasingly important specialty, anyone flexible enough to move where the jobs are can find one.

qualifications: You need an elementary school teaching certificate and coursework in the pedagogy of reading—even certification in the specialty in some states. Some classroom teaching experience is often required.

characteristics: People who can think and plan on a large scale, yet will become immersed in the details of one student's problems, will enjoy the opposing demands on a reading specialist. Oh yes, you ought to love books and reading, too.

Pat Trevi *is the reading specialist at an elementary school in the suburbs of a large city in the East.*

How did you get the job?

Before she was a teacher, Pat was a secretary. "I think it's important for people to work in business for a few years before they become teachers," she says. "It helps you to understand how businesses work and what kinds of skills your students will need to get jobs."

Pat taught all subjects and at every elementary grade level; then after about 10 years she decided she loved reading and teaching reading most of all. "Teachers have to participate in continuing education, and I kept focusing on reading," she explains. "Then I enrolled in a special program at the University of Pennsylvania that certified reading specialists.

"Now, I happened to be working in a school district that needed reading specialists and I knew this as I was taking the courses," Pat continues. "If that

> "IF YOU FIND A SPECIALTY YOU LOVE, PURSUE IT. THEN WORRY ABOUT WHERE YOU CAN PUT IT TO USE."

hadn't been the case, I would have had to be content to stay in the classroom or apply for a job in another district."

What do you do all day?

The school year begins for Pat with a test. "Each September we test all of the incoming students and place them in reading classes matched to their level," she explains. "Reading is the one subject in which we believe students benefit from being with others at their level."

After the students are placed in appropriate groups, Pat takes a turn in each classroom at various points during the semester

to teach specific reading skills. "Our district uses a whole language approach to reading," she says. "Learning phonetics [how to sound out letters and words] is just part of the process. We teach the students to read in many different ways."

Students with reading difficulties receive special attention from Pat. "When we have a student in trouble—either academically or behaviorally, and many times those are related problems—we get together an instructional team of the student's teachers, an administrator, an Instructional Support Leader, and myself and we brainstorm ideas on how to help that student in their regular classroom," she says. "We have two meetings in the beginning to develop ideas and watch the progress of the students in the program, and we meet with the students' parents as often as necessary." Pat has worked on the plights of as many as 75 students (in a student body of about 400) during a single school year.

The books students read are an essential part of every reading program, so Pat carefully selects both the textbooks and

paperbacks the school orders each year. She also orders the reading tests used in her school and monitors their usefulness. "We are always trying to make our programs more effective," she says.

When she has a few moments away from the reading, Pat utilizes her camera to take pictures of the school's Students of the Month, which are hung near the cafeteria. "We just love to give our students recognition," she says. "And they love to see their pictures on the wall."

Where do you see this job leading you?

"When I was working on my master's degree, I thought a lot about where I would go from there, and I realized that if I got a doctorate I could go into administration, but I decided I definitely did not want that," Pat says. "I love working with the children, and administration would take me away from them. What I do takes me out of the day-to-day classroom work, but still keeps me involved with the kids. That's ideal for me."

68. Recruiter

description: Many publishing companies, especially those outside the big-city media centers in the United States, contract with executive search firms to locate qualified candidates to interview for vacancies on their staffs. These "headhunters," as they are often (somewhat) affectionately called, study the company and its competitors, and contact potential candidates and prepare them for the interviews. The headhunters also approach the goal of placing people in jobs from the other direction: they maintain contact with available candidates and search for positions that are suited to those people. More experienced recruiters often give presentations to companies whose business they seek.

salary: Recruiters earn a draw—usually between $25,000 and $35,000 a year to start—plus a commission that is generally a percentage of the salary paid to an employee they have placed with a client firm.

prospects: The larger search firms specializing in publishing jobs tend to be in New York, where there are many. You'll find regional ones in other major cities. You'll have no trouble getting an entry-level position with a search firm if you can prove yourself hard-working, reliable, and willing to start at the bottom.

qualifications: To get a job at a search firm, you need to speak very clearly and effectively to candidates and clients, and to write (letters and resumes) almost as well. You must also be able to sell—your candidates to your clients, your services to potential clients—and you'll have to understand, and/or be quick to learn about, the publishing industry.

characteristics: Resourceful people who engender trust with other people, who like talking on the phone, and who are astute judges of other people will be successful as recruiters.

Sara Nolfo *is an executive recruiter specializing in entry-level publishing jobs for an agency in New York City.*

How did you get the job?

After eight years as an assistant vice president in marketing and planning at a major bank, Sara decided she "couldn't do the job one more day." So Sara, who has a bachelor's degree in marketing and management and a master's in business administration, joined a group called Careers for Women, which helps its members find corporate sales positions. She used the group's network— "talking to other people about their jobs, making contacts, and asking questions"—to find her current job.

"The reputation of the company that I work for was very important to me," she says, "so I talked to the company's clients and the candidates it was working with before I took the job. I wanted to get involved with a company that was well regarded by the people it served."

Sara's advice to the candidates she's helping to place and to anyone who wants to get into the recruiting business is to learn as much as possible about potential employers. "The more you know about the industry in general and the company in particular, the smarter your choices will be," she says. "Finding a job is a job in itself and to do it right, you need to do your homework."

What do you do all day?

Sara's homework begins with getting to know her clients. "When companies hire us to find the right employees for them, we have to know as much as we can about their business, their markets, and their corporate culture," she explains.

Once recruiters learn as much as they can about their clients, they try to get to know the candidates. "We start with

> **"THIS IS A SALES JOB—I'M SELLING CANDIDATES TO COMPANIES, BUT THE COMPANIES WANT PEOPLE TO FILL THE JOB. MAYBE IT'S MORE LIKE MATCHMAKING."**

people on our list, who we know are looking for new positions—I'll get 50, 60, up to 70 calls a day from people looking for work. We find out their goals, their needs, their strengths and weaknesses," Sara explains. "My specialty is entry-level people, so when I identify ones who I think make good candidates, I take some time to help them prepare their resumes or portfolios, I work with them on their interviewing skills, I coach them on their whole presentation."

Once Sara has a group of suitable candidates, she calls the client and sets up interviews. If none of those are a good match, she begins again, looking beyond the list of available people. She works the phone, calling people with jobs to gauge their interest in a new position. "I fill a lot of sales positions, so I am often contacting people outside publishing— like [employees of] consumer products companies—to see if they'd like to sell advertising for a magazine, for example."

Sara also devotes time to keeping up on the news in the industry. "Of course, I read the classifieds to see where new openings are," she says. "I also read the industry journals— *Adweek, Folio,* and others—to find out who got promoted, which publisher is starting a new imprint, who's starting a new magazine—that kind of information you can use. This is not a job where you can wait for things to come to you; you have to look for opportunities."

Where do you see this job leading you?

"This is a very stressful job—it encourages manic-depression— but I'm not ready to leave it yet," Sara jokes, adding, "I don't have any ambition to start my own agency or to run my own business. I think with the skills I've learned here I could be a good literary agent. And I do think about all the jobs that I place people in.

"Some recruiters leave this business to go work in human resources at a corporation. That doesn't appeal to me at all. If I'm going to recruit, I think I'm in the best place to be doing it."

69. Religious Textbook Editor

description: Working with church councils, ministers, and theologians, religious textbook editors conceive of ideas, find and assign writers, edit the copy, and lay out and coordinate the printing of tracts, brochures, pamphlets, books, and other course materials designed to convey the teachings of the faith to kids and adults. While the functions of a religious textbook editor do not differ vastly from those of an editor of other kinds of textbooks, the context, working conditions, and orientation of the religious textbook editor are unique to the job.

salary: Religious textbook editors working for a large publisher or church organization earn about $25,000 a year to start; those employed by smaller organizations make less than $20,000. Editors working in bigger cities and those with advanced degrees will likely earn more.

prospects: The Nashville, Tennessee, telephone directory alone lists eight religious textbook publishers. You'll find other pockets of religious publishing wherever church councils are headquartered. The resurgence of organized religion in America has opened lots of opportunities for people devoted to their faith who have the interest and the ability to convey the message to the flock.

qualifications: You don't need to be a minister or even a theology major to be a textbook editor. What you do need are strong word skills, a degree in the humanities or education, and a thorough understanding of the particulars of the faith. Experience or training in editorial production will make you even more valuable to your organization.

characteristics: A devout belief in your faith, an ability to teach and even subtly persuade people, and diplomatic skills to help negotiate with people holding strong, disparate views on important issues will all help you succeed as a religious textbook editor.

Garland Pierce *is a minister, a divinity student, and the curriculum resource specialist for a church council's Christian education department in the South.*

How did you get the job?

Garland has been involved in church activities all of her life, so her career choice and her decision to major in religion at Furman University in South Carolina were easy. "I've wanted to study theology and become a leader in the church for as long as I can remember," she says. Since her graduation, she's been a student at Vanderbilt University in Nashville, working toward her doctor of divinity degree. During Garland's first year at Vanderbilt, she was a graduate research assistant at the Kelly, Miller, Smith Institute on the Black Church, where "we worked to facilitate dialogue among churches, scholars, and divinity schools," she says. "I also worked with local congregations on documenting their history.

And I gained a lot of experience in project management by helping to plan and implement a national conference on black churches."

Based on that experience, Garland was hired by the church's education department to edit and manage the production of Sunday school textbooks. For two years, she's worked with the church's director of education, integrating her word skills with his teaching expertise, to create texts used in Sunday schools at churches all over the country.

What do you do all day?

The ideas for the teaching materials produced by the education department come from their meetings with pastors, Christian educators, and youth leaders, and are then executed by Garland and her colleagues. "My favorite part of the process is the brainstorming of ideas," she

says. "But there's also a special satisfaction in seeing the ideas come to fruition."

After the ideas are agreed upon—"which can take a lot of work, a lot of back and forth, until we all agree"—Garland contacts bishops around the country for suggestions of authors who'd be suited to each project. The church also publishes a quarterly magazine through which she solicits authors. Then she assigns, edits, and prepares the copy for the printer.

Each of Garland's days is filled with all of those tasks and others, including office management and research into future ideas. "If you are committed to Christian education, you know that everything you do to further it is valuable."

> "MOST CHURCH PUBLISHERS DON'T HAVE A LARGE STAFF; YOU'LL HAVE TO WEAR A LOT OF HATS."

Where do you see this job leading you?

Garland Pierce is a minister who sees her work in developing Sunday school texts as part of her calling. "I always thought I would teach theology at the college level when I earned my doctorate," she says, "but I've come to believe that I could fulfill my mission by developing educational materials, too."

70. Reporter, Magazine

description: The function of reporters at national magazines differs from that of newspaper reporters in one crucial way: magazine reporters do not write articles, they research them. Reporters work with writers to dig up leads, gather background information, comb through research materials, and conduct interviews, all of which they give to the writers to use in composing articles. Reporters are also called upon to go back over a writer's work and double-check facts. At some magazines, reporters get credit lines for the articles they work on; at others, they do not. Reporter is often a stepping stone to a writing job.

salary: Reporter is an entry-level (or slightly beyond entry-level) position at a national magazine, and it pays about $25,000 a year. Experienced reporters can earn up to $40,000.

prospects: Jobs at national publications—the news weeklies, the business journals, the major monthlies—are highly coveted. They are opportunities for the best and the brightest to break into the big time. Does that describe you?

qualifications: An impeccable academic record and lots of experience—through either campus publications or internships—are necessary to be considered for this caliber of job. Knowledge and experience of the particular field covered by the magazine—business, politics, health—will enhance your resume.

characteristics: Enthusiastic, detail-oriented, self-directed journalists who work well in support of others will enjoy success as a national magazine reporter.

Joyce E. Davis *is a reporter at a business magazine in New York City.*

How did you get the job?

Joyce devoted a lot of energy and time to laying the foundation for her career. While working toward her degree in print journalism with a minor in marketing/management (which she earned in 1993) at Howard University in Washington, D.C., Joyce held several internships. "I spent two summers at *The Atlanta Daily World* and one at *Essence* magazine," she says. "And I spent a semester at the Bureau of National Affairs, which produces 80 different publications on the relationship between business and government, and another semester at Communications Daily, an organization that publishes newsletters on all aspects of the communications industry."

At the end of her senior year at Howard, Joyce was offered a position as an editorial assistant at Communications Daily. But earlier that year she had sent out 150 letters to magazines she had an interest in; 10 of those letters resulted in interviews, all of them in New York City. In the succeeding months, she traveled back and forth on the bus from Washington to New York, going through the interview process. "I interviewed at [one of the major business magazines] at the end of a very long day," she recalls. "I had had three other interviews that day and I was ready to go home." But Joyce stuck it out and was offered a three-month paid internship and then the job of reporter.

What distinguished Joyce from the other candidates? She believes it was her solid, real-world experiences, the business courses she took at school, and the time she took to research the magazine and its parent company before she came in for the interview. "It didn't hurt that I am an African-American," she adds, "especially since there were only two others on the staff when I arrived."

What do you do all day?

Joyce primarily spends her time helping the magazine's staff writers compile information for articles on which they are working. "That can mean conducting interviews, gathering data for charts, or reading annual reports and other financial documents," she explains. "A reporter, above all, needs to be detail-oriented and thorough. You have to stay one step ahead of the writer you are working with and on top of the story you are working on."

> **"BE SURE TO GET SOME EXPERIENCE FIRST: 9.999 TIMES OUT OF 10, YOU WON'T GET ANYWHERE IN THIS MARKET WITHOUT HAVING AT LEAST ONE INTERNSHIP."**

Some of Joyce's time is also spent fact-checking stories that have been written. When she's got a free moment—which doesn't seem to be often—Joyce adds to her idea file and suggests stories she'd like to write. "Every so often we get a chance to show off our writing skills with a short department piece or one-pager," she says.

Where do you see this job leading you?

Though Joyce appreciates the opportunity, and values all she's learned on the job ("you can only really learn about journalism through experience," she says), she's also discovered that the business press is not for her. "I am now freelancing for other publications and I hope to get an assistant editor position somewhere else in the next two years."

71. Researcher, Magazine

description: Magazine writers turn to researchers to help them dig up and verify the facts needed for complex stories. Researchers play a critical role at magazines that address issues of health and science, and can be essential to any periodical that publishes in-depth nonfiction articles. Important as research may be, it is done in virtual anonymity—only the rare magazine credits a researcher as well as the writer of an article. Researchers do, however, often get an opportunity to write short articles for the magazine's departments (as opposed to the features). Deadline pressures for researchers are directly related to how overdue the article is.

salary: This is an entry-level job that can earn a qualified person a salary in the mid-$20,000 range; experienced research editors earn $35,000 a year or more. The more technical the magazine and the bigger the city it's in, the higher the pay.

prospects: Not every magazine has full-time staff researchers—though most that deal with complex issues in depth do; many more use part-time or freelance help. But research in many cases is a starting point for magazine journalists, so opportunities can be available regularly as people are promoted to other positions on the staff.

qualifications: Training or experience in journalism and some knowledge of the topic (medicine, fashion, travel, etc.) are the essential elements of an application for a job as a researcher. Strong writing skills are important, too.

characteristics: A detail-oriented, persistent, resourceful person who learns quickly and asks a lot of questions will succeed as a researcher. To be happy at it, you need to have a well-contained ego.

How did you get the job?

"I took this job to pay for my health-care insurance," Catherine says without equivocation. But, of course, her education and experience were leading her to the job from the first. She has bachelor's and master's degrees (and beginning work on a doctorate) in behavioral science, and she worked for 12 years as a freelance researcher, writer, and editor of medical textbooks. So when she decided it was time to have a full-time, permanent job with benefits and answered the ad for her current position, the editors of the health-oriented magazine she works for had no doubts about her qualifications. "I'm sure my medical background distinguished me from the other candidates," she says. "Knowledge of the topic is very helpful, but expertise is not necessary. In fact, knowing where to look for answers to your questions is more than half the battle."

Now Catherine's co-director of the department, supervising a staff of up to six freelancers, a position she earned by being quick, accurate, and reliable.

What do you do all day?

Research work comes in two forms: fact-checking stories that have already been written, and helping collect primary information for stories in progress. "On health stories, it's important to be comfortable with

> "WORKING IN THE RESEARCH DEPARTMENT IS BETTER EXPERIENCE THAN BEING AN EDITORIAL ASSISTANT: NONE OF YOUR WORK IN RESEARCH IS CLERICAL AND THE PAY IS BETTER."

evaluating scientific studies and interviewing technical sources," Catherine explains. "You have to be able to ferret out interesting, relevant, and significant information that might not be in the study's summary; and to make sources feel comfortable giving you detailed information. It helps to speak their language, so you can translate the information for the reader."

Fact-checking is often less challenging and interesting than primary research, says Catherine, but she recognizes its value to the magazine. "The job mostly involves making phone calls to sources, making sure that the basic information is correct and hasn't changed since the writer interviewed the sources," she says. "What you don't do is allow sources to edit themselves, to rewrite their quotes."

Catherine and the other researchers at her magazine do rewrite information that is incorrect. "It doesn't require a lot of style. You just have to write clearly, accurately, and accessibly," she says, adding that "every researcher here has also written short items for the magazine."

Where do you see this job leading you?

If Catherine could just keep that insurance paid for, she'd go back to freelancing in a minute. "Actually, I'd like most to teach scuba diving in the Caribbean," she says. "But since that's not high on the list of profitable, secure career choices, I'll probably stay right where I am.

"Research is a great way of learning a lot about your magazine's subject," she continues. "It's excellent work for a writer or someone who wants to learn to be a writer."

72. Resume Writer

description: In an age when people stayed in one job for most of their careers, they rarely needed a resume—and when they did, it was little more than a straightforward recounting of employment history. But the transience of the labor market, corporate downsizing, and increased competition for scarcer jobs has forced lots of people to devote time and money to crafting resumes that give them an edge on the competition. Professional writers can help people at all levels of the job market—from entry-level to high-powered executive—create resumes that will catch the attention of decision makers. Resume writers usually are self-employed, though some work for career counseling centers and outplacement services.

salary: The complexity of the service provided dictates the fees charged by a resume writer: as little as a few dollars a page for proofreading, up to $300 for writing, proofing, and printing a resume and cover letter from start to finish. Resume writers who also provide career counseling and job search services can earn even more lucrative fees.

prospects: Those aforementioned trends in the job market seem unlikely to change anytime soon, creating a growing demand for resume writers, especially in those regions where the population exceeds the availability of jobs or where the job base is changing dramatically. In short, if you market your resume-writing service effectively, you should be busy.

qualifications: You must write concisely, in the language of business and the client, but also with the verve that will distinguish your work—to your clients and to their potential employers. Certification, available through the Professional Association of Resume Writers, is sure to lend credibility to your abilities as a resume writer.

characteristics: Can you be supportive, yet ask the tough questions? Are you effective at selling yourself and your skills? If so, then you should succeed as a professional resume writer.

Mary Roberts *is a certified professional resume writer in the Midwest.*

How did you get the job?

Though many professional resume writers start as secretaries, Mary says, she did not. She jumped right in when she answered an advertisement placed by an executive recruiting firm looking for a staff resume writer to help clients improve their resumes. Before long, she was out on her own, handling just about all the work she could manage.

Mary has been seeking a master's degree in career counseling, but she believes you can prepare for this work in many different ways. "Studying mass communications, English, literature, creative writing, and journalism is a great foundation," she says. "Psychology, sociology, marketing, and other business courses will help you do this work better. In fact, you'd have to look long and hard to find any kind of schooling that wouldn't eventually be useful in resume writing.

"Join the Professional Association of Resume Writers and get certified. They can be reached at 800/822-7279," she advises. "You'll learn a lot from other professionals that you'd otherwise take a long time to learn on your own, and certification will help your clients choose a more qualified resume writer."

If you're just getting started, Mary recommends that you study some of the books on writing resumes available today—"There must be more than 250 of them," she says. And find someone established in your area, she suggests, and "get them to mentor you. It's a great way to learn the craft. PARW just recently began a mentoring program to assist less experienced writers."

What do you do all day?

Mary's clients—who find her through print advertising and, more often, through referrals—receive a free half-hour consultation before they contract her. "The free consultation allows the clients to assess me and my work," she says, "and it allows me to size them up. I try to determine how much the potential clients have already done with their resumes and what they want me to do for them."

> "COMPUTERS HAVE MADE IT POSSIBLE FOR PEOPLE TO HAVE MORE THAN ONE RESUME FOR DIFFERENT POSITIONS THEY'RE APPLYING FOR. THAT MEANS MORE WORK FOR RESUME WRITERS."

Most clients who sign up after the consultation go home with an assignment from Mary. "I like my clients to be as involved in the process as possible so they are better prepared in the interview," she explains. "To start, I give them a blank sheet of paper—not a form—and ask them to jot down some notes that focus on their accomplishments and achievements with measurable results. If they require help with this, I schedule an interview session.

"The resume is a self-marketing tool, not just a chronological history," she continues. "The question a resume must answer is 'What can you do to make or save the company money?' I try to get my clients to answer that question for themselves and then we work on getting it down on paper."

Writing a resume usually takes from a couple of days to a couple of weeks, Mary says, and she will do cover and follow-up letters, too. She proofreads them, computer-checks the spelling, and will print them on her laser printer, too.

Where do you see this job leading you?

Mary is busy enough to pay her bills, but she wouldn't mind if her referrals increased—and let her decrease her advertising costs. But she's not intending to change anything else about her career. "I've developed a comfortable niche for myself here," she says. Her work as the '95–'96 chairperson of the professional organization's international certification board fills whatever free time she has.

73. Romance Novelist

description: A romance novelist's work is essentially the same as that of other fiction writers: mining the imagination for characters and plots that will captivate the reader. But a romance novelist must adhere to a style—some would say formula—and arrive at a finish that meets the particular expectations of the romance reader. And unlike other fiction writers, a romance novelist who finds an audience can usually rely on readers to continue to buy his or her work faithfully.

These writers rarely use their own names; at certain publishers it's not even permitted. Novelists set their own schedules—both daily work hours and deadlines in many cases.

salary: Romance publishers pay little for a first novel—in one case just $500, but more commonly $2,500 to $5,000. Authors with a strong repeat audience can earn 10 times that and more in royalties.

prospects: One well-known company alone publishes 800 titles a year, and there are dozens of romance publishers, producing works in many different styles, from horror to historical romance, intrigue to realistic novels. That's a lot of opportunities to see your work published. However, the biggest and best-known publishers buy just 10 percent of their releases from new authors. And, to support yourself when you're getting started, you'll need to write three to four books a year to earn a comfortable living.

qualifications: You need no special training or degree to be a romance novelist, just the ideas and writing skills to compose stories that reach an audience. You can learn about the conventions used by romance writers and tactics for submitting your work by taking courses sponsored by the Romance Writers of America.

characteristics: You need a vivid imagination to write romances, and you have to believe in what people in the industry call "the magic," a faith that love will overcome all. Self-discipline is also essential: while you'll have deadlines to meet, you will be your own boss. And a good marketing sense helps a writer to understand what romance readers want and to deliver it.

Tara Taylor Quinn *is the name used by a Harlequin Romance writer living in the Southwest.*

How did you get the job?

After earning her bachelor's degree in English literature from a small college in Ohio, Tara worked as a stringer for the *Dayton Daily News* and later as a freelance advertising and public relations copywriter. "I had always written for a living, but I never thought about writing a novel until I came up with the idea for my first book," Tara confesses. "I didn't dream of writing the Great American Novel or anything."

She found the address of her current publisher in an advertisement in an issue of *Writer's Digest.* "I had no idea there was an organization that could help me prepare my manuscript and guide me to receptive editors, so I just submitted my idea to the publisher," Tara says. "A month or so later, I got a call from an editor saying she wanted to buy my idea." Tara has now written 15 books, she says, of which six have been published. She's sold two more ideas and is working to complete those two books.

What do you do all day?

"My books are not pure fantasy; I base all of my characters in reality," Tara says, "so I spend a lot of time thinking about how they would behave in real life." Once she has her story outlined—"I basically know the direction the story will go when I begin"—she writes while her daughter is in school, working all day, every day, to ensure that she meets her deadline. "I work with the editor to set a reasonable deadline for each book, but when it approaches, the pressure is still on to make it." Tara takes about four months to write each book, "though I've written one in as little as six weeks and taken as long as a year on another."

After a book's finished, Tara's editor and the copy editors send the manuscript back with suggested revisions; Tara makes some changes of her own, too. A manuscript typically undergoes three rounds of revisions, she reports.

Tara also devotes time to answering readers' letters. "Romance readers are very devoted to their favorite authors, and I believe this is an important trust that the author ought to respect," she says. "So I answer every reader personally."

Where do you see this job leading you?

Tara has what she considers her dream job. "I do believe in the magic and I think that what I do makes readers feel better in their own lives," she says. "My only goal is to keep growing my readership and giving the readers who stick with me a lift whenever they read my books."

> **"TO EARN A LIVING WRITING ROMANCE NOVELS, YOU HAVE TO WRITE THREE OR FOUR BOOKS A YEAR. ONLY THE MOST POPULAR AUTHORS CAN AFFORD TO WRITE JUST ONE BOOK A YEAR."**

74. Scriptwriter

description: Hollywood feature films are just a small—albeit the best-known—portion of the video market. Many consumers buy self-help tapes, schools use educational ones, and corporations show multimedia presentations to employees, customers, and shareholders. Just as with feature films, scriptwriters create the raw material from which these videotapes are produced. Some production companies have staff writers, while others rely on freelance scriptwriters. In either case, writers both generate ideas and accept assignments. Writing these sorts of scripts often requires extensive research along with imagination. This kind of scriptwriting is not the normal avenue to Hollywood fame and fortune, but it is steady, creative work.

salary: Staff scriptwriters earn from $25,000 to $50,000 a year—more going to people with in-depth knowledge of popular film topics. Highly productive freelancers won't make much more than $15,000 during their first year, but they can build their clientele and their income in subsequent years.

prospects: Look in catalogs, libraries, and stores, and you'll see a lot more "nonfiction" films than you'd think. With skill, patience, and determination, you will find scriptwriting work in almost any part of the country. The expansion of multimedia offers even more opportunities to scriptwriters.

qualifications: You don't need special training or experience—you just need to be able to tell engaging stories with words and pictures. Knowing how to research thoroughly and to write your ideas succinctly will help you find work and do it well.

characteristics: It's the out-of-the-ordinary combination of verbal and visual sense that makes a good and successful scriptwriter. You'll do even better if you work quickly and can produce under pressure.

Aaron Heinric *is a freelance scriptwriter living on the West Coast.*

How did you get the job?

Aaron earned a bachelor's degree in broadcast journalism, but began working in public relations after college. "I was creating audiovisual presentations for clients and on a freelance basis right from the start," he says. "After several years in the business, I decided to get a master's degree in scriptwriting.

"I don't believe everybody needs a master's degree to be a scriptwriter, but you do need to take a few classes to learn the fundamentals and about the process and mechanics of creating a script," Aaron goes on. "I've taken a lot of seminars over the years—lots of them not very good. You have to look for classes given by people who have produced scripts to their credit."

Once Aaron truly understood how to write a script, he began researching production companies and their areas of interest, then sent out relevant ideas and samples of his work to them. "It helped me that I had

> **"JOIN WRITERS GROUPS ONLY IF THEY ARE STRUCTURED TO GIVE POSITIVE FEEDBACK, RATHER THAN NEGATIVE CRITICISM. YOU SHOULD JOIN THE INDUSTRY AND PUBLIC RELATIONS GROUPS—THOSE ARE FULL OF PEOPLE WHO NEED YOUR SERVICES."**

already had scripts that had been turned into finished video from when I worked in public relations," he says. "But the companies always want to see scripts, not tapes—a lot, both good and bad, can happen to a script during the filming."

With a solid track record and an extensive network of contacts, Aaron rarely pitches ideas anymore—he has plenty of offers coming to him. "That's when your freelance career takes off," he says.

What do you do all day?

Every script, no matter how simple, begins with research. "I recently did an eight-part series for educators on how to mentor high-risk youths, and I spent weeks reading books and articles, and interviewing experts and kids before I started writing," Aaron explains. "I've also just finished the script for a 15-minute corporate video brochure on recycling programs. For that one I spent a couple days talking to people at the company and a few local officials."

Writing a first draft can be equally drawn out or swift. He cranked out the script for that eight-part series under pressure in three and a half weeks—he'd have preferred two months. The corporate video he had no trouble writing in just two weeks.

Then come the revisions. "Most clients—especially corporate ones—don't have a clear-cut idea of what they want

when they assign you," Aaron says. "So the first draft is often just a starting point. After the clients review it and decide what they like and don't like, I'll do a set of major revisions and then another set of minor revisions before the script is ready to be shot."

Because of Aaron's experience in the entire production process, he's often asked to serve as director and producer of scripts he's written. "That can be rewarding," he says, "but I prefer to write."

Where do you see this job leading you?

Aaron is eager to grow beyond the comfortable niche he has carved out for himself: he has several feature-film scripts circulating at Hollywood studios and television networks. "The scriptwriting I have been doing is interesting and fun for me," he says, "but I want to shoot for the big time."

75. Software Documentation Writer

description: Before computer users put programs to work, documentation writers try them out and then write instructions for everyone else to follow when using them. These writers often check the programs for bugs and in some cases work with the engineers during the design of the programs. A documentation writer may also participate in training people (or the trainers) on the software. Documentation writers get to try out new software before anyone else does, but they are rarely credited for their work. Many companies hire technical writers on a contract basis, though some have full-time staff.

salary: Inexperienced contract writers can charge about $15 per hour; more seasoned ones get $25 to $40, depending on how much seasoning and the complexity of the job. Staff writers earn from $30,000 to $50,000 a year, depending on the amount of experience and the company's values.

prospects: If you're qualified, you won't have trouble finding work as a contract writer wherever there are computing service companies. In the areas where high-tech companies have clustered, you'll have an easier time finding a staff position.

qualifications: A degree in technical writing—or even just a course or two—will help you get an opportunity, but is so far not required by most companies. The ability to write clearly and concisely, to understand engineer-speak, and to run software without a guidebook to turn to are the essentials of this job.

characteristics: The single most important quality is the capacity to think like someone who doesn't know what they're doing long after you have developed some expertise in the field. And you'll have to be somewhat diplomatic and selfless to work with programmers to whom everything is obvious.

Sherri L. Cole *is a documentation writer for a government agency's in-house computer programming department in Texas.*

How did you get the job?

Sherri earned her bachelor's degree in journalism with a concentration on magazines at the University of Texas, but she went right to work in the computer field after graduation. She first wrote and edited newsletters for computer vendors, then spent two years working for an agency that contracted her technical writing services to various software producers in the area. "Those jobs taught me how to work on my own and the interviewing and research skills I need to do this kind of work," she says. "And they prepared me to jump right in on a project without any background or support."

That last lesson has been especially important since she was hired by the government agency where she now works.

"The whole documentation process here was a mess," she says. "They needed someone who had experience and who wouldn't need their hand held to get going."

What do you do all day?

Sherri's customers are a captive audience—they are 3,000 employees of various state agencies that must have customized programs (to track water permits, for instance). But that doesn't mean she takes their needs and concerns for granted. "First I learn a system backwards and forwards, and check it for bugs," she explains. "Then I meet with the people who are going to use it to get a sense of their computer skills and their applications for the system. Only after I understand all of that do I start writing." From the insights Sherri gains from talking to the customers, she can include specific examples and instructions on how they'd use the software in their own particular jobs.

The manuals range in size from four to 100 pages, and the writing process can take from two to four weeks. "I submit the finished documentation to the programmers for revisions," Sherri says. "I don't have any cohorts to help me edit for grammar and style; that's my responsibility solely." After the manual's content is approved, Sherri prepares the final document to be given to the users.

> **"JOIN THE SOCIETY FOR TECHNICAL COMMUNICATION; YOU MAKE GREAT CONTACTS AND LEARN ABOUT WHERE THE JOBS ARE."**

"I'm a one-woman shop here," she says. "I write, edit, and design on desktop."

Sherri also works with the agency's training department. "We work very closely on preparing the courses for the users," she says. "We are working for the same goal of helping the customers use the software." In her little spare time, Sherri edits a bimonthly newsletter for the agency's computer users.

Where do you see this job leading you?

Sherri's background may be in journalism, but all of her experience with computers has enticed her to sign up for a course in programming and to contemplate even more technical work. "I think I might like a job as a systems manager," she says.

76. Software Reference Writer

description: Computer software packages usually include a reference book and on-line help files, in which users can find the answers to their specific questions.

The reference writer learns all the nuances of the software and studies the particular users of the software, then organizes and presents the information at a level of sophistication and with a logic that suits the users. The writers work closely with the programmers so that they understand the application thoroughly and can guide the users to tailoring the system to their needs; reference writers also collaborate with the training manual writers to ensure that all of the users' potential questions are answered.

salary: Entry-level software reference writers start at about $28,000 to $35,000 a year, depending on their knowledge of programming and the specific field served by the software.

prospects: The business world's ever-growing dependency on computers and the need for customization virtually assure plenty of jobs for people who can turn complex technical concepts into everyday language that computer users can put into action. The jobs are found all over the country—wherever software producers sprout up.

qualifications: You don't need to be a computer programmer, but you have to understand programmers' talk and be able to work well with computers. And you must write clearly and succinctly about topics that are often complex. A basic understanding of the businesses to whom the software is sold is necessary, and will strengthen your application and help you serve them better.

characteristics: To succeed as a reference writer, you must work well as part of a team yet be able to perform your duties basically on your own. And, most importantly, you'll have to be able to put yourself in your audience's place, to anticipate their questions and make sure they are answered in the reference materials.

Erich Lukas *is a technical writer on the East Coast for a developer of customized software for hospitals.*

How did you get the job?

Internship is the short answer to that question—but hang on, there are relevant details. First, Erich was one of the very focused few who know just what they want to do when they're searching for a major. "When I knew that I wanted to be a technical writer, I chose the University of Delaware's technical writing undergraduate program because of its excellent reputation," Erich says. "I had courses in audience analysis and documentation design that I put to use every day." He had no intention of being a programmer, but he took two courses on how to write computer code.

Most importantly, Erich signed up for a summer internship program during the summer of his senior year. "I had a full-time internship for three months at the company where I now work," he explains. "The managers got to see how I work and I got to see how the company is—it was like a three-month interview." That interview must have gone well, because Erich

obtained the first open position in his department upon completion of his internship. And the main reason, he believes, "is that I took responsibility wherever I could. I didn't wait for work to come to me."

What do you do all day?

More than 60 people are in the technical writing department of the company where Erich works. That ensures that each writer has a very specific job. For Erich, that means writing reference guides and on-line help screens for software systems custom-designed for hospitals. "The more you know about how a product is built, the clearer and more helpful you can be to the users," he says, "so I try to get as much hands-on experience with each system as I can."

Once Erich knows the system he's been assigned to reference through and through, he interviews the users to determine how much they know about computers in general and to get an idea of their particular needs. Then, step by step, he writes the manual and help screens with those users' per-

spective in mind. "For example, if the people using a certain product are experienced data processors, they don't need documentation full of basics on data processing," Erich says. "What they need is details on how to customize the application to fit their needs." Erich's finished copy is first edited for technical accuracy by the programmers, and then for its grammar, spelling, and style by staff editors in the documentation department.

Erich didn't stop seeking out responsibility after he got the

> **"YOU HAVE TO GO INTO THIS KNOWING THAT YOUR WRITING HAS TO BE CONCISE AND STRAIGHTFORWARD AS CAN BE—PEOPLE DON'T READ DOCUMENTATION FOR ENTERTAINMENT. THEY JUST WANT ANSWERS TO THEIR QUESTIONS."**

job, either. He volunteered to teach business writing to his colleagues through an initiative sponsored by his company's human resources department and he helps out the education department in training customers on products that he documents. "That helps me to learn more about our products and our customers," he says. "Teaching business writing has helped me network with other people in our company," he adds, "and it's fun."

Where do you see this job leading you?

The way Erich sees it, he could advance into a management position. "I will strive to advance within my own department and climb the ladder into management," he says. "I can devote more of my time to training. I can also take more courses in programming and systems design to enhance my technical knowledge.

"For right now, I enjoy the variety of things I do," he concludes. "It makes work interesting and fun and keeps it challenging."

77. Speechwriter, Corporate

description: Speechwriters prepare presentations given by executives of large corporations to trade associations, employee groups, stockholders, analysts, and the press. The speechwriter researches the topic and the audience, writes and edits the text together with the executive giving the speech, suggests and gathers graphics to be used in the presentation, and helps the executive with the delivery.

salary: With a couple of years of experience in the press or in public relations and a basic knowledge of the company's industry, a speechwriter can earn $50,000 to $60,000 a year to start. A proven speechwriter might command a $150,000 yearly salary.

prospects: Every successful corporation is acutely aware of the importance of clear, focused communications with its customers, employees, and the public at large. So large corporations are devoting more resources to keeping trained communicators on staff, making prospects for speechwriting very good—particularly in high-profile industries.

qualifications: Training and experience as a journalist will develop your ability to produce on a short deadline, thoroughly research a topic, organize and present information in a logical structure, and turn an interesting phrase. Basic knowledge about the industry you'll be working in will boost your chances of landing a job, too.

characteristics: Speechwriters must be able to communicate clearly and productively with the executive giving the speech and engender trust with that executive. Patience through frequent rewrites and a selfless devotion to doing an uncredited job well are essential. The speechwriter must also have the capacity to conceive of an entire presentation—graphics and demonstrations as well as text.

John Bukovinsky *is the director of communications operations at a well-known high-tech company on the East Coast.*

How did you get the job?

John logged a couple of years as a reporter at a daily newspaper in New Jersey after earning his bachelor's degree in journalism at Rutgers University in New Brunswick, New Jersey, but he quickly moved into jobs at two different trade associations. "The first job was great fun, a lot of laughs," he says. "But the hours were lousy and so was the pay."

John's second trade association job—at the state's builder's association—introduced him to the challenges of speechwriting. "The organization was involved in a lot of issues that required the officers to give testimony to the legislature," he says. "I helped the leadership prepare their statements both to the legislature and to the press."

That intensive workshop in public presentations gave John the experience he needed to win a job as a speechwriter at one of America's best-known technology companies.

> **"BUILD UP A BOOK OF SKILLS THAT INCLUDES REPORTING, WRITING UNDER DEADLINE, AND UNDERSTANDING GRAPHICS, ALONG WITH SPEECHWRITING."**

What do you do all day?

"Good speechwriting begins with solid research," John says. "So before I meet with the person who is to give the speech, I invest the time to find out exactly what type of audience will be hearing the speech, who else is on the program, where the speech will be given, and anything else I can find out that will help us compose the speech." With those facts in hand, John meets with the "client" (his department is a service to the corporation, so each executive who uses a speechwriter is the client) to discuss "the strategic points the speaker wants to make in the presentation."

Then John gathers as much information as he can about the topic, constructs an outline that makes the points with logic and information, and presents that to the client. "The key to a successful writer/speaker relationship is trust," John emphasizes. "And doing your homework reassures the speaker that you're going to make him or her look good." When writer and speaker agree on the outline, the writer will assemble a draft and then show that to the speaker. "If the speaker approves the draft, then the revision process begins," John goes on. "With some teams, that can mean sending the script back and forth every day for two weeks.

If the writer and speaker work well together, it can be as few as two or three rounds before the speaker is comfortable with it."

Where do you see this job leading you?

John Bukovinsky is headed out to sea after this job. "I'll retire after this job and spend my days in my ocean kayak," says the 47-year-old. "But probably not anytime soon." John's worked in all facets of his company's communications operations: in-house advertising agency, employee communications, the company's internal television network, and press relations, as well as speechwriting. He'll be happy to keep writing speeches—and managing other speechwriters—until he can't resist that kayak anymore.

78. Sports Information Director

description: College athletic departments have on-staff specialists who manage coaches and student-athletes' interaction with the media, provide facts and figures to the press, help promote the school's athletes for awards and other forms of recognition, produce special publications used by the department, and serve as the team's historians. SIDs and their assistants travel with their teams to assist with media coverage. In some instances, sports information directors serve as commentators for broadcasts of games.

salary: Assistant sports information directors—the entry-level full-time job—earn from the mid-teens to high $20s at colleges with modest-size athletic departments. The top job at those schools pays into the $40s. Larger programs may pay substantially more.

prospects: The majority of colleges have just two to three paid staffers in their sports information departments—student-interns help out in many cases. That means there are a limited number of positions—but some regularly become available as people move on to other jobs.

qualifications: Sports information directors must write well, speak in public comfortably, handle reporters diplomatically, and support the school's teams devotedly. Experience as a student-intern is the most common avenue into a full-time job.

characteristics: You love sports—and not just the big-three team games, but all sorts of sports. That's the kind of passion that makes sports information directors happy and successful in their jobs.

Tim Harkins *is the assistant sports information director at a large university in the West.*

- -

How did you get the job?

Tim earned his bachelor's degree in journalism from the University of Kansas. He worked as a student assistant for one semester at KU and later served as a graduate assistant at the University of Tulsa and the University of Utah.

"Almost everybody in sports information was an intern or grad assistant at one time," he says. "You learn so much as an intern and there are enough

> **"IF YOU WANT TO WORK IN SPORTS INFORMATION, YOU'LL ALMOST HAVE TO SPEND SOME TIME IN A DEPARTMENT AS A STUDENT-INTERN OR GRADUATE ASSISTANT."**
> - - - - - - - - - -

interns around that there's very little reason why a director would hire an assistant SID who has no experience."

Note, however, that interning does not ensure you a position at your school. Loyalties to your alma mater aside, people in sports information must be willing to move to find full-time positions. After Tim left Kansas, he worked at another university for a few years before he took his current job with a rival school in the same conference. "The more experience you have, the broader your perspective is," Tim says. "And you get more experience by seeing how different departments are run."

What do you do all day?

Tim breaks down his job into three main components: "It's a combination of public relations, working at events, and maintaining records and historical facts," he says. "The first two take up most of our time."

Before the start of each season, the sports information

department compiles the media guide. "It has all the background, facts, and figures for each team and its players," Tim says. For reasons that have to do with the National Collegiate Athletic Association's control over recruiting of athletes, the media guide must adhere to NCAA guidelines.

Sports information departments typically produce other publications such as schedule posters and special All-America publications. "If we have an athlete qualified for All-American recognition, our office will create special publicity materials to send to sportswriters and others who will vote," Tim says. "The department will issue press releases on that and other topics as well."

On game day, the sports information department serves as host to the media—providing statistics and other pertinent facts, setting up interviews with coaches and players, and generally responding to other requests from the press. "If a

football game played on our home field is to be broadcast on a television network, for example, we're responsible for lining up workers the network can hire for the day," Tim says.

In quieter moments, Tim, like other sports information directors, keeps track of the school's records.

Where do you see this job leading you?

Tim, who has been in sports information for about five years, would like to head his own sports information department sometime soon. Assistant SIDs without designs on the top job often move from the athletic department to other areas on campus—such as university relations for the school.

79. Sportswriter

description: Sportswriters report the news, just like other reporters. But while most reporters rarely know when the news they cover will occur, sportswriters can just look at a schedule to know when their news will happen. And the outcome of sports news, in most cases, is predictable: someone wins, someone loses. The challenge for sportswriters, then, is to get the news back to their newspapers as soon as possible (because readers can get the simple facts of wins and losses from broadcast news), and to add enlightening detail and analysis to the scores and statistics. Sportswriters get to attend games that other people pay to see, but they must work while others are merely enjoying the competition.

salary: An entry-level sports reporter will start out earning $25,000 to $30,000 a year at a newspaper in a midsize city; experience will open up opportunities in larger markets, and increase the writer's earning power.

prospects: Just about every local newspaper reports on the teams—high school, college, and club, as well as professional—in its coverage area. In many cases, these newspapers rely on part-timers and stringers (writers paid per assignment) to report on games that full-time staff members do not have time to attend. This is a great way for inexperienced sportswriters to break in. Once you're experienced, you'll be able to find lots of opportunities.

qualifications: You don't need a journalism degree to land a job as a sportswriter, but you must develop the skills that all journalists rely on: the insight to ask the questions your readers want the answers to, and the ability to write concisely, often under rigid deadline pressure.

characteristics: You have to love sports enough to work evenings and on weekends, the times when many games are played. And you have to sustain that passion long after the glamour of covering sports wears off, and it becomes your job.

Phil Anastasia *is a sportswriter at a regional daily newspaper on the East Coast.*

How did you get the job?

Phil was exposed to the journalist's life early by his older brother, who is a reporter at a major metropolitan newspaper. "He's 11 years older than me," Phil explains, "and I was impressed by his job when I was still in junior high."

He studied literature at a small liberal arts college, "because I've always loved reading and writing," and he got an education in sportswriting by reading the reporters in his local papers. "I read all the sports sections, and knew all the writers," Phil says. "I wasn't studying them consciously, but I was absorbing a lot about their writing styles, and that helped me develop my own."

To complement what Phil was learning in school and from reading, he worked during the summer as a clerk for the sports desk at the newspaper where he's now employed—"taking scores over the phone, and doing other important but unexciting work like that," Phil recalls. It was time well-spent. "When I graduated, the editor offered me a job as a beat reporter covering the local college teams."

Of course, he took the offer and never looked back. Two years later, he was promoted to covering the professional football team in a nearby city. After 10 years on that beat, Phil was given a 1,000-word column to write four times a week—which he has been doing for more than two years.

What do you do all day?

As a columnist, Phil has the luxury and the challenge of writing about whatever he wants. "I meet with my editor once a week to discuss what I'd like to do with the column, but I'm more or less free to write whatever I want," he explains. Some days that means attending games and rendering opinions about the local teams and players; on other days he addresses issues of interest in the world of sports. "I try to mix it up both for my sake and the reader's sake," he says.

On those days when Phil's not at a game, he takes his time writing the column in his office at home. "I may work for a couple hours, go to my kid's baseball game for fun, then go back to my desk and rewrite and edit until I am satisfied with it," he says. When Phil does go to a game—a night game in particular—he has to write with a deadline pointed straight at him. "My column must be in no later than 10:45 P.M.," Phil says. "I've been to a hockey playoff game that didn't end until nearly 10:30, and I was writing as the game was still being played, and finished in the stadium before I left—then I filed it electronically before I went home.

"I don't think I do my best work under that kind of pressure, but it's an important part of the job," he explains. "And after years as a beat reporter, you get practiced at writing that quickly."

Where do you see this job leading you?

Phil considers himself fortunate to have a job that combines his two great loves—reading and sports—and he is in no hurry to change. But he would like to get more involved with radio and television sportscasting. "I've done a little bit of sports talk radio, and I enjoyed it," he says. "But I would not want to do that full-time."

> **"EVEN THOUGH YOU'RE WRITING ABOUT SOMETHING FUN AND BASICALLY NOT EARTH-SHAKING NEWS, YOU HAVE TO APPROACH SPORTSWRITING WITH A SERIOUS COMMITMENT TO DOING THE JOB RIGHT."**

80. Story Analyst, Movie Studio

description: "Readers," as Hollywood insiders refer to story analysts, read scripts and write synopses and brief commentaries on them so that the studio's or production company's executives don't have to study each page of a script. Some readers work in an office on the studio lot, and some work from their homes. The readers at the major studios belong to Local 854 of the International Alliance of Theatrical Stage Employees (I.A.T.S.E.); smaller studios and production companies often hire less experienced, nonunion readers for less pay.

salary: A freelance story analyst will earn from $35 to $50 per script. Readers who belong to the union and have some experience in the film industry—as many readers do—generally start at around $40,000 per year. Reliable analysts with years of service make six-figure salaries, with overtime pay.

prospects: There's freelance work for story analysts at smaller production companies, where they can build their skills and reputations before joining the union and seeking out jobs at major studios. But the movie business is competitive and no job in Hollywood is won without good luck and good timing, a strong network of connections, and dogged determination.

qualifications: You can get training in script analysis through both credit and noncredit courses at colleges in the Los Angeles area, but what you really need is the ability to assess movie scripts and to write concisely and constructively about a script's strengths and weaknesses. Membership in the union is a prerequisite for working at a major studio and experience is the prerequisite for joining the union. So what you must do is find work at a small, nonunion story department or a production company.

characteristics: Reading movie scripts is, no surprise, work for movie lovers—but only dispassionate lovers who are willing to play an important role in a movie's production for the least amount of credit. A strong literary background helps, and you have to be able to read fast, too.

Jana Carole *is a staff story analyst for a major movie studio in Hollywood.*

How did you get the job?

Jana's background in the theater continues to be the key to her resume. After graduating with a double major in theater and film (with an emphasis on screenwriting) at a state college in her home state of California, she went to work as a stage manager for a summer Shakespeare festival in Oregon. A few years later, she moved to Los Angeles for a position as a producer's assistant for a film and television production company. "It was fast-paced, exciting work, but I never got comfortable with constantly being in and out of a job—you never know where your next check is coming from," she says.

So, in search of some stability while still working in the entertainment industry, Jana took the steady but unexciting job as an assistant at a talent agency and then at a production company. "I didn't like the people I was working for, so I took a step down from what I was doing to become a clerk/researcher in the story department of the studio where I work now," she says. It wasn't long before she was stepping back up, creating the position of assistant story editor, working with readers. "But I liked 'labor' better than management," she goes on. "I enjoyed the details of developing a story and I didn't want to become a studio executive. So I remain a reader by choice."

What do you do all day?

Jana's work involves, plain and simple, reading scripts and writing commentary about them. She attends meetings at which the week's best scripts are reviewed, then takes hers home and spends about two to four hours a day taking them in line by line. "A typical screenplay is about 120 pages long," she explains. "So I read about eight of them a week." Then she writes the "coverage," which includes a page of summary of the script, a page of her comments about the script's strengths and weaknesses (with suggestions for improvements if she has them), and an evaluation grid rating its premise, dialogue, etc., on a scale of poor to excellent.

"The same reader works with each draft of a studio-optioned screenplay as it progresses through development into a film," Jana says. "That way, you can be aware of how it is changing and give the studio's creative executives informed feedback on the screenplay in each stage." Readers often suggest useful changes to studio executives, who then liaison with producers to work with writers struggling to improve their screenplays.

Where do you see this job leading you?

Jana Carole has chosen to be exactly where she is: a reader and mother working out of her home. "Once I wanted to be a Hollywood executive," she says. "But that's a rat race that doesn't interest me now." She does know lots of readers who go on to be studio executives, producers, and screenwriters. She also knows plenty who make very comfortable salaries as readers.

> "FIND A SMALL PRODUCTION COMPANY AND VOLUNTEER TO INTERN AS THEIR READER. YOU HAVE TO HAVE EXPERIENCE TO JOIN THE UNION AND YOU CAN'T WORK FOR A MAJOR STUDIO WITHOUT BEING IN THE UNION. SO GET EXPERIENCE WHEREVER YOU CAN."

81. Story Editor, Movie Studio

description: Every movie starts as a script, and the story editor is responsible for managing its trip around the studio lot. The editor assesses unsolicited scripts, assigns story analysts ("readers" in Hollywood jargon) to read and write synopses of scripts, and makes sure that every department and interested individual receives copies of each script. Story editor is not an entry-level job, but it tends to be the first level of executive at a movie studio or production company.

salary: A new story editor makes between $35,000 to $45,000 a year—more at a major studio, less at a small production company. A higher-level executive with responsibility for the story department can earn six figures and more.

prospects: No hype: the entertainment industry is as competitive as any and jobs at Hollywood studios are hard to come by. But if you have your heart set on working in the movie business, you can break into the story department at a studio or production company, and as junior executives climb the ladder, they will be replaced by eager, hardworking staff people like you.

qualifications: Story editors don't need a specific degree, but they must be highly organized and able to write clearly and concisely, and they should have a broad knowledge of literature and film.

characteristics: You have to be a people person to run the story department at a movie studio or production company: you provide a service to many talented and often self-centered artists. Only a diplomat will survive.

Jennifer Klein *is the story editor at a well-known Hollywood movie studio.*

How did you get the job?

Jennifer has hopscotched through the entertainment industry since earning her bachelor of arts degree in English from the University of California at Los Angeles. She started out as the personal assistant to a popular singer, then went to work in the programming department of a television network, first as a secretary, and moved her way up the ladder to assistant manager of the department. With the help of a former boss, she jumped over to the major movie studio where she now works.

"I can't say enough how it helps to make and keep contacts in this business," Jennifer says. "Who you know is very important, so developing and maintaining relationships—with people you work with, people you meet at parties, virtually anyone—can open doors for you."

Jennifer started out as an administrative assistant, but by getting in early, staying late, and absorbing everything she could about the story department, she became the leading candidate to replace the previous story editor when he was promoted to vice president. "People move very quickly at movie studios," she explains, "so if you get in at any level, you can work for an opportunity for yourself."

What do you do all day?

Every script that comes onto the movie studio's lot crosses Jennifer's desk. "I think of our department as the boiler room of the whole studio," she says. Jennifer's primary responsibility is to assign and distribute the scripts to the readers and to send their "coverage," which is a synopsis and critical evaluation of the script, to the creative executives responsible for the project. "I hold a weekly meeting with the readers and report to them about the reaction to their coverage by the execu-

> **"IF YOU WANT TO MOVE UP IN ANY JOB, START SEEKING OUT THE RESPONSIBILITIES OF THE NEXT JOB. AND DON'T ASSUME THAT YOUR BOSS KNOWS THAT YOU WANT THE NEXT JOB—SAY SO, LOUD AND CLEAR."**

tives," she says. "I think it's important to let the readers know when their work is praised as well as when it is criticized."

A lot of Jennifer's time is spent talking to producers and creative executives, giving them status reports on the more than 250 scripts in development at any time by the studio. She also confers with writer's agents when the studio needs a writer to work on a particular script. "We get to go to a lot of premieres and other Hollywood events, which can be fun and glamorous," she says. "But the rest of the time we work very hard for long hours."

Where do you see this job leading you?

Jennifer Klein has seen the fast rise of others in the movie business, and she's expecting to do the same. "The story department is a good place to see a lot of the business of making movies," she says. "I hope to use it as a springboard to climb the executive ladder." Some of Jennifer's counterparts at other studios combine broader creative responsibilities with management of the story department; some enjoy the processes of the story department enough to stay there without striving to move up.

82. Subsidiary Rights Agent

description: The process of selling books involves more than just getting them onto the shelves of bookstores. Today, publishing companies rely on subsidiary rights—book club, magazine, and international sales—to generate profits. Subsidiary rights agents think about and pursue these kinds of avenues for marketing books. Though a lot of the work is done in person, most of it is done on the phone or in writing. This is not a straight sales job—you are working with other knowledgeable people in the field to keep their pipelines full of books in which their readers will be interested.

salary: Sub rights assistants start out earning $17,000 to $20,000 a year at publishing companies in big cities; agents with solid results earn up to $50,000, department directors up to $100,000 per year.

prospects: More venues than ever before buy subsidiary rights—audiotape publishers, multimedia services, foreign companies, etc.—which means lots of opportunities for capable people willing to learn the business from the bottom up.

qualifications: A well-rounded education, attention to detail, and the ability to express yourself orally and in writing are the essentials for working in subsidiary rights. An understanding of marketing will help.

characteristics: People who enjoy reading and talking about books, are enthusiastic and creative, and are self-motivated will succeed in this field.

Kristin Kliemann *is the subsidiary rights director of a book publishing company in New York City.*

- -

How did you get the job?

Kristin graduated from Trinity College in San Antonio, Texas, with a bachelor of arts in English and sociology. "There were many courses that seemed irrelevant at the time," she says, "but upon reflection I've learned that nearly everything I studied can be called into play in general publishing, since we do books across a wide range of subjects. I even cherish the courses in math—particularly algebraic formulas, which I use fairly frequently."

After graduation, Kristin headed straight for New York, the capital of book publishing in the United States. "I started out as an assistant in subsidiary rights at Harcourt Brace Jovanovich and have worked my way up the ladder since then," she says.

From that prestigious publisher, Kristin went to another, where she was eventually promoted to director of the subsidiary rights department.

> "LEARN TO WORD PROCESS, PHOTOCOPY, AND BE EFFICIENT AT ALL SECRETARIAL SKILLS IN ORDER TO PLEASE YOUR BOSS AND FINISH THE MORE MUNDANE ASPECTS OF ANY TASK, THUS LEADING TO MORE FREE TIME TO PURSUE MORE INTERESTING WORK."

When her current employer—a recent but major entrant into book publishing—was launched a few years ago, she applied for the job of sub rights director there.

"I wanted new challenges. And the opportunity to shape a new publishing company by creating its subsidiary rights department was too good to pass up," Kristin says, adding that she believes she got the job because of "my range of experience, my organized nature, and an eagerness to be a part of it all."

If you'd like to work in Kristin's department, she recommends that you "read everything: books on the best-seller list, classic books, magazines, newspapers. And hang out in bookstores trying to learn what motivates people to buy and read."

What do you do all day?

As a subsidiary rights agent, Kristin thinks about who would like to buy the rights to reprint or reuse the books her company publishes and then markets them to the prospective customers. "That means I spend a lot of time on the phone, at lunch, and at other meetings," she explains, "telling people from other publishing companies around the world, or from book clubs, or magazines, or whatever outlet I can find, about our wonderful books and why they should spend money to license rights from us."

To understand who the potential customers are for any book, the sub rights agent needs to know the book itself. "When I'm not selling," Kristin says, "I'm reading the books themselves in order to determine markets and sell them better and more broadly."

As the department director, Kristin has managerial duties, too. "I have five agents reporting to me, I have a budget to meet every year," she says, "and I work closely with other department heads" such as those managing the sales, marketing, and promotion departments.

Where do you see this job leading you?

Though Kristin has always worked in subsidiary rights, she'd like to become involved in other aspects of book publishing. "I hope this job leads me to another job that utilizes my skills and knowledge of publishing in a broader context," she says. "Not just licensing rights, but working with titles and authors in an overall publishing program."

173

83. Tabloid Newspaper Writer

description: Admit it—you've looked at tabloid newspapers while waiting in the checkout aisle at the supermarket and wondered, "Who writes this stuff?" Believe it or not, professional journalists trained in the particular style of tabloids write the articles in these highly popular periodicals. The writers gather information from sources themselves or work with reports submitted by correspondents, then compose the articles, often under tight deadlines. They must adhere to strict legal guidelines when writing to protect the newspapers from lawsuits. Experienced tabloid newspaper writers usually get bylines in their stories, and are generally paid better than their colleagues at regional daily newspapers.

salary: Entry-level writers (who typically have some experience at a daily newspaper) start out at about $30,000 a year; many of the proven writers earn more than $100,000 a year—in both cases, that's a lot more than comparable positions at daily newspapers pay.

prospects: Like reporters at other newspapers, writers at tabloids move around a lot, though the good pay and pleasant working conditions do keep some of them in place for long careers. Still, if you're willing to live in Florida—where all the major tabloids are based—and demonstrate the capacity to write in the tabloid style, you can break in.

qualifications: This is a newspaper job, so you need the same kind of training in interviewing and concise, active writing as you would for any other reporter/writer position. Newspaper experience isn't absolutely required to get hired at a tabloid, but few people get hired without it. And you'll have to prove that you can write simply and enthusiastically about celebrities, interesting ordinary people, health, and the law—you may have to take a test to demonstrate your writing skills.

characteristics: Successful tabloid writers must approach their work with the same professional attitude as other writers, and they need a genuine feel for the interests of tabloid readers. They also need to keep track of celebrities' careers and lives so that they can place new information in context for the readers.

Bob Smith *(his real name) is an editor at one of America's best-known tabloid newspapers.*

How did you get the job?

Bob studied engineering at the University of Tennessee because he could get a government scholarship to do so, and he worked as an electrical engineer while serving in the Navy. "But I always hated engineering," he recalls, "so when I got out, I went down to the local newspaper and asked if there was any job I could do. I was hired as a copy editor.

"I was aggressive in trying to expand my responsibilities and enthusiastic about everything I did, and I quickly moved up to general assignment reporter," Bob says. "Eventually I worked in just about every department you can think of: hard news, sports, features." In fact, Bob was so good at the job of a reporter that he had to leave the paper after 10 years. "I wrote a series of articles about corrup-

tion that involved the police and judges that made a lot of people very angry with me," Bob explains.

Bob answered an ad in *Editor & Publisher* that was placed by the tabloid where he currently works. "Once again, I was enthusiastic about what I was doing, and aggressive in seeking out more to do," Bob emphasizes. "Those are the keys to getting a job, and doing it well, at any newspaper."

What do you do all day?

Mostly, Bob confronts deadlines—he writes an average of 20 articles for each weekly issue, and then follows those stories through the paper's production cycle until they're ready to go to the printer. "Each day of the week a different section of the paper is laid out, and we must have the articles for that section done," he explains. "Some stories come together

over several days—or even longer—while for others we have as little as 20 minutes to rewrite before they go to press."

The celebrity stories that Bob primarily works on come from correspondents who interview the sources. "The reporters in the field have contacts who know the celebrities, and they get information from interviews with those contacts," he says. "The reporters then submit the stories to us, and we rewrite them so that they are bright, accurate, and readable, with all the essential facts included.

"The one part of our approach that many people doubt is that our stories must be accurate, but it's true," Bob stresses. "We have a legal department that must approve every celebrity story to protect

> **"MAKE YOURSELF INDISPENSABLE— ENTHUSIASTICALLY TAKE ON JOBS NO ONE ELSE WANTS."**

us from lawsuits. If we can't substantiate our information, the legal department will kill the story."

When Bob is not writing about celebrities, he's looking at medical journals for new health information that will interest the newspaper's readers. "We take complex scientific research reports and turn them into stories that our readers can understand and use in their lives."

Where do you see this job leading you?

Bob has worked at his newspaper for more than 20 years, and he has no intention of going to work anywhere else. In his tenure, Bob has seen former colleagues go on to careers in "reality-based" television shows, to book publishers, and to other nationally circulated newspapers. Bob has also written a couple of books in his spare time.

84. Teacher, English as a Second Language

description: America may be in some ways a multi-ethnic society, but in most respects it is a country with one language: English. Immigrants who want quick entry into the job market enroll in classes that teach English to non-native speakers. The teachers of these classes are rarely trained educators—more often they are people with a strong command of the language and the desire and natural ability to share that with others. The teachers may get involved in helping the students attain very specific goals, such as reading job applications. The classes are often held in the evening, though the teachers can have some input into the scheduling.

salary: ESL teachers typically earn $15 to $20 an hour, depending on where in the country they are and what institution (college, university, private sector) sponsors the classes.

prospects: The steady flow of immigrants to America from all over the world virtually assures that there will always be a need for ESL teachers. Of course, the demand is inevitably highest where the most immigrants are—in the areas along the Mexican border and in large cities.

qualifications: You must have a bachelor's degree in most cases to get this job, but the degree can be in nearly any subject area: a well-educated native speaker can teach basic English as a Second Language. If you have any experience in front of a class, your application is that much more appealing.

characteristics: Patient, supportive, and lively people make the best ESL teachers.

Lela Khan *teaches English as a Second Language at a community college in Texas.*

How did you get the job?

Lela was born in America and is married to a man from Pakistan. She had been trained as a social worker, but she had taught preschool while she was raising their children. When a neighbor who had been teaching English as a Second Language told Lela about the work, she was intrigued. "The way she described her classes, they sounded so rewarding, they sounded like fun," Lela says. "Our kids are still in school, so I wanted a job that had a flexible schedule. This seemed perfect."

She applied to the local community college and was asked to work as a substitute to gain classroom experience. After a few months, she was offered an opportunity to teach a mid-level ESL course. "The college supplies teacher's manuals and resource materials to go with the course," Lela says. "The manual leads you step by step through the process of the course and gives you lots of ideas for exercises you can do with the students."

After a few semesters teaching various course levels, Lela has moved up to the more advanced level. "Once you have experience in the classroom and a more technical knowledge of English grammar, you can handle the advanced class," she says. "Those classes are even more fun, because of the verbal interaction among the students."

What do you do all day?

The students in Lela's ESL classes reflect the flow of immigrants to the United States. "We get people from all over the world," she says, "but most of them are from Latin America or Asia.

"Even in the mid-level class, many of them speak English fairly well already—some are very well educated, with advanced degrees in the sciences, engineering, and medicine," Lela continues. "But they want to understand, read, and speak English as it is used by native speakers. They want to communicate on an equal level with their co-workers."

Lela's class meets at a local high school—"it's closer to my house than the community college campus, so I chose to teach there"—for two hours twice a week for a 15-session semester. The class is conducted exclusively in English and includes "a lot of oral practice, along with written exercises," Lela says. "I put people in groups—I like to get people of different nationalities together—and they help each other with the exercises we do."

Lela relies on the teacher's manuals to help generate ideas, but she also devotes her own time to reading books she finds

> "THIS JOB PAYS REALLY WELL FOR PART-TIME WORK THAT IS ALSO VERY, VERY REWARDING IN OTHER WAYS."

in the library and at bookstores on the teaching of ESL. "The more I do this, the more I want to do for the students," she says. "The students are so grateful for everything you can teach them. It's just so satisfying."

Where do you see this job leading you?

For Lela, teaching one class a semester is an ideal arrangement she has no intention of changing anytime soon. "I think this job is just perfect," Lela says. "You meet people from all walks of life, from all sorts of cultures and experiences, who still believe in the American Dream. And you learn so much from them, too. It's fantastic."

85. Teacher, Program for Schools in Disadvantaged Areas

description: Many programs around the country seek to bring college graduates who were not education majors to teach in schools in economically disadvantaged areas. Participants in the program receive training in the fundamentals of teaching, but the program managers believe a well-rounded education and basic language skills are the most critical factors in the ability to teach students to read, write, and think. Typically, the teachers are asked to make a two-year commitment when they agree to participate in the program.

salary: In an urban area, you'll start at the basic teacher salary of $25,000 to $30,000 a year; in rural areas, the base level is more like $18,000 to $20,000, or even less. If you have a master's degree, you'll earn slightly more. Experienced teachers with master's degrees can earn $50,000 to $60,000 per year or even more.

prospects: You'll find lots of opportunities for teachers in inner-city and deeply rural schools, especially in the South and West. And programs that connect college graduates with schools in need are always looking for candidates.

qualifications: You need nothing more than a bachelor's degree in virtually any subject area and some basic training in teaching techniques, which the program will provide to you.

characteristics: A rapport with children and the confidence to stand up in front of a classroom of kids are essential. You'll also be well served if you have the capacity to keep some distance from your work: many of the students you'll be teaching live in nearly impossible circumstances with little hope for the future. You can't be taking that home with you every day or you'll become an emotional burnout.

Abigail Breiseth *taught language arts to third- and fourth-graders at a school in South-Central Los Angeles.*

How did you get the job?

Abigail selected general studies and humanities as her major at the University of Chicago because she wanted to delve deeply into American culture and history from several different angles. "The general studies major allows students to design their own major and to learn what they want to know," she explains. "I created an American studies program that included history, literature, and education." She hadn't planned on teaching, but when she graduated in 1990 she felt a powerful moral draw to the Teach for America program, which brings college graduates without education degrees to be teachers in economically disadvantaged areas. "Teaching was the only thing I was certain I wanted to try, and I wanted to be with the most interesting kids in the country—kids who also happen to be the most needy."

After eight weeks of training that included five weeks of student teaching and introduction to curriculum and classroom management, Abigail received what are known as "emergency credentials" and was assigned to an elementary school in Los Angeles. She stayed for three years (a year longer than the required commitment).

What do you do all day?

The teacher who stands in front of the class and drills the students all day long on the alphabet is thankfully long gone as the model for teaching reading and writing. Today, students work in groups and individually to unlock the keys to literacy. "My role was much more as a facilitator than a lecturer," Abigail says. "The kids would work at centers at their own pace, and I would help them to find resources to answer their questions, and I made sure they were making progress. We used an interdisciplinary approach, so our reading projects connected with what they were learning in math, science, and social studies wherever possible.

"We also wrote in and read from journals and had a story hour every day," she goes on. "But the most amazing thing we did was what we called the 'magic stick.' It was a stick that got passed to each kid and whoever had it could talk about themselves—no one else could say anything about them. I was in Los Angeles during the period right after the riots and these kids were very deeply affected by what had happened in their neighborhoods. They were scared and they needed to talk about it. Being interested in what they had to say was the most important thing I had to do."

Where do you see this job leading you?

Abigail Breiseth left the Los Angeles school district after three years and spent a year teaching conversational English to high school students in Hungary. Now she's taking art classes to become qualified to teach art to developmentally disadvantaged students. "I may move around until I settle on one thing," she says, "but I know I'll always be involved with kids who need help."

> "TEACHERS MUST BE STRONG ENOUGH MENTALLY TO COME BACK DAY AFTER STRESSFUL DAY AND STRONG ENOUGH PHYSICALLY TO HOLD UP TO ALL THE GERMS THEY'RE EXPOSED TO EVERY DAY."

86. Technical Writer, User's Manuals

description: How do you learn to use all the features of your new television, stereo, computer software, or car? Read the user's manual. Technical writers use the products, talk to the engineers who designed them, and then organize and compose the manuals in terms the user can understand. The writing needn't be dry or boring; in fact, the best make the user want to read the manual. Many manual writers also design or help design their work. These writers are almost always anonymous to their readers.

salary: At the entry-level—with training or experience in writing and some facility for the products you'll be writing about—you'll earn about $25,000. As you progress, you'll likely have more input into the products' design, which will earn you more, up to $75,000 with large companies.

prospects: Wherever you find companies making sophisticated products, you'll find technical writers. Many high-tech firms employ staff writers; others use outside contractors. As more people buy home electronics and the information age alters how we all live, more technical writers will be needed to explain how to use the high-tech equipment in our homes.

qualifications: Besides good basic writing skills, you need to have excellent verbal skills to communicate with the engineers who design the products, and you must ask clear questions to get clear answers about the products with which you're working. You should also have some facility with the kinds of products you'll be dealing with, but you do not need to be an engineer yourself.

characteristics: The ability to reduce complex instructions to usable directions is the essence of a technical writer's work. Though you will become increasingly familiar with the products you're writing about, you must always be able to imagine yourself in the place of the user.

Peter Woodley *is a customer communications designer for a consumer electronics company on the East Coast.*

How did you get the job?

After earning a master's degree in journalism at William Patterson College in Wayne, New Jersey, Peter worked as a stringer for a local newspaper, taking assignments to cover local zoning and school board meetings. He quickly decided he'd be more enthusiastic about writing advertising copy. He answered a help wanted ad to be a copywriter at the large book publishing company Prentice Hall. "I took an ad copywriting test, which I apparently failed," he now recalls with a laugh, "because they offered me the job of production editor." He calls that job "the best place to start you could imagine: I got to do a little of everything there is to do in publishing: write, copyedit, design pages, work with the printer. Really, everything."

Among the books that Peter worked on were a number of early computer books for consumers, a topic that piqued his interest. He took his experience in publishing, his more polished writing skills, and that new-

> "IF ALL YOU'VE DONE IS WRITE, THEN YOU WILL HAVE A HARDER TIME GETTING IN THE DOOR WHEN THE COMPANY NEEDS A PRODUCTION PERSON OR AN EDITOR OR, MORE TYPICALLY, A JACK-OF-MANY-TRADES."

found interest in technology to Bell Communications, where he temporarily worked as a contractor on documentation, and to Burroughs (which later became UNISYS), where he had a full-time position writing manuals for its computer operating system. "When I arrived at Burroughs in the early 1980s, the company believed that the engineers who designed the system were the best people to explain the products to the users. The editors were there mostly to proofread and check grammar," Peter explains. "But we slowly earned the respect of the engineers and developed a more collaborative working relationship that made the manuals more understandable by laypeople." His proven capacity to work on a team with engineers was key to his landing his current job for a well-known home electronics manufacturer.

What do you do all day?

"My job first started with me working on the manuals when the products were nearly finished," Peter explains. "Now I sit in with the engineers, the industrial designers, the package designers, and the marketing department through every phase of a project. I feel like I'm the users' representative on the team. I'll question any decision that makes it hard for the average person to use the machine."

When Peter's not meeting with the design team, he's busy putting the latest product through its paces, trying out all its features and devising the clearest way to explain how to use it. He writes and designs the manuals himself, using a desktop publishing program called FrameMaker. "I always keep in mind, the last thing anyone wants to do is read the manual," he says with unflinching objectivity. "So I've got to be brief, clear, and above all, useful."

Where do you see this job leading you?

Peter Woodley's already headed in the direction he wants to go. "I never wanted to be pigeonholed as simply a technical writer who translated for the engineers," he says. "I've been striving to make engineers understand the user, to help them design and build products that are intuitive to the rest of us. And I'd like to become involved in product and package design earlier in the process and more effectively."

87. Television Listings Editor

description: What's on tonight? Well, you can waste time channel-surfing or you can find out quickly and easily by checking the newspaper television listings. And while you're at it, thank the paper's listings editors for calling your attention to the day's highlights. The listings editors at a newspaper compile daily and Sunday schedules tailored to the specific areas served by the paper and write brief synopses of many programs. They often write longer reviews for the daily edition and features for the weekly television guide included with the Sunday edition. These editors must meet strict daily deadlines, but they get to watch a lot of television on the job, too.

salary: Listings editor is an entry-level job that typically pays $6 to $10 an hour—more in big cities and for other contributions the editor makes to the television coverage.

prospects: Almost every large daily newspaper in the U.S. includes television listings, but the staff for the television department tends to be very small—typically just two or three people. These are entry-level jobs, frequently vacated by editors/writers moving up into other departments of the newspaper. Opportunities exist, but not in great abundance.

qualifications: No type of degree or training is required, but a background in journalism will help you move out of merely compiling listings to the more fun stuff of television coverage. You must be able to write concise, engaging summaries and have a facility with computers, which are used to do the compiling.

characteristics: Listings editors are detail-oriented and work quickly, even under pressure. And they need to be able to focus amid the noise of a newsroom. They ought to like interacting with the public and probably should like to watch television.

Jan Currie *is a senior news assistant and layout assistant for the television and cable section of a daily newspaper in a large Midwestern city.*

How did you get the job?

After Canadian Jan Currie earned her degrees in journalism and English (bachelor's from York University and master's from the University of Western Ontario), she worked as a free-lance business writer and learned the importance of meeting deadlines. She later served a brief spell on the staff of a public relations agency. "I found out when I was working in PR that I handled the public fairly well," she says. "That's come in handy in my current job." While Jan was honing her writing skills at the public relations agency, she was also discovering her interest in layout and design. "I liked doing the newsletters and brochures that we did there," she explains. Her experience in writing helped Jan get a job in the television section that she had seen advertised.

What do you do all day?

"The three listings editors here are each responsible for one zone that the paper covers," Jan says. "I handle the metro area, and one of the other editors handles the east zone and the other the west zone." Jan and her colleagues compile channel-specific listings for their areas from press releases submitted by broadcast and cable networks and local stations; the Macintosh computers used by the paper have templates set up for each region, so all Jan and her colleagues have to do is type the listings into the format.

After the listings for each day are sent to the paper's composing room (by 9:30 A.M. for the following morning's edition), Jan writes the briefs for her "Today's Best Bets" column based on shows she's previewed (that's when she gets to watch television on the job) and those that catch her attention

> **"ONCE YOU'RE IN A NEWSPAPER, YOU CAN CHOOSE YOUR PATH. TAKE AN ENTRY-LEVEL JOB LIKE LISTINGS EDITOR AND BUILD FROM THERE."**

from the descriptions in the press releases. She also selects germane stories that come from the wire services the paper subscribes to and edits those for the daily television page. About once a month, Jan interviews and writes a feature about a television personality for the paper's "TV & Cable Week" insert for the Sunday edition. "That is, obviously, the most fun part of the job," she says. "But the truth is, I like the challenge of putting the puzzle of the listings together and writing about my best bets, too."

Another important part of Jan's job is answering the public's questions. "I'll get about six phone calls from readers each day," she says. "They tend to ask questions about what's coming on their favorite shows or how to contact the studios."

Where do you see this job leading you?

Layout is where Jan is headed. "Not many people make listings editor their end goal—it's just a way into the newspaper and to learn about the different paths to take from there," she says. "For many people that's into more reviewing and feature writing. But I've found I really like production, design, and layout. I'm aiming for layout editor."

88. Television News Producer

description: Producers of television news programs function a lot like the editors of newspapers or magazines: they decide the lineup of stories, assign the coverage to different reporters, manage the writers, and do some writing themselves. At stations in smaller cities, the producer may write most of the copy.

Producers, like most people in television news, work odd hours preparing programs broadcast throughout the day. In most cases, a producer is not an entry-level job, but assistant producers and staff writers learn the business and craft of television news on their way to the position of producer.

salary: Writers and assistant producers start out at stations in small cities, earning as little as $15,000 per year. But with a year or two of service and a jump to a bigger market, they can make nearly double that.

prospects: Even behind-the-scene jobs in the world of television are coveted. But opportunities to break in regularly arise because people are almost constantly seeking work in bigger markets. Writer and assistant producer jobs may be less competitive than on-air spots.

qualifications: People in the television business are quick to say that you don't need to be trained in broadcasting to work as a writer or assistant producer—the ability to write concise, lively copy quickly and to think on your feet are the only requisite skills—but broadcast journalism programs graduate so many students that you'll find it tough to get an interview without the same education.

characteristics: You have to move fast, work well in a team, be a newshound, have catchy ideas both visual and verbal, and be flexible about where you live to make it in television news.

Dan Stadler *is executive producer of the news at a television station in the Midwest.*

How did you get the job?

Internships and working at small-town stations are the building blocks of a career in broadcast news, Dan says. "Those first experiences teach you a little about a lot of different aspects of putting on a news broadcast," he explains. "That's where you find out where your strengths lie—in reporting, writing, editing, or producing."

Dan's own odyssey took him from college internships at stations in Columbus, Ohio—while earning his bachelor's degree in broadcasting at Ohio State University—to full-time jobs in Knoxville, Tennessee, and Norfolk, Virginia, and then to the station back in Ohio where he works now. "Flexibility about where you live is critical to making it in broadcasting. Moving around is generally the only way to move up," he says. "But you don't have to stay in those small towns long; after a year or two, you've established yourself and learned all you need to get out of them."

> "TO BE A NEWSHOUND DOESN'T MEAN JUST KEEPING UP ON CURRENT EVENTS. YOU HAVE TO BE CURIOUS, RESOURCEFUL, AND INSATIABLE IN PURSUIT OF A STORY, ANY STORY."

What do you do all day?

By the time Dan arrives at the station at 2:30 P.M., the day's news is already taking shape. The assignment desk has been sending out reporters and camera crews to cover breaking stories all day. When Dan comes in, he meets with the news director, assistant news director, assistant producer, assistant editor, and reporters to decide the 11 P.M. program's rundown: specifically, in what order the stories will be reported and how much time each one will be allotted. "That meeting is the executive producer's primary function," he says. "From there, it's just a matter of keeping everybody on track."

Often that means writing copy or editing videotape himself. "You do what you have to do to make sure that everything is done," Dan says. On what passes for normal days, the show's ready to go an hour before airtime—all the copy written and tape edited—but normal days are punctuated by times when late-breaking stories can claim a place in the lineup moments before the show goes on. "We have people here," he says, "who can write a good-quality news story in less than two minutes. That's writing under pressure, and sometimes in television news that's what has to be done."

Dan differentiates writers from assistant producers this way: writers take the information reporters bring back from the scene of news or that they've gathered from telephone interviews, and then compose the words the anchors—the on-camera people in the studio—will read. Assistant producers write some copy, too, but they also work with videotape editors to create a story complete with words and images.

Where do you see this job leading you?

After eight years in broadcast news, Dan knows there's only one way to go up in his field. "I've worked at four stations in eight years," he says, "and I know I will work at some more. Eventually, I'd like to be the news director of a major metropolitan station, but that's probably a couple jobs away yet." Lots of the people Dan works with take some time to find their niche, working as writers, on-air reporters, editors, assignment desk assistants, and producers before settling on one of them. "It's not a negative on your resume for you to try different positions—in fact, it's really a positive."

185

89. Television News Reporter

description: A television reporter is more than good looks and well-styled hair appearing on camera to give viewers the specifics of a news story. The reporter goes to the scene of news events and questions public officials, eyewitnesses, experts, and any other source that will help the audience get a full picture of the story. Then the reporter distills all the information into a brief but captivating account that can be either taped beforehand or delivered live.

salary: Most television reporters start out at stations in small towns and cities, where they can make as little as $12,000 a year, but more commonly $18,000 to $25,000, depending on the city. You can quickly double that by gaining some experience and then moving to a slightly larger market—in as little as six months to a year after starting out. Star reporters at local television stations earn $150,000 to $200,000 in the country's largest cities.

prospects: More television channels + more on-the-scene news coverage = more opportunities for reporters. And as reporters graduate from the smallest markets to the larger ones, entry-level jobs continually open for newcomers. But being on television is still alluring to many people, which makes for a lot of competition for those jobs.

qualifications: It is better to be good than to look good. So you'll have to learn how to cultivate sources, ask questions, organize information, and write with style and interest—in short, to learn the craft of journalism—to get an opportunity to be a television reporter. Your application is even stronger if you know the technical facets of television broadcasting: how to work with a camera (you don't need to be able to work it, just know how to present yourself to it), edit tape, and narrate along with images. When they apply, successful candidates for television reporter's jobs submit a videotape that demonstrates all of those capabilities.

characteristics: Dogged in pursuit of the most relevant facts of the story, irresistible in persuading sources to talk on camera, and clear and engaging in speaking to the audience are the essential attributes of television reporters. You'll also need to be a reliable team player because reporters work with camera technicians, producers, editors, and other reporters on many stories. And, to be frank, good hair and teeth don't hurt.

Debra Quintana *is a reporter for an independent television station in an East Coast city.*

How did you get the job?

"I was lucky to find a paying internship at a station in San Antonio that was looking to put someone on the air right away," recalls Debra, who earned her journalism degree from the University of Texas. "While I was there I saw firsthand everything that went on at a television station. I found out what I should be concentrating on at school and what I could pick up on the job. And I got some tape together that I could use when applying for a position when I graduated." That experience was the key to winning a spot on the staff at a station in Austin, Texas, where she worked for six months before moving on to Tampa, Florida, for one and a half years and then to Denver. "The great thing about small stations like the ones I worked at in Austin and Tampa is that you learn everybody's job," she says. "Then you go to a bigger station and you have it all in perspective."

Two years after she went to Denver, Debra moved to New York for personal reasons. There she made contact with people at the various stations in the city, including one she had worked with in Tampa. "He remembered me," Debra says, "and when the station needed a reporter to come in and quickly turn around a story, I was offered the chance to do it. I've been working for the station ever since."

What do you do all day?

In a big city like the one where Debra works, the news is happening all the time; the reporters merely have to go out and cover it. "When I get to the newsroom in the morning— usually between 9 and 10 A.M.— the assignment editor already

> **"MAINTAIN YOUR CONTACTS: WHEN A STATION NEEDS A REPORTER IN A HURRY, THEY'LL ALWAYS TURN TO A KNOWN QUANTITY."**

has a story for me to cover, so I just head out with a camera person right away," she says. "And I can spend all day getting the background, asking questions, gathering comments, and filming about 15 to 20 minutes of footage, which will be edited down to one and a half to two minutes of tape for the news broadcast.

"Some days, I can take all day to put together a great story, then come back to the station to write it, cut and track (that's what we call narrating over the pictures) the film, and have it be finished when another, more important story breaks," she laughs. "And then I have to prepare a report on another story in a half hour and the first one is scrapped."

Where do you see this job leading you?

"To move up in television news, you can either specialize in investigative journalism or in a particular beat like business or politics, or you can aim to be an anchor, or you can shoot for one of the network jobs," Debra says. "None of those appeal to me as much as what I am doing now. I love the news and I'm not interested in focusing on only one area. I don't want to sit inside and read news someone else did the work on, like an anchor does. And I don't want to travel away from my family as much as network reporters do. I just love what I'm doing right now and can't imagine doing anything else."

90. Television Series Writer/Story Editor

description: Week after week (or even day after day in the case of soap operas), characters appear on television in stories created by writers working alone and together, on staff with the production company or freelance, experienced at the art or getting their first big break. The executive producer is commonly the head writer, and staff television writers are often referred to as "co-producers," "supervising producers," or "co-executive producers." These writers together must generate a finished script for every week of the broadcast season—which is 22 to 32 episodes long for a prime-time series, but twice that for those daytime programs which never take a summer hiatus and produce shows daily.

salary: The fee for a script is set by an agreement between the television networks and the Writer's Guild of America: $22,500. In addition, story editors (entry-level staff writers who help manage the script) earn $4,500 an episode, producers make $12,000 to $20,000 per episode, and executive producers pull down $30,000 to $75,000 per episode.

prospects: Television series producers are eager for useful story ideas and scripts, so anyone with them can get an opportunity. However, lots of people think they have the talent, and producers are inundated with submissions. But be assured, if you've got the ability and are determined to do it, the odds are in your favor—especially with all the new broadcast and cable networks producing original shows in need of material.

qualifications: You need talent and the determination to get your ideas in front of the people who need your work. You'll be best prepared by studying the programs you want to write for. You can also read one of the many books that outline the proper format for a television script and offer hints on getting your script read.

characteristics: To survive as a staff writer/producer you have to be able to work well under steady pressure, to function as part of a team, and to be willing to rewrite to the demands of the networks, directors, actors, and other members of the production team. Freelance writers need to be disciplined enough to produce without any pressure to do so.

Steve Wasserman *is the executive producer of a popular television show.*

How did you get the job?

Steve was working as a news cameraman for NBC 15 years ago, when he decided to take a shot at writing for television. "So I wrote a script for a show that I liked and submitted it to an agent," he says. "The agent thought it was good, so he sent it to a producer. The script was sold and I began to get assignments to write scripts for the show."

The consistently high caliber of Steve's scripts earned him a staff producer job for the company he now works for, and eventually brought him to the position of executive producer for a very popular show. He is certain his path to the job is the best avenue for anyone who wants to write for television.

"The best preparation for becoming a television writer is to be an astute consumer of the medium. Watch and try to understand what the producers are doing with the characters and stories in the series," he says. "When you're ready, write a finished teleplay and send it to an agent. If you have talent, you'll get an agent, who will send your work to people who buy them, people like me. If you're consistent, you'll get assignments, and then maybe an opportunity for a job."

What do you do all day?

Steve is the producer of a dramatic series with stories that continue from one episode to the next, so the show's producer/writers begin to prepare scripts by developing ideas for those stories. "We describe in paragraph form what we call 'story arcs' that are two, four, and six episodes long that we pitch to the network and to the head of our production company," he explains. "They send those back with notes, which we incorporate when we turn those paragraphs into an outline of scenes—of which there are 35 to 40 in each episode. The network and our boss read the outline and send it back with more notes. We incorporate those into a shooting script, or teleplay, which again is sent out to be noted. When the network and our boss has approved the teleplay," he says, "we send it to the show's director, crew, and cast."

Steve says a teleplay is typically rewritten four to eight times before it is approved—though in some cases he and his staff of five producer/writers have revised a script 18 to 20 times before taking it to the "studio floor," where it is filmed. But that's not the end of the rewriting.

"Once a teleplay is finally approved, we don't change the story lines or the major details," Steve says. "But we make lots of other minor changes to the script during preproduction because certain ideas don't work for the production team. A script is almost never finished."

Where do you see this job leading you?

Steve enjoys overseeing the writing of the show he's currently involved in and he expects to keep doing it for a while. But, like many other writer/producers, he hopes to create and run his own shows someday. "Working on someone else's shows is satisfying," he says, "but the challenge of creating and running your own is very appealing to me."

> **"IF YOU WANT TO WRITE FOR A COMEDY SHOW, WATCH LOTS OF COMEDIES AND WRITE A SCRIPT FOR A COMEDY; IF YOU'RE INTERESTED IN DRAMA, WATCH DRAMAS AND WRITE A SCRIPT FOR A DRAMATIC SHOW."**

91. Textbook Editor, English as a Second Language

description: The textbooks used to teach English to adult non-native speakers (in what are referred to as ESL programs) are structured to guide students and teachers through the process of learning the language—rather than to be read outside the classroom and discussed during the class. The editors of ESL books work with experts in the field to develop ideas and produce manuscripts that provide teachers and students at all levels with materials covering a broad range of skills and content. And the editors are involved with the process of producing the books once they are written.

salary: Editorial assistants (the entry-level job for people with little or no teaching experience) earn $20,000 to $25,000 a year; editors with some classroom experience earn $5,000 to $10,000 more. Acquisitions editors make $40,000 to $50,000 per year.

prospects: At this time, only a few major publishing companies produce almost all of the ESL textbooks used in the United States—which means that opportunities to break into this field are limited. But people with strong credentials—editorial sensibility and teaching experience—are rare as well. If you're qualified and committed to working on ESL books, you can find work.

qualifications: The first candidates hired in any search for an ESL editor are sure to be those who have master's degrees in education and some teaching experience. Equivalent foreign language skill is also desirable. People with English degrees and no teaching experience fill editorial assistant and assistant editor (there is a difference) roles.

characteristics: To enjoy success working as an ESL textbook editor, you must care about the teaching process, be able to work as part of a team, and be adept at juggling lots of projects in different stages of development.

Frank Black *is the executive editor of the ESL division of a textbook publisher.*

How did you get the job?

Ten years of teaching experience, and the ability to understand how materials work in classrooms, helped set the stage for this editor's career. "We've found that the best editors are those that know the field and have a great deal of personal commitment to it," Frank says. "To develop useful ESL books, you have to understand the pedagogical process, and, it seems to me, people with field experience know it better and can put that into action more effectively than those that haven't been in the field."

On the way to his current job, Frank worked as a textbook reviewer (not as a critic in the newspaper sense but as a professional in the field who assesses a manuscript's value) and developed manuscripts on a freelance basis. Then he found full-time work in textbook publishing, editing college and later ESL texts.

What do you do all day?

The acquisitions editors that Frank oversees have a long list of responsibilities, managing a book from inception to completion. "Our editors regularly review our list of books to look for gaps that need filling, then seek out authors to write books that will fulfill the need," Frank explains. "When an author submits a manuscript, the editor assigns freelance professional reviewers to evaluate it to ensure its quality.

"Writing and line editing are not acquisitions editors' responsibilities generally, but we expect that our editors be able to step in and fix problems in the manuscript when necessary," he continues. "And an editor might write a teacher's guide to a book for certain titles."

Bear in mind that content development is only part of the job. "The editors are working with the marketing and promotion staff throughout the process, so that those departments' efforts are on target, too," he continues. "And the editor must manage the project's budget."

"The real function, summed up simply, is to be each project's guiding light. To remind everyone, from beginning to end, what the book is supposed to be, and to be sure that everyone follows through."

Editors can be working on 20 or more books at one time, and still must find time to assess unsolicited manuscripts and keep up with trends in language education by reading professional journals.

Where do you see this job leading you?

"I could aspire to move up the corporate ladder here, but that would only remove me from the work I enjoy most. What I have now is a hybrid of business functions and working with editors on list development. I like that mix and am not eager to change it at this time."

> "IF YOU DON'T HAVE TEACHING EXPERIENCE, THE BEST WAY TO LEARN ABOUT THE TEXTBOOK MARKET IS TO WORK AS A SALES REP FOR A FEW YEARS. THAT GIVES YOU A SENSE OF THE MATERIAL. THEN YOU CAN COME BACK AND WORK IN EDITORIAL AND HAVE A BASE OF KNOWLEDGE TO BUILD ON."

The few people who leave jobs editing ESL textbooks usually find new ones at other textbook or foreign language publishers, according to Frank. "People who have the credentials to get into textbook publishing," he says, "tend to stay in the business."

92. Tour Guide

description: At museums, national parks, historical monuments, and other places of cultural interest, tour guides lead visitors through the sites' highlights, telling stories, relating facts, and answering questions. Tour guides must have in-depth knowledge of the site and a lively way of sharing that knowledge. They also have to be able to manage a crowd. At publicly owned sites, tour guides are civil service employees—they work for federal, state, or local government. Tour guides are typically employed only during busy seasons, though in some cases that may be nearly year-round. They frequently are required to work on weekends and at night.

salary: Civil service workers are usually paid on a scale negotiated by a union; for tour guides, the scale generally ranges from $10 to $25 an hour, depending on the site and the person's years of service. Private organizations pay similarly, though guides with more expertise will earn more.

prospects: These jobs are highly sought after during the peak of the tourist seasons in the summer and over the holidays. But because the jobs are often temporary, many of the experienced tour guides will move on to more permanent positions, creating opportunities for new people.

qualifications: Excellent public speaking skills and knowledge of the site and related topics are the key components of the job. A well-rounded education and experience in handling people will make you more attractive to the person responsible for hiring tour guides.

characteristics: Enthusiastic people who like working with the public, who can be firm but polite, and who can absorb a lot of information and enjoy sharing it with others will make good tour guides.

Bruce Brown *is the supervisor of the guides at a well-known landmark on the West Coast.*

How did you get the job?

Bruce started as a tour guide while he was a speech communications major at a nearby college—just like many of the guides he now supervises. "Our busy season here coincides with the schedules of college students and teachers," he says. "We are most in need of guides during the summer and the month or so around Christmas."

After 12 years of leading tours at the site, Bruce became the supervisor of guides—"The job just sort of fell into my lap," he says—and he continues to hire speech majors from nearby colleges. "You need to be comfortable talking to groups of people. And speech majors are trained in just that," he says. "But I believe that anyone who has experience working with the public—people who have

> **"YOU HAVE TO LIKE PEOPLE TO BE A GUIDE, BUT YOU ALSO HAVE TO BE WILLING TO BE FIRM WITH PEOPLE."**
> ----------

worked in retail or as a waiter or waitress—has many of the qualities we're looking for, too."

Those offered jobs as guides where Bruce works undergo 144 hours of paid training before they begin leading tours on their own. "That training includes polishing their public speaking skills, introductory classes in art history, architecture, horticulture, and history, and techniques for managing crowds," Bruce says. "The training is conducted on weekends from January through May, so that the guides are ready for our busy times.

"Because this is a state-owned operation, each guide

must take the state civil service exam," he continues. "But to take the exam you must have experience. So we created the guide trainee designation so that the trainees can get the experience they need to take the exam while they learn the job."

Just 12 people have permanent full-time jobs as tour guides working for Bruce, but about 100 have what he calls "permanent intermittent" positions. "The permanent intermittents work at least 1,500 hours a year," Bruce says.

What do you do all day?

Bruce manages the more than 100 guides on the premises during the height of the season, coordinating schedules, answering complaints, and generally keeping his hand on the tiller. The guides lead tours of one to two hours, from the most basic to the more in-depth.

"We have five tours we offer, and a guide must work here for a full year before they can begin training for tour five," Bruce explains. "The fifth tour is very elaborate—it's longer, we go into parts of the building that aren't included on the other tours, we have people dressed up in period costumes—and we only do it in the evenings. Only experienced guides do it."

Where do you see this job leading you?

Bruce didn't put in more than a decade as a tour guide to leave the job when he got promoted to guide supervisor. "I love being a guide," he says. "I learn a lot, I meet a lot of interesting people, this is a fantastic environment to work in every day."

Many of the guides Bruce now supervises are teachers who come back year after year; others are students who move on into other fields when they complete their degrees.

93. Trade Magazine Editor

description: When businesspeople need news and points of view about their industry, they turn to trade magazines. The editors of trade journals develop ideas for articles, then write and/or edit them in much the same way that newspaper journalists do. The difference is that the trade magazine's world is defined by the industry: every story is evaluated based on its relevance to the trade, every angle focused on how it will affect people in the industry. And the editors of a trade magazine must walk a delicate line: the companies that support the magazine with their advertising dollars are often the subject of editorial coverage in it.

salary: Entry-level trade magazine editors earn $20,000 to $25,000 a year, maybe slightly more at journals covering high-tech industries and in larger cities. Top editors can make $40,000 to $70,000, based on their knowledge of the field and their experience in it.

prospects: Every industry in the American economy has a trade magazine covering it; many have several. From *Advertising Age* to *Veterinary Pharmaceuticals and Biologicals,* no niche is uncovered. And you'll find trade magazines headquartered all over the country. If you'd like to work in magazines and have an interest in or knowledge of a particular industry, this is a very accessible avenue of entry.

qualifications: Writing and interviewing skills are primary necessities in journalism of any kind, and trade journalism is no exception. Knowledge of business in general and the magazine's industry in particular will strengthen your application.

characteristics: Successful trade magazine editors can engender trust with sources, are innately curious, aren't afraid to say "I don't know" to people who know more about their industry, and have a positive outlook on people and business.

Chuck Day *is editor of a trade magazine published in a big city in the Southeast.*

How did you get the job?

Chuck Day considers himself lucky to have landed a job as a sportswriter at the *Cleveland Press,* a now defunct daily newspaper in his hometown, right after graduating from Albion College in Michigan with a history degree. "Most new reporters become general assignment reporters and then get a chance to specialize later on," he says. "But I had some experience as the sports editor at the college paper and the sports editor at the *Press* needed a new reporter. As is often the case in any business, being in the right place at the right time can be all the difference." It seemed that Chuck's good fortune expired when the paper folded seven years later.

He took a job as an assistant editor at *Industry Week,* a trade journal, and worked his way up to being editor-in-chief there.

While still in that position, he was asked to give a presentation at a meeting of the American Business Press Association. That presentation was attended by the publisher of *SportsTrend,* a recently relaunched magazine serving sporting goods retailers, who was looking for a new editor. "Again, I happened to be in the right place at the right time," says the devout baseball fan reunited with his favorite topic. "By the same token, the extra work involved in giving a presentation and overcoming the fear of public speaking paid off for me."

What do you do all day?

The trade magazine editor's primary responsibility is to stay abreast of what's important to the readers' businesses. "Most of our time is spent cultivating sources, asking them questions and listening to what they tell us is happening in their corner of the industry," Chuck says. "And then our unique service is to synthesize that information into perspectives that our readers can use to be more successful."

When trade magazine editors are not talking on the phone to sources or writing and editing articles, they also attend conferences where they can meet face-to-face with their audience. "You often get your best insights, the most valuable information, outside regular working hours," Chuck points out. "And having a drink with someone at a conference is one of the best ways to meet people after hours and get the skinny."

Where do you see this job leading you?

"When I worked for *Industry Week,* I heard an executive from Ford say, 'I have approached every job I've ever had as if it will be the last one I'll ever have.' That sentiment has always worked for me," Chuck says, while allowing that he could imagine himself as publisher of his own magazine or an executive with broader responsibilities at the publishing company where he now works.

> **"IF YOU WANT TO SIT IN FRONT OF A SCREEN ALL DAY AND WRITE CRITICAL ESSAYS, STAY AWAY FROM THE BUSINESS PRESS. NOBODY CARES."**

94. Traffic Reporter

description: In every city, wherever commuters sit idle during rush hour and wonder what's the holdup, radio stations broadcast traffic reports. Most stations don't keep their own traffic reporters on staff, but rather contract a service to provide regular traffic reports during the rush hours. Traffic reporters working for these services gather some of the traffic information and assimilate it with information compiled by other watchers, then deliver it to the listeners of many radio stations in the market. Some traffic reporters broadcast from helicopters, while some remain on the ground.

salary: In a midsize market, traffic reporters start at around $6 to $7 an hour. Salaries rise along with experience.

prospects: Traffic reporting is a prime way to break into on-air radio work, so lots of people who want to get into radio are hustling for traffic reporter jobs. But because traffic reporting is an entry-level position, reporters come and go frequently, which means there are often openings.

qualifications: There's no specific training needed to be a traffic reporter, but you must be able to speak clearly, react quickly on the air and put often complex information into simple, useful reports. Experience with communication and radio technology will help.

characteristics: Successful traffic reporters can endure the odd hours, can banter comfortably with disc jockeys, and have lively personalities.

Susan Thomas *is the assistant director of operations for a traffic service in a major metropolitan area in the Midwest.*

How did you get the job?

Susan didn't begin her career anywhere near the broadcasting business. After graduating from the University of Tulsa with a bachelor of arts in communications, she worked as a public relations rep for an insurance company. "I wrote and edited three newsletters—one for our staff, one for our brokers, and one for our clients," she says. Her desktop publishing skills led her to a job at a copy shop franchise, where she wrote and designed resumes, brochures, and other printed materials. But she knew she hadn't yet found her niche, and one day she realized, "I should use this voice," a bright, lively, and clear speaking tone.

After a year of training at a broadcast trade school, Susan took a job as the news director at a small radio station in Georgia. "It was a real small-town operation," she recalls. "I *was* the news department." Six months later, the station's owner decided on cutbacks and Susan headed back home. A friend told her about an opening with the traffic service she now works for, and her training and broadcast experience got her the job.

What do you do all day?

"I wake up at an obnoxious hour and give my first report at 6:04 A.M.," Susan says. Even at that early hour, Susan has to be sharp. "In the morning I sit in one of the top floors of a high-rise overlooking a bridge into downtown, with a pair of binoculars, a two-way radio, a phone, and a computer, and I radio into our central center what I see on the bridges," she explains. "Then I do six or seven reports an hour on the news that I collected and other information that I read off the computer screen." At 8:40 A.M., Susan gives her last report, then goes home to sleep until she has to awake to return in time for her first evening report at 3:40 P.M.

In the afternoon her reports are broadcast on three stations (the morning report is on only one), so she doesn't do any spotting. "With three stations I'm on every few minutes in the afternoon," she says. "I'm also responsible for managing the whole place—including other reporters in the afternoon."

Where do you see this job leading you?

Susan's job as assistant operations manager keeps her busy enough, but she wants to move into news broadcasting, so she works as a writer and occasional on-air reporter for a local television station. Lots of her colleagues are weekend disc jockeys or news reporters. "Traffic reporting is a good way to break into radio and television," Susan says. "Not many people want to stay in it forever."

> **"I'M NOT SURE EXACTLY WHAT I WANT, BUT I KNOW I WANT TO STAY IN BROADCASTING. SO THIS IS GREAT EXPERIENCE FOR ME."**

95. Translator

description: English has become the language of the global economy, but American businesses and individuals still rely on translators to make critical documents available in foreign languages. Translators are often employed by agencies that specialize in these services, though some translators market themselves directly to customers. In either case, successful translators are more than fluent in the language they are working in—they must know legal or other technical terminology. Translators generally enjoy the freedoms and suffer through the uncertainties of being a freelancer. Translators are typically paid according to the number of words in the document, though they are also paid a flat fee for the job in some instances.

salary: You can be paid as little as $150 for a simple divorce decree up to $1,500 for a lengthy and complex business proposition. The only way to make a living is to keep up a steady flow of work.

prospects: In big cities, in border areas, in regions where international businesses cluster, you can find steady work as a translator. You'll be most in demand if you can work in Japanese, Chinese, and/or Middle Eastern and Eastern European languages. Spanish can be valuable, too.

qualifications: To do the job, you must be fluent in English and another tongue, and in the languages of business, engineering, and/or the law. To do it well, you must pay attention to details, work quickly, and handle deadline pressure.

characteristics: This is painstaking work done on your own, often to exacting standards. Self-motivated perfectionists are invited to apply.

Carol Myers *is the owner and project manager of a translation agency in the Southwest.*

How did you get the job?

Carol Myers has always had a facility for languages. She grew up in Germany, where she learned to speak English and the native tongue. She came to the United States to go to college, where she majored in—you guessed it—languages. There she studied Spanish and began to recognize her calling.

After college, Carol took on translation jobs when they came her way. Word-of-mouth brought her a steady flow of business, so, eight years ago, she launched a business that provides a full range of translation services to companies in her area. "Most of my new business still comes to me by referral," she says. "And most of the other customers are repeat business."

To help her translate into languages in which she does not have expertise, Carol contracts with people in her area who do. "I prefer to work with native speakers," she says. "Even people who have studied at the college level do not have mastery of the nuances in every language that native speakers do.

"I require strict attention to detail—I'm a stickler for things like accents being proper," Carol adds. "That's why I'm most comfortable when we're working with a language I can check myself."

What do you do all day?

One thing Carol does not spend any time on is soliciting work—as she said, referrals and repeat customers are the bulk of her business, and her advertisements in the Yellow Pages and local legal directories and her membership in the local chamber of commerce provide plenty of work.

> **"YOU SHOULD CONCENTRATE ON ONE PARTICULAR INDUSTRY AND LEARN ALL YOU CAN ABOUT IT. THE MORE YOU KNOW ABOUT YOUR CUSTOMER'S BUSINESS, THE BETTER AND MORE VALUABLE YOUR WORK WILL BE."**

"We do many, many contracts," Carol says. "I like business involved with mining most. I'm interested in the topic, I've learned a lot about it, and I think the translations are best if you're comfortable with the topic."

Carol's days—and often nights—are devoted to keeping track of the jobs she has accepted and making sure the translations are done on time and right. "We do all of our work by hand—no computer-assisted translations," she stresses. "The difference is as big as the difference between a Yugo and a handcrafted Rolls-Royce."

Carol and her translators do use computer word processors to format their work and provide finished documents to the customers. And they rely on all the resources they can find to help them write precisely and accurately.

"It is all about quality," Carol says. "The customer trusts you to get it exactly right—and you must."

Where do you see this job leading you?

Carol is just trying to keep up with what she already has. "I don't want to get so big that I can no longer check the work and control the quality," she says. "I'm already at my limit."

96. Travel Guide Writer

description: A travel guide is a work in progress—in need of updating at regular intervals to remain useful to readers. Year after year, the writers visit hotels, restaurants, and attractions at their assigned destination to describe and rate them. While traveling for a living may seem to be nothing but pleasure, thorough guide writers spend as much time checking out hotel rooms as they do seeing the sights. Some writers see all the places themselves, while others hire assistants who recheck some of the old spots while they look for new ones. A few writers become brand names, with faithful readers who never travel without their guide.

salary: Writing and updating a major country guide pays between $10,000 and $80,000—expenses included—depending on the publisher and the size of the country. An assistant may earn $2,000 to $15,000 (depending on the same factors) for three to six weeks of traveling and one to three months writing.

prospects: More and more travel guidebooks—filling an array of niches—are published each year. Freelance travel writers and students can find work as assistants. Experienced, reliable assistants can work their way up to be the lead writer.

qualifications: You generally must understand the language and culture of any foreign country you cover. You also need to be a keen observer, curious interviewer, and a concise, matter-of-fact writer. Strong physical stamina is essential. Usually, only experienced travel writers need apply.

characteristics: Resourceful people with a sense of adventure and the drive and energy to keep moving for weeks on end succeed as travel guide writers. You'd better be prepared to travel alone, too.

Marita Adair *lives in Texas and is the lead writer for a travel publisher's guides to Mexico.*

How did you get the job?

Marita fell in love with Mexican culture when she was 11, during a spur-of-the-moment day trip to a Mexican border town. It took some time before she found work to pay her for her passion. She majored in history with a focus on Latin America and minored in Spanish in college, then went to Washington, D.C., to work for a diplomatic organization representing 21 countries in Central and South America.

But that job offered her little opportunity to travel to Mexico or the rest of Latin America, so Marita moved to Texas, where she taught at a racially mixed school, then married and went to work at her husband's business and later at a local university library—all the while reading and writing and traveling to Mexico whenever she could.

"After a visit to Pátzcuaro during their Easter celebration, I wrote an article and sent it to the Sunday supplement editor of our local newspaper with photographs from the trip," she says. "He bought it and introduced me to the paper's travel editor, who invited me to submit other stories."

Soon Marita learned about sending the same story to different newspapers in different regions. "Once I learned about multiple submissions, I got out of my hometown," she explains, "and I began to develop a reputation as an expert on Mexico."

That reputation brought her offers to go on trips for travel writers organized by the Mexican government and resorts—which she took. On one, she met a woman who was working for a travel guide publisher. "We stayed in touch," Marita says, "and eight years later she recommended me to her publisher to update the company's series of travel guides to Mexico.

"I got the job because I knew Mexico—I had been going there for more than 20 years already," Marita says. "And I'd had experience working as an assistant to a writer who was working on another company's guide. I understood the job."

What do you do all day?

Marita spends one-fourth to half the year in Mexico, sampling meals, looking at rooms, recording admission prices, searching for bargains, finding out whatever travelers need to know—all to get the latest information for each new edition of her six guides.

"Good research gives the books their value," she says. "That's why you must speak the language to do the work. People speak English in many places nowadays, but you have to be able to get beyond the superficial with your information, you have to ask questions of the people in hotels, restaurants, and tourist attractions that require answers with more depth than their knowledge of English goes."

The rest of Marita's year is spent writing, rewriting, and integrating the work of the two to three assistants she's now using. "I place a lower priority on writing, in my selection of assistants, than fluency in Spanish and quality of research," she says. "I can reorganize the writing, but I can't go back and redo the research after the fact." Though, of course, the next year, Marita will be back.

Where do you see this job leading you?

No job could be more suited to an inveterate traveler and Mexico-phile than writer of travel guides to the country, and Marita knows it. "I feel like I've been aiming for this job all my life," she says. "It can seem repetitive, but I haven't grown tired of it yet." When she does find the time, Marita would like to travel more in other parts of Latin America—she's already visited some of it—and write about those places.

> **"IF YOU THINK YOU WANT TO BE A WRITER, THEN WRITE. AND WRITE ABOUT WHAT YOU KNOW BEST. IF YOU'RE GOOD, EVENTUALLY SOMEONE WILL BUY YOUR WORK."**

97. Typefont Designer

description: These days, how words look is almost as important as what they say. In advertisements, logos, magazine layouts, book covers, and other media, the letters are artfully styled to make an impression even before they are read. Designers create new fonts, or type styles, by deconstructing the letters of the alphabet and recasting the parts to suit their vision. Much of this work is performed on desktop computers. The designers are relatively anonymous (even though their work may be recognized by millions of people—think of the Coca-Cola logo script), but they do get to name the fonts they create.

salary: An entry-level designer at a font foundry starts out earning about $25,000 a year. People in the field say that the upper limit for a successful designer is well into six figures.

prospects: Though new typefonts have been developed steadily since the invention of the printing press, the proliferation of desktop publishing and computers have dramatically increased the demand for fonts. Very few design firms are devoted solely to this pursuit, but if you have the talent and the desire, you can find a job with a design firm—one that either specializes in new typefonts or offers font creation as a part of its services.

qualifications: Creativity is foremost, followed by knowledge of traditional typesetting methods and contemporary computer design programs. Experience as a designer—at a design firm, an advertising agency, or a publishing company—will help you understand the needs and interests of your potential customers.

characteristics: Only imaginative people willing to break rules and reinvent something as familiar as the alphabet need apply.

Andy Cruz *is the cofounder of a small but quite successful type foundry on the East Coast.*

How did you get the job?

Andy chose to attend a vocational high school that had a strong commercial art program. And while he was still a high school student he sought out practical experience—which started him on his career path.

"I worked at a co-op job at a local design studio during my junior and senior years. I was offered a full-time position by the studio when I graduated in 1990," Andy says. "I took the job because I thought I'd get more out of working full-time than I would get out of going to a college for design."

While at that firm and then another, Andy worked on logos, posters, packaging, and lots of other design projects. One thread seemed to run through much of his work. "Type and experimentation with out-of-the-ordinary printing techniques became strong design elements in most of our jobs," Andy says.

After two jobs working for other people, Andy and a colleague, Rich Roat, decided to strike out on their own, forming their own firm. "After a few months in the 'service' business of graphic design, we decided we needed a product to sell," Andy says. "One day I came in with the idea to sell typefaces. We had a few custom fonts left over from design projects we had done and a third partner had a few fonts he had designed. We slapped together 10 fonts, a postcard-size catalog, and the next thing we knew we were a font foundry."

What do you do all day?

Andy and his partners approach their work with one overarching principle: "Check out what all the other font companies are doing today, then go 180 degrees in the other direction," he says. "I get at least one pro-

motion or catalog a week from a 'new' font company that is simply ripping off another type design and trying to call it their own."

These designers look throughout the culture for inspiration for their work—from graffiti and comic books to industrial design, ancient Greece, and virtual reality. Once inspired, they try out their ideas on paper.

"I'd say that 99 percent of our fonts begin as sketches on paper," Andy explains. "Then we scan these rough outlines in and clean them up in Adobe Illustrator [a graphics program for Macintosh computers]. The next step is placing the characters from Illustrator into Fontographer, where all kerning and mastering takes places," which refers to adjustments made in the proportions of the letters and other details. Once finished, the fonts appear in the firm's catalog, from which art

> "I THOUGHT I'D GET MORE OUT OF WORKING FULL-TIME THAN I WOULD OUT OF GOING TO COLLEGE FOR DESIGN."

directors at advertising agencies, magazines, and other media can order them to use in their designs.

Where do you see this job leading you?

Andy goes for the frankest of answers to this question. "Someplace where people will appreciate my work," he says, "and will pay me a little cash for it." Once established in this field, most people choose to design fonts and market them on their own.

98. Video Catalog Editor

description: Producers of educational videos and CD-ROMs market them through information-dense catalogs organized by topics. The editors choose the works to be offered and compile the catalogs. Some editors even become involved in developing products. The job demands a variety of different skills and an in-depth understanding of the customers in the markets targeted by the catalog. Editors have near-total responsibility for their subject areas, though they work with other people in the production of the catalogs.

salary: An assistant starting out in this field will earn about $20,000 to $25,000 a year, depending on where the company is and how profitable the particular line of products you're assigned to is. Editors generally earn less than $40,000 a year until they break into management.

prospects: Companies that produce, buy, and sell training and self-help videos are located throughout the country. You can get into this industry if you're capable and determined.

qualifications: With the ability to write clearly and concisely, and a demonstrable understanding of marketing (either through education or experience), you'll get an interview. Add to those dexterity with a budget and your abundant ideas for new products and you will be able to do the job well.

characteristics: People with a complementary mix of creativity and business sense, an attention to detail, and a capacity to think about the big picture will succeed in the job. Interest in learning about educational topics in depth will help you enjoy it.

Juliana Lord McKowen *is a product development editor for an educational video marketing company in the East.*

How did you get the job?

Juliana studied marketing and management at a college in Massachusetts, with a practical eye on the future. "While I always enjoyed writing, I planned on a more business-oriented career and took only required writing classes," she says. "My position now demands both writing skills and business sense. If I had it to do again, I would have taken more electives involving writing."

After earning her bachelor's degree, Juliana worked for a market research and development firm. "I did market research and wrote reports about it for our clients," she says. Juliana learned a lot about both the struggles and rewards of a job well done in that position. But she wanted time to learn more about her own goals.

"I took three years off to live at the beach and wait tables," she explains. "My friends and family thought I had completely lost my mind, but it really was time well spent. I learned a lot during that time—that I needed challenges, wanted to use my mind more, and what it's like not to be able to afford sunscreen."

Through a family member, Juliana found out about her current employer and came to

> "DEVELOP YOUR OWN NICHE. EACH OF THE CATALOG EDITORS HAS BECOME AN EXPERT IN A SPECIFIC AREA."

its offices for an informational interview; the company had no openings at the time.

"Two months later I was hired for a full-time temporary assistant position while someone was on maternity leave; I was told there was a slight possibility that it might become permanent," she says. "I later found out that I was selected from among the candidates because I had experience selecting and working with printing companies at the market research firm.

"I believe I got the job because I was willing to take a chance on the temporary part and the low pay accompanying it," Juliana continues. "I treated the job as a permanent one and proved that I could handle more work and responsibilities than I had been assigned."

What do you do all day?

Juliana is responsible for the company's career guidance and home economics catalogs, which offer a wide range of educational videos, CD-ROMs, books, and posters to individuals and organizations. Juliana handles nearly every aspect of producing those catalogs. She chooses products to be included in the catalogs, writes the cata-log copy, and designs and lays out the pages. She also creates new products for the catalogs.

"My success in this position depends on my knowledge of our markets and my ability to develop scripts in areas that are big sellers," she says. "When I find a topic for a video that I believe will sell well, it's up to me to get it on our production schedule and write a script or find a writer." Juliana has written scripts for videos and CD-ROMs, as well as contributed to workbooks and posters.

"In this field, you have to be flexible and take initiative," she says. "I write about different subjects and often switch gears several times a day. We always have several projects in the works simultaneously and must juggle our time to keep them all moving."

Where do you see this job leading you?

"Currently, I spend a large part of my time writing scripts for multimedia CD-ROM projects," Juliana says. "I hope to someday work on CD-ROM development full-time."

99. Web Page Master

description: The World Wide Web is the most active element of the Internet right now, and many businesses are rushing to create their own "home pages," where Net surfers can find information about their products and services. The people who create the content of those pages are not programmers, but writers/editors who come up with ideas that programmers execute. Web page masters manage and update the information on the pages to retain the freshness essential to the medium. And not only do Web page masters have a very happenin' title, but they're in on the ground floor of what could be an important media of the future. Then again, maybe it's just a fad.

salary: No standard has been set for this job yet, but newspaper writers turned Web page masters for their publications are earning more—about $400 a week versus about $300—than their print-bound colleagues.

prospects: The rush is on now. Anyone adept with computers, particularly in using the Net, and having strong ideas for content will be able to find work managing a Web page, especially in those high-tech centers around the country. Again, this seems like a medium that will grow, but no one can say for sure.

qualifications: There is little formal training in Web page management available right now, but computer skills combined with editorial ideas and knowledge of how a print publication is put together are almost certain to get you an interview. If you can program at all, you may be able to write your own ticket.

characteristics: You have to be flexible and enjoy taking chances, like to work as part of a team, and be invigorated with new ideas to succeed as part of the development of this new medium.

Harley Jebens *is the Web page master for a Texas newspaper's World Wide Web page.*

How did you get the job?

Ever since Harley was a little boy ... OK, maybe Harley had no idea that the Web would even exist, but he has been building his career step by step in this direction for some time. He graduated with a bachelor's degree in magazine journalism from the University of Texas, then served in internships at *Texas Monthly* and Whittle Communications in Knoxville, Tennessee. "Those jobs didn't offer me much opportunity to write, so I took a job as a general assignment reporter at a daily newspaper in Base City, Texas," Harley says. But when the paper hit hard times, he was laid off. "So I headed back to Austin, because that's where I had the most contacts."

To pay his bills while waiting to find the right job, Harley worked as a bartender in clubs around town. That experience, believe it or not, prepared him

to take on a job at Austin's daily newspaper, his current employer. "I was hired as an entertainment clerk," he explains. "I compiled the calendar of events listings and wrote a 'best bets' column for the entertainment section. They hired me, in part I believe, because I knew my way around the club scene in town."

When that job appeared to be a dead end, Harley applied to graduate programs specializing in technical writing. Though he was accepted at several schools, he was offered an opportunity to learn about that topic at the newspaper. "We're in a high-tech town, so the editors of the paper decided to produce a reg-

> **"DON'T THINK THAT ANY EXPERIENCE IS USELESS. MY WORK AS A BARTENDER GOT ME THE JOB THAT LED ME TO THE ONE I HAVE NOW."**

ular electronic entertainment section and they asked me to produce it," he says. "When they decided to take the newspaper on-line, I was the logical person in their minds to represent the editorial side."

What do you do all day?

Right now the paper is just beginning to create its presence on the Web, so Harley sees his job as "facilitator between the programmers and the newsroom." Mainly that means selecting stories for trial on the site. "What we're hoping to do, for instance, is to take the week's club listings and add some links to them so that readers can get more information about events they're interested in," he explains. "If you're interested in seeing a certain band, say, you can find out where they're playing, then read reviews of other performances and listen to a sound bite of one of their songs."

Harley believes this will be even more valuable with the

hard news, so that readers can catch up on any topic in the current news with all the stories that have been printed about it. And in Harley's view, someday each reporter will have his or her own page and readers will also have their page to post their views about topics in the news. "The paper, any paper, is often criticized as being monolithic, as having its own agenda," he says. "I think this will tear that down and make it a forum for everyone's views."

Where do you see this job leading you?

Harley doesn't have a chance to even catch his breath to consider this one. "We're just getting this started," he says. "I want to get it up and running before I think about the next thing.

"I'm excited about learning all I can about electronic communications," he adds. "I think it will be quite a while before I exhaust it."

100. Wire Service Correspondent

description: A wire service, such as Associated Press or Reuters, is the source most newspapers rely on for news of national interest. That is, because most newspapers cannot afford to keep correspondents in far-off cities, the papers subscribe to a wire service, whose reporters gather news and write articles that each paper can tailor to its particular audience. In effect, wire service correspondents work for hundreds, perhaps thousands, of newspapers around the country and the world, reporting the news in their region to readers elsewhere.

salary: The entry-level salary for a wire service correspondent is between $25,000 and $30,000 per year, but the wire services generally hire only reporters who have two years or more of experience at a daily newspaper. Top reporters in large cities earn up to $80,000.

prospects: Print reporters move around a lot, which opens lots of positions on a steady basis at the wire services. The most opportunities for relatively inexperienced reporters tend to be in small markets, as reporters graduate to larger and larger news centers. And there are wire service bureaus in more cities than ever before. Still, lots of reporters with a couple of years' experience at their hometown newspaper seek the broader exposure that comes from working on a wire service, so positions are competitive.

qualifications: A broad-based education with an emphasis on critical thinking and writing skills is most important. And again, you'll need at least two years' experience as a reporter on a daily newspaper to land a job with most wire service bureaus.

characteristics: Chief correspondents at wire service bureaus value natural curiosity and assertiveness in their reporters, as well as self-motivation and the ability to write quickly, concisely, and frequently. Innately outgoing people have an advantage in engendering trust in sources, which leads to more revealing interviews and more in-depth stories.

Robert Naylor *is the correspondent in charge of a wire service bureau in a state capital in the Deep South.*

How did you get the job?

Robert Naylor has handled the news from several angles, but he came back to daily reporting, where he began, out of true love for newspapers. "I got a job as a general assignment reporter at my hometown newspaper, *The Meridian Star,* right after graduating from Jackson State College," says Robert, who has a degree in mass communications with a focus on journalism. "But after a few years I was attracted by what I saw as the glamour of being a press aide to the governor of Mississippi." Two years later, Robert took a job as the assignment editor for a local television news program, but was wooed back to *The Meridian Star,* where he rose to the job of managing editor for a brief tenure. An offer to do the same at a daily newspaper in Columbia, South Carolina, lured him out of state, but he came back just a few years later to work as a correspondent for the wire service. "The wire service offered the caliber of journalism that I am interested in," he says simply.

Robert served as a correspondent in the service's important Washington, D.C., bureau before earning the job of chief correspondent at the bureau where he now works. "The wire service is a meritocracy," he says. "You move from small bureau to larger bureau, from correspondent to chief correspondent by proving yourself day in and day out at your job."

What do you do all day?

Wire service reporting is about the daily deadline. "The pressure is always on to get any story out on the wire as soon as possible; we have no luxury of time to develop a story," Robert explains. "But accuracy remains critically important for our reporters because the newspapers that subscribe to the wire service have almost no way to

> "IT SEEMS THAT PEOPLE HAVE LESS TIME TO TEACH YOU THAN EVER BEFORE. STUDY NEWSPAPERS AND OTHER REPORTERS' WORK ON YOUR OWN; THERE'S LOTS TO LEARN FROM THEM."

verify the stories that they pick up. They rely on us."

Wire service correspondents are typically assigned particular "beats" to cover, such as the statehouse, the major industry in the area, or the district's federal court. The reporters check in every day at their beats, cover scheduled events like press conferences, interview sources about significant occurrences,

and write brief articles about their findings as soon as possible. "In an office the size of ours, a reporter may have several beats to cover and will spend some time at the rewrite desk preparing stories from our local papers to go out on the wire. At larger bureaus, many reporters spend most of their time cultivating sources who will give them access to deep information when big stories break," Robert says. "All of us are spending less time on spot news stories and more on generating articles that have unique angles or that explain important news events."

Where do you see this job leading you?

Robert Naylor's direction has been upward through the ranks as his career progresses. He is content to manage the wire service bureau where he's at for now, though eventually he'd like to take on an even larger one. But he resists looking that far ahead. "I'm focused on our daily deadlines," he says. "I rarely get to look too far beyond that."

RESOURCES

These organizations offer professional training, hold conferences, publish newsletters, compile salary surveys, and, in some cases, maintain job banks.

American Association of Law Libraries, 53 W. Jackson Blvd., Suite 940, Chicago, IL 60604; 312/939-4764

American Association of School Librarians, 50 E. Huron St., Chicago, IL 60611; 312/944-6780

American Medical Writers Association, 9650 Rockville Pike, Bethesda, MD 20814-3998; 301/493-0003

American Society of Indexers, P.O. Box 386, Port Aransas, TX 78373; 512/749-4052

American Society of Journalists and Authors, 1501 Broadway, Suite 302, New York, NY 10036; 212/997-0947

American Society of Magazine Editors, 919 Third Ave., New York, NY 10022; 212/872-3700

Association of Professional Writing Consultants, 3924 S. Troost, Tulsa, OK 74105; 918/743-4793

Copywriter's Council of America, Communications Building 102, 7 Putter Lane, Box 102, Middle Island, NY 11953-0102; 516/924-8555

Editorial Freelancers Association, 71 W. 23rd St., Suite 1504, New York, NY 10010; 212/929-5400

International Association of Business Communicators, 1 Hallidie Plaza, Suite 600, San Francisco, CA 94102; 415/433-3400

Medical Library Association, 6 N. Michigan Ave., Suite 300, Chicago, IL 60602; 312/419-9094

National Association of Science Writers, P.O. Box 244, Greenlawn, NY 11740; 516/757-5664

Professional Association of Resume Writers, 3637 Fourth St. N., Suite 330, St. Petersburg, FL 33704-1336; 813/821-2274

Radio-Television News Directors Association, 1000 Connecticut Ave. NW, Suite 615, Washington, DC 20036; 202/659-6510

Romance Writers of America, 13700 Veteran's Memorial Dr., Suite 315, Houston, TX 77014; 713/440-6885

Society for Technical Communication, 901 N. Stuart St., Suite 904, Arlington, VA 22203; 703/522-4114

Society of American Business Editors and Writers, University of Missouri, P.O. Box 838, Columbia, MO 65205; 314/882-7862

Society of Children's Book Writers and Illustrators, 22736 Vanowen St., Suite 106, West Hills, CA 91307; 818/888-8760

Read these trade journals to learn about current issues in their particular fields. Some include help wanted advertising.

Advertising Age, Crain Communications, 220 E. 42nd St., New York, NY 10017; 212/210-0259

Adweek, 1515 Broadway, New York, NY 10036; 212/536-5336

American Bookseller, 828 S. Broadway, Tarrytown, NY 10591; 914/591-2665

Editor & Publisher Weekly Magazine, 11 W. 19th St., 10th Floor, New York, NY 10011-4234; 212/675-4380

Folio, the Magazine for Magazine Management, 4 High Ridge Park, Stamford, CT 06905; 203/358-9900

Publishers Weekly, Cahner's Publishing Co., 249 W. 17th St., New York, NY 10011; 212/645-0067

ABOUT THE AUTHOR

Scott A. Meyer has been a reporter and editor at weekly newspapers and trade magazines. He is currently a senior editor at Organic Gardening *magazine and is a contributor to several other national and regional publications. He has written one other book before* 100 Jobs in Words *and is already working on another. He spends his spare time doing nothing of any purpose with his beloved wife, daughter, and son at their home in Pennsylvania.*

NOTES

NOTES

NOTES

NOTES

NOTES

NOTES